ReFocus: The Films of Susan Seidelman

ReFocus: The American Directors Series

Series Editors: Robert Singer, Gary D. Rhodes and Frances Smith

Editorial board: Kelly Basilio, Donna Campbell, Claire Perkins, Christopher Sharrett and Yannis Tzioumakis

ReFocus is a series of contemporary methodological and theoretical approaches to the interdisciplinary analyses and interpretations of neglected American directors, from the once-famous to the ignored, in direct relationship to American culture—its myths, values and historical precepts

Titles in the series include:

ReFocus: The Films of Preston Sturges Edited by Jeff Jaeckle and Sarah Kozloff

ReFocus: The Films of Delmer Daves Edited by Matthew Carter and Andrew Nelson

ReFocus: The Films of Amy Heckerling Edited by Frances Smith and Timothy Shary

ReFocus: The Films of Budd Boetticher Edited by Gary D. Rhodes and Robert Singer

ReFocus: The Films of Kelly Reichardt E. Dawn Hall

ReFocus: The Films of William Castle Edited by Murray Leeder

ReFocus: The Films of Barbara Kopple Edited by Jeff Jaeckle and Susan Ryan

ReFocus: The Films of Elaine May Edited by Alexandra Heller-Nicholas and Dean Brandum

ReFocus: The Films of Spike Jonze Edited by Kim Wilkins and Wyatt Moss-Wellington

ReFocus: The Films of Paul Schrader Edited by Michelle E. Moore and Brian Brems

ReFocus: The Films of John Hughes Edited by Timothy Shary and Frances Smith

ReFocus: The Films of Doris Wishman Edited by Alicia Kozma and Finley Freibert

ReFocus: The Films of Albert Brooks Edited by Christian B. Long

ReFocus: The Films of William Friedkin Steve Choe

ReFocus: The Later Films and Legacy of Robert Altman Edited by Lisa Dombrowski and Justin Wyatt

ReFocus: The Films of Mary Harron Edited by Kyle Barrett

ReFocus: The Films of Wallace Fox Edited by Gary D. Rhodes and Joanna Hearne

ReFocus: The Films of Richard Linklater Edited by Kim Wilkins and Timotheus Vermeulen

ReFocus: The Films of Roberta Findlay Edited by Peter Alilunas and Whitney Strub

ReFocus: The Films of Richard Brooks: A Literary Cinema Edited by R. Barton Palmer and Homer B. Pettey

ReFocus: The Films of William Wyler Edited by John M. Price

ReFocus: The Films of Wes Craven Edited by Calum Waddell

ReFocus: The Films of Susan Seidelman Edited by Susan Santha Kerns

edinburghuniversitypress.com/series/refoc

ReFocus:
The Films of Susan Seidelman

Susan Santha Kerns

EDINBURGH
University Press

Edinburgh University Press is one of the leading university presses in the UK. We publish academic books and journals in our selected subject areas across the humanities and social sciences, combining cutting-edge scholarship with high editorial and production values to produce academic works of lasting importance. For more information visit our website: edinburghuniversitypress.com

© editorial matter and organisation Susan Santha Kerns, 2023, 2025
© the chapters their several authors 2023, 2025

Edinburgh University Press Ltd
13 Infirmary Street,
Edinburgh, EH1 1LT

First published in hardback by Edinburgh University Press 2024

Typeset in 11/13 Ehrhardt MT by
IDSUK (DataConnection) Ltd
A CIP record for this book is available from the British Library

ISBN 978 1 3995 0305 1 (hardback)
ISBN 978 1 3995 0306 8 (paperback)
ISBN 978 1 3995 0307 5 (webready PDF)
ISBN 978 1 3995 0308 2 (epub)

The right of Susan Santha Kerns to be identified as the editor of this work has been asserted in accordance with the Copyright, Designs and Patents Act 1988, and the Copyright and Related Rights Regulations 2003 (SI No. 2498).

Contents

List of Figures vii
Notes on Contributors viii
Acknowledgments xi

    Introduction: Ahead of the Curve 1
    Susan Santha Kerns

Part 1 Building a Foundation

1 The Making of Ms. Right: Susan Seidelman and the Persistence of "Women's Films" 11
    Maya Montañez Smukler
2 Susan Seidelman's *Sex and the City:* TV Authorship and Feminist Possibility 28
    Elizabeth Alsop
3 "I've Always Been a Voyeur": An Interview with Susan Seidelman 45
    Susan Santha Kerns

Part 2 Embodied Spaces

4 "Who is This?" *Smithereens*, Susan Seidelman's Auspicious Debut Feature 69
    Susan Santha Kerns
5 Swapping the Suburban Housewife for the NYC Feminist: Susan Seidelman and her Personas 85
    Ruth Wollersheim
6 Original *She-Devil* Ending Screenplay Pages 105
7 Unsettling Domesticity: *Desperately Seeking Susan*, Madonna and the Voyeuristic Politics of MTV Stardom 111
    Michael Reinhard

8 Directing a City: Susan Seidelman's New York 127
Josephine Maria Yanasak-Leszczynski
9 Making Frankie Stone: Feminism, Post-Romance and *Making Mr. Right* 141
Vanessa Cambier

Part 3 Making Room

10 Electric Melodrama: Susan Seidelman, Childhood and the Girl Next Door 159
Debbie Olson
11 Age, Disability and Agency in the Late-Period Films of Susan Seidelman 171
Cole Bradley
12 And You Can Dance! Movement, Mobility and Magic in *Musical Chairs* 185
Warren Holmes
13 Death, Illusion and the Hijab in Susan Seidelman's *Cut in Half* 200
Stacy Thompson

Bibliography 216
Index 226

List of Figures

1.1	Susan Seidelman on the *Desperately Seeking Susan* set, 1985.	3
2.1	Still of Wren (Susan Berman) in *Smithereens*, 1982.	35
2.2	Still of Carrie Bradshaw (Sarah Jessica Parker) in *Sex and the City*, 1998.	35
3.1	Susan Seidelman directing *Yours Truly, Andrea G. Stern*, 1979.	47
4.1	Susan Berman (standing) and Susan Seidelman (squatting) on the set of *Smithereens*, 1982.	81
5.1	Juxtaposed stills from *Confessions of a Suburban Girl*, 1992.	87
5.2	Juxtaposed stills from *Confessions of a Suburban Girl*, 1992.	87
5.3	Susan Seidelman and Susan Berman on the set of *Smithereens*, 1982.	92
5.4	Roseanne Barr in the ending shot of *She-Devil*, 1989.	98
5.5	Carrie Bradshaw (Sarah Jessica Parker) and Lancy (Dana Wheeler-Nicholson) talk on the phone during "The Baby Shower" episode of *Sex and the City*, 1998.	101
6.1	Final pages of original *She-Devil* screenplay.	106
6.2	Final pages of original *She-Devil* screenplay.	107
6.3	Final pages of original *She-Devil* screenplay.	108
6.4	Final pages of original *She-Devil* screenplay.	109
6.5	Final pages of original *She-Devil* screenplay.	110

Notes on Contributors

Elizabeth Alsop is Assistant Professor of Communication and Media at the CUNY School of Professional Studies, as well as a faculty member in the M.A. in Liberal Studies program at the CUNY Graduate Center. She is the author of *Making Conversation in Modernist Fiction* (2019), and her essays on twentieth-century fiction, film and television aesthetics, feminist media studies and contemporary television storytelling have appeared in *Feminist Media Studies*, *The Journal of Film and Video*, *[In]Transition*, *Narrative*, *College Literature*, *The Atlantic* and *The LA Review of Books*. She is currently writing a book on the films of Elaine May.

Cole Bradley is a writer and filmmaker based in Brooklyn. He has directed several short films, including *Modernity* (2019), *dirtbags!* (2018) and *Caroline* (2016), and he has worked for a number of film festivals, including the Chicago International Children's Film Festival, Boulder International Film Festival and Chicago Feminist Film Festival. He received his Master's degree in Cinema Studies from New York University, and his research focuses on American independent cinema and exploitation film.

Vanessa Cambier is a feminist scholar and Graduate Program Academic Advisor at the University of Minnesota. Her research focuses on the intersections between feminist activism, experimental cinema and the politics of multimedia animation from the 1970s to the current moment. Her work has been published in *The LA Review of Books* and the journal *Animation Studies*. Vanessa earned her PhD in Comparative Studies and Moving Image Studies from the University of Minnesota, where she also taught courses in cinema and critical theory.

Warren Holmes has a Master's in Film and Television Studies from The University of East Anglia and a Master's in Social Work Practice from Manchester Metropolitan University. He is the author of "On the Cutting Edge" in the *Auteur* volume dedicated to Tim Burton and has written for charity publications, including Lifelines' *The Wing of Friendship*. A tutor with over seventeen years of experience in a range of settings, he currently teaches sociology at a UK Academy School.

Susan Santha Kerns is Associate Professor of Cinema and Television Arts at Columbia College Chicago, Associate Provost of Faculty Research and Development and an award-winning filmmaker. Her scholarship on feminism and film festivals has appeared in the *Journal of Film and Video*, the *Routledge Handbook of Contemporary Feminism* and *Cuaderno*, and she has published on embodiment in popular culture in *Amputation in Literature and Film*, the *Routledge Companion to Gender and Sexuality in Comic Book Studies*, the *Journal of Graphic Novels and Comics* and *Nip/Tuck: Television that Gets Under Your Skin*. She produced the documentary *Manlife* and has produced or directed numerous short films. She holds a PhD from the University of Wisconsin-Milwaukee.

Debbie Olson is Associate Professor of English and Coordinator of First Year Writing at Missouri Valley College. Her research interests include images of African and African American children in film and television, critical race theory, childhood studies, cultural studies, African film and New Hollywood Cinema. She is the author of *Black Children in Hollywood Cinema* (2017), as well as editor of *The Child in World Cinema* (2018), *The Child in Post-Apocalyptic Cinema* (2015) and many others. She has co-edited, with Adrian Schober (Australia), *Children, Youth, and American Television* (2018) and *Children in the Films of Steven Spielberg* (2017). She has written numerous book chapters, most recently "On the Innocence of Beasts: Child Soldiers in Cary Fukunaga's Beasts of No Nation" in *New Perspectives of African Childhoods*, edited by De-Valera Botchway, Awo Sarpong and Charles Quist-Adade (2019). She is currently working on her next book, *Counterculture Cinema: Youth in Transition*.

Michael M. Reinhard is an NEH postdoctoral fellow working on the *Rediscovering American Democracy* initiative at Montclair State University. He is also a Lecturer at Rutgers University (New Brunswick). He holds a PhD in Cinema and Media Studies from the University of California, Los Angeles, as well as an A.M. (Humanities; Film) and A.B. (English Language and Literature) from the University of Chicago. He has taught courses on US film history, youth culture and television as these subjects intersect with questions of style, media industry and social politics. His work has appeared in *Velvet Light Trap*,

Intersectional Feminist Readings of Comics (2021) and *Feminist Media Studies*. His upcoming research will also be featured in edited collections such as *Viva Las Vegas: Music and Myth in America's City of Second Chances* and *The Oxford Handbook of American Documentary*. Currently, he is developing his research monograph, *The Diva's Public: Celebrity, Media Activism and the New Cultural Citizenship*, to explore new ideas about citizenship and social activism in contemporary media.

Maya Montañez Smukler, PhD, heads the UCLA Film and Television Archive Research and Study Center. She has conducted oral histories for the Visual History Program at the Academy of Motion Picture Arts and Sciences, including an interview with Susan Seidelman. Her book *Liberating Hollywood: Women Directors and the Feminist Reform of 1970s American Cinema* (2019) is a recipient of the Theater Library Association's Richard Wall Memorial Award. She is also a contributing author to *ReFocus: The Films of Elaine May* (Edinburgh University Press, 2019).

Stacy Thompson is Professor in the English Department at the University of Wisconsin-Eau Claire, where he teaches courses in film studies, critical theory and rhetoric. He has published the monograph *Punk Productions: Unfinished Business* (2004) on punk rock, as well as articles on film, ethics, Marxism and psychoanalysis. He holds a PhD from Purdue University.

Ruth Wollersheim is a tenured faculty member at Century College in the Minnesota State system where she teaches courses in humanities, film and gender studies. Most of her writing and research focuses on the mediated construction of the American housewife, and her chapter "Feminism's Reoccurring Nightmare: Monstrous Patriarchy, Pulp Horror and The Stepford Wives" appears in the anthology *Horror Comes Home: Essays on Hauntings, Possessions and Other Domestic Terrors in Cinema* (2019).

Josephine M. Yanasak-Leszczynski is an author, film critic and photographer working as the Rights and Reproductions Specialist for the Publishing Department of the Art Institute of Chicago. Her scholarly work has appeared in *Ties that Bind: Love in Fantasy & Science Fiction* (2020), while her creative writing includes her novel *A Coven in Essex County* (2016) and her short story "Córka Rusalka," which appeared in the fiction anthology *Decoded* (2019). Her additional writing has been featured in *Gayly Dreadful, FemHype, The Startup, Auteur, Heated* and others.

Acknowledgments

This book would not be possible without the support of Columbia College Chicago and my department, Cinema and Television Arts. I am indebted to my graduate assistant, Kateryna Sazonova, and to David Tarleton for allowing her to work with me. Thanks also to department chairs Eric Scholl and Thelma Vickroy, cinema studies coordinator Zoran Samardzija and my colleagues for incessant cheerleading: Visda Goudarzi, Ruth Leitman, Michael Niederman, Grace Overbeke, Sharon Ross, Rachel Rozycki, Mehrnaz Saeedvafa, Molly Schneider, Joe Steiff, Wenhwa Ts'ao and Michelle Yates. Thanks especially to Ruth Wollersheim, a contributor to this collection, for being brilliant, always eager to jump in and one of the best people I know. She says that I am Susan to her Roberta, but instigators need willing friends to come along for the ride. I am ever so appreciative that she is a pal and a confidante.

My parents, Jim and Santha Kerns, and my brother, Jason Kerns, have provided emotional and financial support over the years to assist my academic and creative endeavors. I also rely on my partner, Jay Beckman, who listens to initial brainstorms and continues listening when I over-extend myself. While my chihuahuas, Gary and Wyatt, are on my lap when I write, Jay formats images, tracks down hard-to-find movies and even paid for the indexer of this volume. He has unending curiosity about and enthusiasm for cinema, and I cannot overstate how grateful I am for his kindness, humor, patience and assistance.

Finally, I must acknowledge Susan Seidelman's vast contributions to this collection. Her body of work is the foundation for everything here, but she also became a collaborator. We met several times via zoom to complete her interview, which she generously added to by email, providing additional articles, images and screenplay pages to round out production and reception histories. I am sincerely grateful to her, and I hope that we have done right by her legacy with this initial volume on her work. Thank you, Susan, for bringing to life so many films and television shows that have inspired us, dared us to dream bigger and encouraged us to keep looking.

Introduction: Ahead of the Curve

Susan Santha Kerns

In 1985, my best friend Kara and I went to our local mall to see a matinee of *Desperately Seeking Susan* with two boys we were "going with": I with Chad and Kara with Steve or Troy (probably Steve, but I can't remember, and it definitely does not matter). We had just graduated from sixth grade, and this was my first date. Sitting in the back row, Chad awkwardly put his arm around me and whispered: "I'm desperately seeking Susan." I froze, looked straight ahead and hoped he would not say it again. But he did, distracting me from the world in which I wanted to live for ninety minutes – the New York where Madonna wandered the city wearing over-sized bows, too many bracelets and colors and clothing that defined, and still define, what it meant to be alive in the 1980s. Growing up in Iowa, New York was an urban fantasyland, a dream I only saw in movies where stylish women – Madonna and Rosanna Arquette, Susan and Roberta – ran free. Sure, men chased them, but first and foremost they tracked their desires, hunted their destinies. It was a sight I saw too infrequently on screen. That summer, Chad moved to Florida, and Kara and I drifted apart as we transitioned schools, pursuing different friend groups. My bonded relationship with *Desperately Seeking Susan*, however, remained; looking back, several early Seidelman characters influenced my teenage self, including Wren of *Smithereens* and the titular Cookie. Like Wren, I floated in and out of music and art scenes. Like Cookie, I carried a Le Clic camera in my purse, documenting my friends' lives. I did not connect Cookie, Wren and Susan to Susan Seidelman at the time, but the films encapsulate a period of my adolescence. Seidelman was ahead of Hollywood in bringing these characters to the screen, and I hitched a ride.

About a decade later, in the late 1990s, I again connected with Seidelman's women, as so many people did, with the release of *Sex and the City*. Like those who came before them, these new characters – Carrie, Samantha, Miranda and Charlotte – crisscrossed New York pursuing their desires, sharing them now in newspaper columns and chats over brunch or cosmopolitans. These characters were older, more polished and financially secure, but they still did not have it all figured out. I was a decade behind them, allowing me to follow along and dream bigger. And again, these characters bonded my girlfriends. While working at summer camp, my co-worker's mom, Edna, sent VHS tapes of *Sex and the City* to camp for Beth, Mary and I to watch during "me time." In summer 2001, my friend Kim and I moved to New York. On my cab ride into the city, a billboard read: "Welcome to the playground for the fearless." Beside it, another advertised *Sex and the City*. My brother, Jason, lived in New York then, so we got together on Sundays to watch. It was a summer of being an insider, and although Seidelman was no longer directing episodes, I still felt her fingerprint on the show.

What I did not realize was that Seidelman had been blazing trails I was not following. Her first feature out of graduate school, *Smithereens*, sidled its way into competition at the Cannes Film Festival, a first for any independent American feature. *Smithereens*' success put her on the map, allowing her to secure an agent and be selective about her second project, an uncommon situation for women directors at the time. She waited to make a move until she read the script for *Desperately Seeking Susan* – and then had the foresight to cast an emerging musician, Madonna, in the title role. Certainly, the serendipitous timing of *Desperately Seeking Susan*'s release coinciding with Madonna's skyrocketing popularity could not have been planned (although many marketers since have tried), but where many early career directors would have cast a known star whose name could carry the project, Seidelman intuited that Madonna was perfect. In casting Madonna as Susan, Seidelman showcased her prowess for recognizing nascent talent and giving it room to grow. She gave more musicians acting opportunities, like Ann Magnuson in *Making Mr. Right*, but cast established and emerging actors in roles that utilized their talents in new ways. *Making Mr. Right*, for example, also showcases John Malkovich's comedic abilities in two roles – as Ulysses, a robot, and as Dr. Peters, his creator – at a time when Malkovich was only known for dramatic roles. Cast alongside him were his then-wife Glenne Headly and Laurie Metcalf (who also had a bit part in *Desperately Seeking Susan*), all of whom were transitioning from theater to Hollywood. Seidelman's next film, *She-Devil*, again sees her taking intuitive casting risks. Here, Meryl Streep, in her first comedic film role, stars opposite television comedian Roseanne Barr in her first feature film. Seidelman continued casting up-and-coming talent in later films – for example, Laverne Cox as Chantelle in *Musical Chairs*, one of Cox's earliest feature roles – while spotlighting older actresses – for example, Dyan Cannon, Brenda Vaccaro and Sally Kellerman in *Boynton*

Figure I.1 Susan Seidelman on the *Desperately Seeking Susan* set, 1985. (Photograph by Andrew Schwartz. Courtesy of Andrew Schwartz and Susan Seidelman.)

Beach Club and Brooke Shields, Daryl Hannah, Wanda Sykes, Camryn Manheim and Virginia Madsen in *The Hot Flashes* – illustrating how her knack for casting includes making space for actors to continue shining.

While all of this was occurring, Seidelman's authorial interests developed: exploring tensions between women's opportunities (romantic, professional or otherwise) in city centers versus the suburbs. Often this was explored through genre-bending narratives that insert unusual women into well-tread story structures – interests thoroughly explored throughout the chapters in this volume. Simultaneously, Seidelman's focus on women uninterested or unwilling to adhere to generic standards often left critics puzzled, most of whom at the time were male. In the interview included in this collection, Seidelman notes the strong influence that a very small number of 1980s film critics held; appealing to their tastes seemed crucial for career longevity. But certainly women directors were subject to harsher critiques than their male counterparts and their failures more pointedly marked, sometimes ending careers. While Christina Lane notes that Seidelman was "arguably the most successful feminist, crossover, indie-commercial filmmaker of the 1980s"[1] having directed four studio films in five years, in an interview from the 1990s, Seidelman admits: "I think the failure of *Mr. Right* was noticed more because I'm a woman."[2] Seidelman also explains that some difficulties in making *Cookie* were compounded by *Making Mr. Right*'s disappointing box office returns:

"I was pressured because I was coming off a flop. One failure in this business, and they look at you differently."³ As with women directors before her, opportunities began arising in television as her relationship with studios waned.

Rather than see this career trajectory as one of limitations, however, Seidelman explored wide-reaching opportunities. In addition to directing the documentary *Confessions of a Suburban Girl* for BBC Scotland, she made *The Dutch Master*, part of *Tales of Erotica*, a German-produced series of shorts by esteemed directors, for which she was nominated for an Academy Award for best live-action short film. She also directed an episode of *Early Edition* and the Disney remake of *The Barefoot Executive*. Seidelman notes that these decisions were, in part, based on the desire to make life easier: "When you're directing a feature, it's really a full-time job. It's really hard to have another life and [. . .] I had worked pretty much extensively through all the eighties, and was ready to take a rest."⁴ Opportunities like these also released Seidelman from some responsibilities that generating her own projects had required: "I was now in a period where, when a project came my way, if it was something interesting, I'd say, sure, I'll try it."⁵ Although Seidelman had made films about little girls, she had not yet made children's entertainment. That changed when Disney approached her with *The Barefoot Executive*: "I would never have thought I would have been interested in doing [*The Barefoot Executive*]. But at that time, having a five-year-old kid, I decided, why not?"⁶ It is common for women directors to move into children's programming at some point. Women filmmakers with wide-ranging backgrounds have directed children's films mid-career: Penelope Spheeris, who was known for her punk films *The Decline of Western Civilization* and *Suburbia*, directed *The Little Rascals*; Euzhan Palcy, who, after the success of *Sugar Cane Alley*, made the Oscar-nominated *A Dry White Season*, the first film directed by a Black woman and produced by a major Hollywood studio, then directed Disney's *Ruby Bridges*; and Agnieszka Holland, who built her reputation with Polish political films, including the Oscar-nominated *Angry Harvest* and *Europa, Europa*, made *The Secret Garden*. It is outside the scope of this introduction to speculate why high-achieving women directors especially are invited to move into children's programming, although I have some guesses. Nevertheless, like episodic television, it provides another outlet for women to keep working.

Seidelman then had another massive hit on her hands, although she received little credit for this one: directing the pilot of *Sex and the City*. While directing several episodes for the first season, Seidelman began balancing directing episodic television with independent films, such as *Gaudi Afternoon*, and made-for-cable movies such as *A Cooler Climate*, *Power and Beauty* and *The Ranch*. This range of production models and outlets allowed her to continue pushing new representations of under-represented women on screen. Much of Seidelman's post-*Sex and the City* work focuses on middle-aged and older cis-gendered women. However, Seidelman also started exploring queer narratives, transgender characters and alternative ideas of family and community through *Gaudi Afternoon* and *Musical Chairs*, which also foregrounds disability. Even *The Ranch*, her SHOWTIME film about sex workers, expanded the well-tread "hooker with a heart of gold" storyline to turn sex work into plain-old work while exploring interpersonal dynamics within a community of women. Disappointed IMDb user tuttletail88, for example, explains that "apart from the bare breasts of many of its leading ladies (which earns this movie its four points)," the sex is . . .

> . . . a letdown to men who watch it to be titillated [. . .]. The strong female bonding aspect of the movie could just as easily have been portrayed without trying to gain access to the male demographic who [. . .] thought it [would include] some decent soft-core action.

While tuttletail88 is not a vetted film critic, his assessment speaks to years of critics wanting Seidelman's films to meet them on their terms, not hers, another thread seen throughout this collection. Moreover, these kinds of stories likely would not have been possible in 2000s Hollywood studio productions. Seidelman says: "Cable is an excellent alternative to film especially when commercial films seem so geared toward teenage boys."[7]

Seidelman's survival instincts included not just adapting to the times but making the most of opportunities by not being afraid to try things. Moving back into independent film, via independent financing, allowed Seidelman once again to take control of the stories she told while cultivating her audiences, which she has always insisted exist.[8] Lane writes:

> It is an uphill battle to combat the industry notion that adult women are not worth reaching. This is a strange position when trade research shows that most film and television products need a strong female demographic to survive, the majority of viewing decisions are made by women, many of the biggest industry success stories are female-driven films and television series, and 73% of women aged thirty-five to forty-nine have household purchasing power.[9]

Leveraging her audiences, Seidelman embraced crowd-sourcing and direct-to-consumer distribution models before either were common. *Boynton Beach Club*, *Musical Chairs* and *The Hot Flashes* were "conceived and pushed out into the world [. . .] through crowdsourcing, alternative financing, self-distribution, and travelling exhibitions," and private investors, savvy pitching skills and community support (including things such as borrowed staging spaces) were all utilized in these productions.[10] Popular regional screenings of *Boynton Beach Club*, in part advertised through Seidelman's mother Florence's "grassroots promotional activities" (Florence provided the story idea and wrote a first draft of the film's screenplay) wooed initially sheepish distributors, resulting in a larger release for the film.[11] *Musical Chairs* took this direct-to-consumer approach a step further by streaming free for two weeks through its website to generate reviews and buzz before being picked up for wider release.[12] *The Hot Flashes* also capitalized on social media to promote awareness of the film with Facebook swag and DVD giveaways, leaked cast video interviews and partnerships with cancer fundraising organizations.[13] Lane notes that these shifts "signal an additional burden" on directors, requiring them "to know more about each stage" and "manage every phase" of filmmaking and distribution.[14] Yet Seidelman has kept pace with the industry shifts that necessitate agility, from development to distribution. Her dexterity illustrates the continuous struggle many filmmakers face – one success does not beget the next – imploring directors to stay ahead of the curve.

This collection deeply explores Seidelman's journey. Constructed in three parts suggesting a domestic theme, the first part, *Building a Foundation*, offers more information about Seidelman's background, her play with genre, and how her career trajectory might be used to reconstruct notions of auteurism to include directors moving between production models. Looking at Seidelman's romantic comedies, for example, reveals that generic expectations give way to women's desires, and heteronormative romantic coupling is never the entire goal. Her films suggest something odder and more ambiguous than "happily ever after," giving these films her authorial twist. However, Seidelman's television work also might be looked at through the lens of authorship, if one recalibrates auteur studies to account for work created within industrial production models, such as television production, where directors may not be the key creative force and where women are often employed. This section ends with a candid interview with Seidelman, where she fills in the gaps about her career.

In Part 2, *Embodied Spaces*, the connection between characters and space is explored via the first decade of Seidelman's films. While *Smithereens* lays the groundwork for her interests in women's stories within urban landscapes, the character Wren also acts as something of a double for Seidelman – embodying and traversing the culture of the times while eluding being fully included in artistic movements. The two exemplify a specific time and place but remain canonically untethered, largely because of gendered expectations. Doubles also provide an escape for housewives in Seidelman's early films. Once activated by their doubles, housewives "persona swap" and transform into different versions of themselves. Reproductions of the final five pages of the original *She-Devil* script are included here to illustrate how Seidelman's changes to the original *She-Devil* ending, which closely adhered to the Fay Weldon novel with Ruth becoming Mary, show Ruth coming into her own on her terms. *Desperately Seeking Susan*'s urban/suburban tensions build on this idea while also reflecting sexual and racial anxieties around MTV during the time of Madonna's rise to stardom and release of the film. Additionally, Seidelman's insider knowledge of New York allows her to recreate the city, especially in her early films and *Sex and the City*, as a place of both big-city spectacle and small-town accessibility, allowing female audiences easy access to the fantasy of New York life. Yet, Seidelman's interest in playing with genre remains, as *Making Mr. Right* flips gendered expectations of science-fiction/romantic-comedy hybrids, allowing a career woman, Frankie Stone, to shape her perfect man. Further, career mobility, media influence and the domestic merge via Frankie's red convertible, producing a reconceptualized "home" space encapsulating the disjuncture between the freedoms promised by second-wave feminism and the demands of women's labor.

The third part of this collection, *Making Room*, looks at Seidelman's later films and television work when she begins more deliberately including under-represented populations into her productions. These pieces suggest an expanded focus on much younger and older characters, disabled characters, LGBTQIA+ characters, as well as characters of a myriad of races, ethnicities and religious backgrounds. In her work focused on young audiences – namely, four episodes of *The Electric Company* reboot that Seidelman directed and the short film *Cut in Half* – strong girl characters align with interests seen in Seidelman's earlier films. Dichotomies such as "good girl" and "bad girl" tropes, being seen versus heard, and even reality and belief inform how characters navigate their stories, while other binaries, including gendered notions of nurturers, are overturned. Multigenerational women and their histories are also interwoven in several of Seidelman's later television episodes and feature films. *Boynton Beach Club*, *Musical Chairs* and *The Hot Flashes* also all focus on people with "non-normate" bodies, using Rosemarie Garland-Thomson's term, who endeavor to navigate, if not overcome, limited and limiting cultural expectations of aging and/or disability in America. Characters in these films reclaim confidence, dignity and power; again, genre is key, as sports films and romantic comedies are infused with expansive discussions of gender, aging and disability, while suggesting that aging, disability and impairment are not one-size-fits-all. These shifts reflect Seidelman's awareness of audience, as she tapped into the need for expanded on-screen depictions and a new millennium of spectators calling for fresh stories.

While this collection endeavors to provide both breadth and depth for current and future Seidelman scholars, we hope that it will be the first of its kind, since there is much more to pursue in her rich and interesting oeuvre. For example, while several authors connect the use of voiceover in *The Dutch Master* to the *Sex and the City* pilot, Thompson's chapter on *Cut in Half* also examines the use of voiceover to illustrate friction between speaking and having a voice in that short. Like Teresa (Mira Sorvino) in *The Dutch Master*, who is subject to everyone else's words, Layla (Ajna Jai) in *Cut in Half* struggles to assert her decision about chemotherapy. Both want a say in their destinies, yet their communities – immediate and extended families and friends – instead assert what they think is best. Tension around when and how girls and women communicate, and are or are not recognized as doing so, exists throughout Seidelman's works, suggesting that female voices or desires often must be articulated in extremes to be heard at all. One might plaster her own photocopied image around a city, change herself to embody a she-devil, or disappear into a painting. Others speak via personal ads and newspaper columns or through diaries read by and for others. These ideas have yet to be fully explored. As such, just as Seidelman says that women's stories and communities fuel her creativity, we hope that this volume fuels additional scholarship around her work.

NOTES

1. Christina Lane, "Susan Seidelman's Contemporary Films: The Feminist Art of Self-Reinvention in a Changing Technological Landscape," in *Indie Reframed: Women's Filmmaking and Contemporary American Independent Cinema*, edited by Linda Badley, Claire Perkins and Michele Schreiber (Edinburgh: Edinburgh University Press, 2016), 74.
2. Judith M. Redding and Victoria A. Brownworth, *Film Fatales: Independent Women Directors* (Seattle: Seal Press, 1997), 150.
3. Ibid. p. 149.
4. Ibid. p. 151.
5. Ibid. p. 151–53.
6. Ibid. p. 153.
7. Christina Lane, *Feminist Hollywood: From Born in Flames to Point Break* (Detroit: Wayne State University Press, 2000), 64.
8. Lane, "Susan Seidelman's Contemporary Films," 73.
9. Ibid. p. 73.
10. Ibid. p. 73–79.
11. Ibid. p. 75–76.
12. Ibid. p. 77.
13. Ibid. p. 80.
14. Ibid. p. 76.

PART I

Building a Foundation

CHAPTER I

The Making of Ms. Right: Susan Seidelman and the Persistence of "Women's Films"

Maya Montañez Smukler

Susan Seidelman's formative years as a filmmaker started at a time when independent film production in the United States was expanding with the prominence of domestic film festivals and showcases including the Sundance Film Festival and the Independent Film Market, distributors such as Miramax and the ascendancy of home video distribution. Coming of age professionally in the early 1980s, Seidelman experienced the gradual impact of the feminist reform efforts that had taken place in 1970s Hollywood: during the 1970s the number of women directing narrative features increased, in small amounts, for the first time since the silent era; during the 1980s those numbers would continue to grow, albeit still gravely below male directors. As a graduate student at New York University in the mid-1970s, Seidelman made multiple award-winning short films. In 1982, her feature film debut, *Smithereens*, became the first independent American film to screen in competition at the Cannes Film Festival; it was picked up by the independent distributor New Line Cinema. In the early 1980s, Seidelman was signed to a three-picture deal by Orion Pictures where she directed the comedies *Desperately Seeking Susan* (1985), *Making Mr. Right* (1987) and *She-Devil* (1989); the feature *Cookie*, also released in 1989, she directed for Lorimar Film Entertainment Company. By the end of the decade, the filmmaker had made five female-driven comedies focused on a protagonist's search for her self-identity.

Seidelman's creative output during these years is situated within her origins as a New York-based independent filmmaker and her transition into commercial filmmaking, directing feature films for small but established companies. While Hollywood during these years is very much defined by the action-themed, blockbuster-franchise model that centered around a male star, the popularity of the era's woman's film, frequently produced as romantic comedies, provided a variation on 1980s gender politics. This chapter examines Seidelman's body of work during the 1980s within the scope of genre – the screwball comedy, the science fiction film, the soap opera, the romantic comedy, the woman's film – to consider the design of her female protagonists, as they are influenced by the punk girl narrative and the unruly woman archetype, who unravel the expectations of heterosexual romantic love to make way for female subjectivity and women's fantasies to flourish.

DOWNTOWN FILMMAKING AND PUNK GIRL AESTHETICS

Susan Seidelman was born in Philadelphia in 1952. When her father's hardware business began to grow, her family, including her two siblings, moved to the suburbs of Abington, Pennsylvania, while she was in grade school. As a teenager growing up in the 1960s, Seidelman was ensconced in the era's pop culture. She and her girlfriends would go to the local television station in Philadelphia and dance with other teens as part of the *Super Lou Show*. From a young age, Seidelman was interested in art, design and fashion:

> I was one of those kids that would buy things and then go to a Woolworth's and look in the button counter and sew buttons on to the top of my shirt or up the side of my socks or get a cording and put it around the hem of my skirt [. . .] it was sort of an artistic outlet.[1]

After graduating from high school, she applied to the Drexel Institute of Technology (now Drexel University) in Philadelphia where she initially studied fashion design, before realizing that she did not have the patience to sit at a sewing machine. She then stumbled across a film appreciation class in the Communications Department where she found her niche. After completing her degree, in 1974, Seidelman applied and was accepted to New York University's graduate film program. Out of the estimated thirty-five students enrolled in her class, five were women.[2]

Seidelman made two short films at NYU: *And You Act Like One, Too* (1976), about a discontented suburban mother and wife during the course of an afternoon, which received funding from the American Film Institute and the New York State Foundation of the Arts and was nominated for a Student Academy Award; and *Yours Truly, Andrea G. Stern* (1979), the story of a ten-year-old girl frustrated with her mother's live-in boyfriend. Both films screened at film festivals and were picked up by an educational distributor. Local independent filmmaking was thriving around her. Filmmakers such as Lizzie Borden, Betty Gordon, Amos Poe, Marisa Silver and those who had studied at New York

University – such as Joel Coen, Sarah Driver, Amy Heckerling, Jim Jarmusch and Spike Lee – were making films, including features. Some were using the landscape of New York City as an intricate part of their work; for many, as first-time filmmakers, a defining influence on their cinematic style. Because of the attention and success of her student films and influenced by her peers, Seidelman felt encouraged to pursue making a feature.

Having gone to school and still living in the East Village and Lower East Side, Seidelman would go to clubs such as Max's Kansas City and CBGB's. There she became aware of a cultural shift taking place in the neighborhood where the hippie counter-culture that defined so much of the 1960s and early 1970s was being replaced by the punk rock and new wave scene that was responding to the disrepair and neglect taking place in New York City. Of particular interest to her were the young women she noticed:

> I started to see girls like the character of Wren in *Smithereens*, groupies or people who just sort of wanted to be a part of that scene, and although I wasn't a groupie, I related to the idea of being a groupie in the sense that I was a girl from outside who came to New York to be part of what was happening in New York.[3]

From these observations, Seidelman began to imagine what would become *Smithereens*. *Smithereens* is the story of Wren (Susan Berman), a fast-talking (and walking) young woman who trolls the punk rock and new wave music scene of Manhattan's East Village, hoping to break in. She has no discernible talent except for her drive to be known and her limitless energy to self-promote. Her day job at a copy shop gives her access to a Xerox machine where she makes collaged pop art flyers with an image of herself and the tagline "Who is this?" These she then papers around the neighborhood and on the subway, using a bottle of dish soap as glue. *Smithereens* utilizes the familiar cinematic love triangle to move the characters around a very loose narrative structure. Wren is chasing Eric (Richard Hell), the handsome, scheming rock star, whose celebrity persona in the local scene she sees as an opportunity to attach her wannabe stardom. Paul (Brad Rinn), an aspiring portrait painter from Montana who lives out of his van, falls for Wren, but what he has to offer is romantic love and commitment, all of which is far too ordinary for her.

Missing the structure and community of graduate school, Seidelman took a screenwriting class at the New School, where she met Peter Askin, another aspiring filmmaker, and the two began work on the initial script of *Smithereens*. Eventually, she brought in another screenwriter, Ron Nyswaner, who was also just starting his career. During this time, Seidelman was engaged to be married. When the relationship broke apart and her grandmother died leaving her around $12,000 for the presumed wedding, Seidelman, using the inheritance, cobbled together an estimated $25,000 to start production.[4] The final budget came to $80,000. Much like the crew, the case members were newcomers to filmmaking. Susan Berman, an unknown actor at the time, was performing in an "off, off, off Broadway" production; Brad Rinn, Wren's wholesome, out-of-town suitor, was spotted by the film's assistant director sitting on a bench reading a book on acting. His inexperience landed him the role. Richard Hell – who was a fixture in the downtown scene and a member of the punk-new wave bands Neon Boys, Television, the Heartbreakers and the Voidoids – was cast as the dashing and conniving musician who seduces and scams Wren out of her own game.

The production started in the summer of 1980; during the first week, Berman, performing a scene on a fire escape, fell and broke her leg, and the shooting resumed, in stages, throughout the summer of 1981. The film's initial budget of $25,000 was stretched by the cast and crew's deferred salaries. Seidelman formed a limited partnership where she took small donations, while DuArt Film Laboratories, where the film was processed, deferred fifty percent of its fees. Economizing costs was further necessitated by the film's unorthodox production practices: official filming permits were forfeited by stealing shots on the subway, using a friend's apartment for a location and striking a deal with the owners of the Peppermint Lounge – Seidelman and crew would provide the band and 300 audience members, while the nightclub would make a profit from the bar tab.[5]

Jimmy Weaver categorizes *Smithereens* within the "female punk narrative" that emerged during the 1980s in American cinema.[6] These films often fall into two types of stories: a backstage musical about a female-centric band, such as *Ladies and Gentleman, the Fabulous Stains* (1982, dir. Lou Adler, Paramount Pictures), or a female protagonist who struggles because of her punk identity and is usually in conflict with a male love interest, as in the case of *Smithereens*. In the 1970s, New York City's punk rock culture opened up a creative space for women to rebel against the more strictly prescribed gender roles rampant in rock'n'roll. The female punk narrative explores social expectations, primarily structured around heterosexual relationships. These pairings function within punk culture under the influence of 1980s consumerism, at a time when second-wave feminism was giving way to third-wave feminism. By focusing on a young female protagonist who is economically disenfranchised and attempting to gain access to the male-dominated punk rock scene as a way to establish herself, these narratives emphasize the character's personal agency and reinforce her outsider status.[7]

At first glance, Wren may seem like a groupie: she is a young woman dressed for the scene in a mini skirt, fishnet stockings and red lipstick, loitering around the male band members and vying for their attention. But quickly it becomes apparent that, while her appearance – wardrobe, make-up, hair – is coded as traditionally feminine, she is too lanky and thin to be a conventionally sexy woman; she walks and talks too fast to be seductive; and she talks too much, and only about herself, to be an adoring fan. There is no question that Wren is annoying, rude, manipulative and narcissistic, but she is not entirely unlikeable. As Seidelman described her heroine, "[Wren is] like a little kid who's selfish. You know, they're not [a] bad, calculating person. It's just that they're so young and they're just going for it, in a confused kind of way."[8] The character's gutsy manner embodies punk rock values that rally against authority and the constrictions inherent in established social systems, and her status as a loner gives her an aura of bravery. Paul is drawn to Wren's confidence, but he wants to soften it with domestic love by living together in his van and planning an escape from New York City to the quiet of New Hampshire. To which Wren quips, "I don't even like trees." Eric sees something of himself in the young woman and her quest for fame at any cost; equally if not more self-centered, the musician is interested in what Wren can do for him.

As she finished editing the film, Seidelman had no plan for what the next steps were in preparing for a theatrical release or how to secure distribution. She sent letters to some festivals and eventually received a response from the Cannes Film Festival, letting her know that representatives would be screening films in New York City and that they were interested in seeing her work. Seidelman dropped off her newly made (and only) answer print of the film and wondered whether she would ever see it again. Soon after, Pierre-Henri Deleau, head of the Director's Fortnight, called to meet for breakfast where he explained to her the necessary costs of taking a film on the festival circuit to cover marketing and publicity materials and the expense of blowing her 16mm print up to 35mm. The filmmaker had access to none of the required funds. Sitting at the next table were Joy Pereths and Jonathan Olesberg, film-sales representatives, who overheard the conversation and were interested. Their company, Affinity Enterprises, took on the film, which was accepted into the Director's Fortnight. Gilles Jacob, the president of Cannes, called Seidelman and asked her if she would consider moving the film into the main competition where it became the first American independent film to be showcased in that event; Seidelman was the only woman director that year included in that category. The film's reception at Cannes was positive and encouraging, and *Smithereens* was picked up for distribution by New Line Cinema.[9]

In addition to her acute perceptions of New York City's emerging cultural trends and artistic movements, filtered through a generational feminist lens, Seidelman's extraordinary experience with the Cannes Film Festival was reflective of the changing circumstances taking place for independent filmmaking in the United States in the early 1980s. With the expansion of the home video market and cable television, the life of a film – especially a small, niche title such as *Smithereens* – had increased. Where previously theatrical distribution and then a possible television broadcast were the primary options for a film, now ancillary markets focused on home video and pay-cable opened up new exhibition sites, resulting in heightened demand for all kinds of content.[10] In the late 1970s, the establishment of a marketplace for American independent film began with film festivals such as the Telluride Film Festival (established 1974) and the US Film Festival (established 1978), which the Sundance Institute (established 1980) oversaw and renamed in 1985, and the non-profit organization, the Independent Feature Project (established 1979). In the 1980s, companies such as New Line Cinema (established 1967), Orion Pictures (established 1978) and Miramax Films (established 1979) – eventually described as "mini-majors" or "major-independents" to reflect their stature in the independent community and their subordination within the larger corporate infrastructure – would begin exploiting these distribution and production options and were instrumental in what Yannis Tzioumakis describes as the institutionalization of American independent cinema.[11]

The positive reception of *Smithereens* created opportunities for Seidelman, and she weighed her options carefully in considering what might be her independent-to-Hollywood crossover project. The pressure for a women director making her second feature was enormous, and Seidelman was fully aware of Hollywood's double-standard in giving male directors more chances to fail and succeed. "Not every movie has to be a hit for a director to keep working," she told the *Los Angeles Times* during the release of *Desperately Seeking Susan* in 1985, "but it seemed like with women, the executives said, 'Well, we gave her a shot, she can't direct – the movie wasn't a huge success'."[12] *Desperately Seeking Susan* is examined in detail in other chapters of this collection. My discussion of the film here is brief and only to describe Seidelman's shift from do-it-yourself independent filmmaking to small, but substantially more expensive commercial productions.

After seeing *Smithereens*, producers Sarah Pillsbury and Midge Sanford sent Leora Barish's script for *Desperately Seeking Susan* to Seidelman, who was drawn to a story about two women: "I liked the idea of a woman becoming obsessed with another woman. We've seen enough movies about guys growing up, and it's about time to see the other side."[13] Pillsbury and Sanford had formed their business partnership in 1980, and *Desperately Seeking Susan* would be the first film that the team produced, but it would take the pair some time to secure financing. A film written, produced and directed by women, starring two women, was a rare package. "All over town women executives were fans of it," said Pillsbury, describing their initial struggle to get the film made. "And it stopped right there. We realized you need a man to say yes."[14] Eventually, Barbara Boyle, who was senior vice president of worldwide production for Orion Pictures at the time, had seen *Smithereens* and liked it. Boyle, who was actively trying to hire women directors, was able to get her boss, Mike Medavoy, to say "yes."[15]

The experience of making *Desperately Seeking Susan* for Orion Pictures was a positive one for Seidelman, and she has consistently, over the years, described her creative partnership with the company in these terms. It was extremely rare for a woman director at that time to sign a multi-picture deal, and even more unusual for her to complete all of the projects with the studio or production company. Orion Pictures, a new company that was not part of a conglomerate trying to compete with larger studios, needed content, and films with small budgets were a risk worth taking. *Desperately Seeking Susan* was made for five million dollars. Furthermore, Orion, which had been founded in 1978 by former executives at United Artists, a studio known for its "hands-off" policy in working with filmmakers, strove to duplicate that philosophy by supporting its directors' creative visions.[16] It is within this industry setting, as well as the popular discourse around the rise of the 1980s career woman on a crash course with modern romance, that Seidelman embarked on her next four films.

THE UNRULY WOMEN OF THE 1980S

Without minimizing Hollywood's rampant sexism during the 1980s, a few women characters during the decade experienced some meaningful representation in designated genres, specifically the romantic comedy and the romantic/erotic thriller. What made these genre cycles notable was their focus on contemporary gender politics specific to a female protagonist who is forced to juggle her professional and personal lives that are in competition with each other. These films exist in almost exclusively white, heterosexual narratives that take place in middle- and upper-middle-class socioeconomic brackets. These characters have lived through the women's movement of the 1970s and are struggling to reap second-wave feminism's achievements in the cut-throat capitalist marketplace of the 1980s. Many of these films were critically acclaimed, and the majority of them were made with studio budgets and casts featuring established stars – women and men – by predominately male directors. For example, the 1986 romantic comedy *She's Gotta Have It* was one of the few independent films in this genre cycle, and with an all-Black cast and Black filmmaker, Spike Lee; in 1987, *Broadcast News*, *Moonstruck*, *Baby Boom* and the erotic thriller *Fatal Attraction* were released, followed by more high-profile comedies including *Working Girl* (1988) and *When Harry Met Sally* (1989).[17]

In many ways, Seidelman's work during the 1980s finds affinity with the romantic comedy-career woman genre. As the characters in her films journey towards self-discovery and a new-found autonomy, some are more concerned with their place in the professional world (*Making Mr. Right*, *She-Devil* and in *Cookie* the business of gangsters), while others are focused on status and style more so than on work ethic (*Smithereens*, *Desperately Seeking Susan*). While all of her films are comedies and most have a romantic component, Seidelman detours from the genre's focus on coupling as the primary resolution for narrative conflict and instead looks to the disruptive transgressions of her female protagonists who consider conventional romance secondary to pursuing ambiguous endings.

The leading themes in Seidelman's work during the 1980s are a female protagonist's search for independence, usually from the smothering expectations of family, the disappointment that she experiences in her attempt at heterosexual romance and the cultural limitations of her physical environment usually framed within the schism between suburbia and the big city, as well as the character's ability to navigate a path of self-discovery between the two. As a teenager, Seidelman was already drawn to this plot twist as she watched Marlo Thomas in the television show *That Girl* (1966–71) and Audrey Hepburn in *Breakfast at Tiffany's* (1961): "I think the reason so many women of my generation and later generations related to [*Breakfast at Tiffany's*]," the filmmaker reflected decades later on those early influences, "is because it's that quintessential story of the girl from nowhere who goes to the city and reinvents who she is and lives out a life she couldn't have had back where she came from."[18]

The restless searching of Seidelman's protagonists draws on Kathleen Rowe Karlyn's theory of the "unruly woman" in cinema, as a character that unsettles social hierarchies by being "too fat, too funny, too noisy, too old, too rebellious."[19] The unruly woman laughs and laughs loudly, disrupting cultural norms associated with women and comedy that deny female subjectivity, for both the female character and the female spectator. The unruly woman's laugh can be an expression of anger or happiness; it is an expression and assertion of female desire that may be sexual, emotional and vengeful. The unruly woman's ability to deliver and respond to a joke makes her a visible spectacle and places her in direct confrontation with the male gaze. The unruly woman is traced to genres historically targeted to female audiences, specifically two types of woman's film: the melodrama, where female desire is mostly experienced in women's suffering, and the romantic comedy, where female transgression is celebrated in joyous heterosexual chaos.[20]

The way in which the unruly woman performs in certain kinds of films opens up opportunities for her to push against gender and genre expectations. In many ways the punk girl narrative of *Smithereens* finds kinship with the unruly woman. Wren is noisy, excessively chatty, and while her body type is slim and petite, almost adolescent, she takes up considerable space with her constant disregard for boundaries by showing up uninvited to Eric's loft, moving into Paul's van and cutting the security line at the Peppermint Lounge with a sense of entitlement that not even the men in front of the club would consider. Like Wren, Susan in *Desperately Seeking Susan* has no regard for boundaries. She steals and takes advantage of her friends (also like Wren); she goes through Roberta's closet and reads her diary. This film redresses the classic screwball comedy of the 1930s and 1940s as a female buddy film where Roberta's personal growth and the platonic obsession for another woman take the place of heterosexual romance. Roberta's unruliness is a little softer as she trips and fumbles, accidentally crashing into places uninvited before deciding that is where she would like to be. Susan does not have to talk as much as Wren; her sexual confidence simultaneously engages and confronts the male gaze as she actively demands to be looked at, in the way in which she dresses, the way in which she walks down the street or across a dance floor, but whether she returns the gaze is entirely on her terms. In *Making Mr. Right* and *She-Devil*, Seidelman blends elements of the soap opera – its emotional excess conveyed through over-the-top acting styles, a strong musical soundtrack, a saturated visual style and multiple overlapping storylines – with the science fiction genre in the former and the revenge film in the latter, to create fantasy-like settings in which the unruly antics of the films' women have full range.

THE REVENGE FILM: ROMANTIC NIGHTMARES AND SHE-DEVIL FANTASIES

She-Devil, based on the book *The Life and Loves of a She-Devil* (1983) by Fay Weldon, was Seidelman's third and final film with Orion Pictures. The film overlaps multiple genres – the marriage comedy, the soap opera, the woman's film – to produce a feminist revenge satire. Ruth (Roseanne Barr) and Robert Patchett (Ed Begley Jr) are an average middle-class married couple with two children, a dog and a house in the suburbs. When Robert, a mid-level accountant, leaves Ruth for the successful and glamorous romance novelist Mary Fisher (Meryl Streep), Ruth plots her revenge on husband and mistress. Seidelman makes use of dueling protagonists, a relationship she often employs, to create narrative tension and character arcs. In *Desperately Seeking Susan*, amnesia is the device that drives the screwball plot and confuses Roberta and Susan's identities, thus giving Roberta the chance to develop her sense of self. In *Making Mr. Right*, Dr. Peters and his android creation Ulysses look identical, which provides another set of screwball antics, while also presenting Frankie with a relationship dilemma about two opposing kinds of men. *She-Devil* brings Ruth and Mary together as opposite in competition – Ruth as the ordinary woman, a downtrodden mother and housewife burnt out by the doldrums of domesticity, who eats donuts in bed while reading romance novels, versus Mary, who has fashioned a lifestyle and persona that mirrors the fantasy of one of her novels, filled with candle light and bubble baths in the many rooms of her pink mansion; Mary is slim and blonde and manicured, while Ruth is overweight, a brunette and disheveled.

Casting was crucial in creating an antagonistic juxtaposition between the female roles. Meryl Streep and Seidelman shared an agent, giving the filmmaker and star access to one another. Streep, who had been nominated for seven Academy Awards, two of which she had won for dramatic roles, would play Mary Fisher as one of her early slapstick comedy endeavors. The actress would bring an added dimension of surprise and shock to the physical humor exhibited by her character by playing against type. In contrast, the casting of Roseanne Barr was on-point for the character of Ruth. Barr, at the time, was known for her stand-up comedy that tore up any idealized notions of housewifery, while simultaneously celebrating mothers and wives as "domestic goddesses." Her sitcom *Roseanne* (1988–97, 2018), the study of a working-class American family praised for its realism, was in its second season and receiving outstanding ratings. During these years, the performer challenged expectations around gender, class and physical appearance, and she had an ample number of fans who applauded her abrasive, crass, un-self-conscious and confident style, as she had detractors who were appalled by it. *She-Devil* would be Barr's first screen appearance, and she brought to the role an authenticity, based on her star persona and success as a comedian, in her portrayal of the disgruntled and neglected wife, mother and woman with the capacity to plot her husband's downfall.

In this film, the unruly woman emerges through the pairing with her rival. Ruth starts off as an agreeable wife. When her husband's infidelity is exposed and he accuses her of not being a woman, but a she-devil, the sky opens up with lightening, and Ruth screams in rage over a dramatic musical soundtrack. She blows up her family's house in an act of destruction and liberation and drops off the children, unannounced, at Mary's fairy-tale mansion, interrupting her and Robert embracing in a pink bubble bath. "I don't know where [I'm going], I guess into my future," she tells Robert. "I've been sorry my whole life." Disappointment and rage sets Ruth free from the oppressive day-to-day as mother and wife. A newfound clarity not only starts her on a revenge plot to destroy Robert, but it leads her to seek out other neglected women, whom she encourages to stuff their faces with cream-filled pastries and laugh out loud.

In the course of Ruth's revenge, Mary undergoes a transformation as profound as her nemesis, which unleashes her own unruly woman. Mary unravels under the pressures of inadvertent motherhood, responsibilities that she is unprepared for and thus overwhelmed by, as they wreak havoc on her fantasy world. When in control, Mary speaks in a breathy whisper and is poised, without a hair or nail out of place. Under pressure, Mary screams and cries; she breaks the record player, slaps the children and sends them to their room. Entirely out of her element and at an emotional breaking point, she even attempts to do laundry. Her outbursts are rageful, physical, sloppy and loud; they are not romantic, and they are not fantasy-making but rather express the nightmare of domesticity.

By the end of the film, both women are changed, inside and out. Ruth, with the assistance of Robert's latest mistress, uncovers her husband's financial schemes and helps send him to prison. Ruth is a successful businesswoman, committed to making professional opportunities for "unloved and unwanted" women, like she herself once was. Seidelman derails the common use of the makeover, especially as a device to tame an unruly woman for the male gaze and has Ruth's appearance change gradually and without much fanfare. Gone are her shapeless floral print dresses, replaced now by a power suit – in white or pink – and the oversized mole on her upper lip, used to mark her as a rebellious woman, is removed, but without a storyline. Mary is also different: exposed to homemaking, she focuses her next novel on the domestic. *Love in the Rinse-Cycle* is a flop, but she has discovered some depth in her desire to write about women's experiences. Her next book, a "docu-novel" about trust and betrayal, is a departure from the romance novel and becomes a success. She is still precious and breathy and on the lookout for male attention, but her color palette has shifted to dark blue and black, and her hair is pulled back, making her less princess-like and more professorial.

Seidelman filed *She-Devil* right alongside its contemporaries in the 1980s woman's film genre, describing the film, at the time of its release, as "a sort of comic version of 'Fatal Attraction,' told as a fable, but there's a core of truth to it."[21] *She-Devil*, a social satire and campy comedy, was far less dire in its message about working women in America (the film makes a concerted effort to represent them in a positive light), and while the unfaithful husband is punished for his betrayal, his lessons are learned by losing both Ruth and Mary and serving time in prison. In dialogue, Christina Lane and Seidelman make a pitch to reconsider *She-Devil*, which was not an enormous success, and to consider how the film was the precursor to *First Wives Club* (1996), a comedy about wives who seek revenge on their husbands who left them for younger women. In retrospect, Seidelman felt that the latter film, which was a box-office hit, was more "palatable" to audiences in 1996 and that "*She-Devil* was extreme to make a point. The film was not simply exaggerated for the sake of humor; the goal was to provide a feminist fable."[22]

SCIENCE FICTION MAKES OVER MR. RIGHT

In *Making Mr. Right*, Seidelman brings together the career woman-romantic comedy and the science fiction film to tell a fable about heterosexual love and sex in the 1980s. Frankie Stone (Ann Magnuson), a successful public relations executive, epitomizes the 1980s cinematic working woman. Always in a rush, Frankie gets dressed on the way to work and applies make-up while stopped at a traffic light; her fashion sense is impeccable, as are her professional skills; she wears her massive client Rolex as a bracelet, showing how the working woman is never off the clock. Moreover, her ability to multitask is impressive: in the morning she breaks up with her philandering boyfriend and then goes to work where she lands the big account with ease. When the all-male crew of engineers from Chemtec Laboratories hire her to rebrand their newest invention, the Ulysses (John Malkovich) android, Frankie's professional skills collide with contemporary gender politics.

As Frankie works to naturalize Ulysses' mechanical origins, by teaching him to be a better human, it is the bot's inventor who presents the bigger challenge to her social science experiment. Dr. Jeff Peters (also played by John Malkovich), Ulysses' creator, is a socially awkward misogynist who rages against Frankie's approach to humanizing the robot. "That woman, what has she been teaching you?" Dr. Peters barks when Ulysses asks if love and sex are the same thing. "Remember," commands the doctor, "you are much more advanced than that woman will ever be. . . she lives in an emotional swamp, but then so do most people!" But Ulysses is interested in life's burning questions about what it is like to be in love and whether he is capable of having children.

Ulysses' human transformation is dependent on his exposure to the feminized marketplace: the bot watches daytime talk shows, rummages through Frankie's purse only to discover her birth control, lipstick and self-help books. When the android, a curious and fast learner, breaks out of the lab and ends up at the mall, the film makes a feminist intervention into the romantic comedy by refashioning the makeover scene, so often used to demonstrate the female protagonist's transformation, on the male character. At a man's dress shop, Ulysses accidentally gets fitted for a tuxedo. In his first set of clothes outside of the laboratory's jumpsuit, he learns that his penis is impressive and that he looks good in a suit. Moreover, he is not only introduced to the concept of a wedding, but also that Frankie needs a date to her sister's upcoming nuptials. Eventually, following confusion caused by the mistaken identities of Dr. Peters and Ulysses, as well as a slapstick fight scene at the wedding, Dr. Peters takes Ulysses' place on the spaceship, and the android unites with Frankie for a happy, romantic ending.

In *Making Mr. Right*, Seidelman uses the conventions of the science fiction film to create a fantasy reality where a robot competes with a human and wins. The 1960s animated television show *The Jetsons* (1962–63) was the filmmaker's inspiration for the film's visual style, a colorful, sometimes cartoonish production design, underscored by the playful nostalgia of the story's setting amongst the pastel palette and Art Deco architecture of Miami. "I wanted 'Making Mr. Right' to be the present but from the p.o.v. of 1962," explained Seidelman of her stylistic choice and her "wink" towards the low-budget, B science fiction films of the 1950s and 1960s, instead of making a film with the CGI technology available in 1987. The comic irony is that a male android has the capability and desire to learn what it is to be human – to love – and becomes a better lover, friend, listener and wedding date than any human man; in turn, his human creator is able to achieve his dream of traveling into deep space, alone, for seven years.

For exactly these reasons, critics did not quite take to *Making Mr. Right*'s final reconciliation between a human-android. Even the few romantic comedies of the decade where the couple failed to come together in the end (for instance, *She's Gotta Have It, Broadcast News*), the character flaws had clearly been explored in human terms. Charles Champlin of the *Los Angeles Times* found *Making Mr. Right*'s message bleak in what he interpreted as no human man being capable of a meaningful relationship and human women being shallow. "It does make for a chilly film, when only an android is capable of tenderness," lamented the critic.[23] Julie Salamon, writing for the *Wall Street Journal*, gave the character of Frankie rave reviews, gushing that "[i]f Mr. Right isn't all he is cracked up to be, his girlfriend is worth a detour all by herself." But Salamon also felt that Frankie and Ulysses, as the final couple, were not plausible, and she was adamant that "you never for a minute believe that this goofy bag of motor parts could be anyone's dream man."[24]

Even Seidelman described *Making Mr. Right* as a failure, citing similar flaws as the critics did in how the film diverted from genre expectation. "Frankie is potentially a great character," she reflected.

> I might have spent more time with her problems. When I saw "Broadcast News," I really liked the Holly Hunter character and they could have been similar. There is something intriguing about a work-obsessed woman in her 30s whose professional life is sort of together but whose personal life is a mess [. . .]. Perhaps if the film spent more time on the "Pygmalion" aspect – what does a woman want from a man in the 80s? – and less on the farce, it would have been a lot more interesting.[25]

However, Frankie's choice to fall for Ulysses is a bold solution to romantic comedies' timeless problem: the incompatibility of women and men. If this career woman's problem is her struggle to find respectful romantic love, then only in the world of science fiction can the insolvable battle of the (human) sexes be skipped over for something with an enormous mechanical heart.

THE FINAL FRAME

In 1989, Seidelman had two movies in theaters, *She-Devil* and *Cookie*, a gangster film told from the perspective of a teenage girl. Cookie (Emily Lloyd) is raised by her single mother, Lenore (Dianne Wiest), the long-suffering mistress of mob boss Dino Capisco (Peter Falk), who has been incarcerated for all of his daughter's life. When Dino is released from prison, Cookie is made to work for the family business, and father and daughter meet their match in a battle of the most stubborn wills: mobster vs teen girl.

Seidelman describes *Cookie* as an "orphan" film: it was produced by Lorimar Film Entertainment and eventually released by Warner Bros. who inherited the project as part of the companies' merger with each other. Because *Cookie* did not originate with Warner Bros., the company did not prioritize the film's distribution plan, dampening its full potential at the box office.[26] While the film may have suffered something in its release, it succeeds in how Seidelman, as she had done with her subsequent movies, takes a familiar genre, the gangster film, and breaks apart its conventions, primarily by upsetting gender expectations and introducing a prominent young female character into the world of middle-aged men. "'Cookie' appealed to me because it's a gangster film told from a girl's point of view," Seidelman explained around the time of the film's release. "Actually, it's a father-daughter story."[27] The film plays with duality, but unlike the filmmaker's previous work, the story focused on the characters' morality as sympathetic anti-heroes spending considerable time occupied with a familiar gangster narrative: a violent power play between mob bosses that involves a complex sting operation intact with car bombs, kidnapping and the domestic reform of the male outlaw.

However, at the film's center is what by the late 1980s had become a familiar Seidelman protagonist: the unruly woman. Cookie has the spunk and rebellious nature of Wren: she is opinionated, meddlesome and talks the most and loudest in any group. Her style is a mix of punk, new wave and mall rat fashion that works against long-standing expectations of young women's appearances, while retaining some traditionally coded feminine embellishments. Cookie is a scrappy rebel dressed in black with a splash of red lipstick and wears a jacket adorned with pins and tags that make her a direct descendent of Susan; her pink Le Clic disc camera is a constant accessory showing off this teen girl's inquisitive and bold nature, just like Frankie's oversized Rolodex marked her as an accomplished female professional.

Consumer-oriented technology and hardware are important resources and accessories to Seidelman's 1980s unruly women. Wren uses the Xerox machine as her means to self-promote; Wren, and especially Susan, constantly document themselves with a Polaroid camera, an inexpensive tool that feeds the characters' narcissism by producing rapid images of themselves for instantaneous self-admiration. Cookie, who is as disobedient as her cinematic predecessors in style and manners, but not as obsessed with self-glorification or vanity, buys a camera in bubble gum pink for ten dollars at the flea market, mostly to document her new mob life and family. The camera is small and easily accessible in her coat pocket, just like a make-up compact. Susan carries with her a portable radio, a necessary accessory for a party girl on the lam; and Mary talks on a pink wireless phone, a literal extension of her romance novel house, just before unravelling under the noise and distraction of her new life as a housewife, and almost destroys Robert's teen daughter's blasting pink radio. These devices are affordable, dispensable and easily forgotten or replaced by flaky girls and women shopping for the next best model.

Feminized pop culture – gossip magazines, television soap operas, the romance novel and newspaper personal ads – are paramount to Seidelman. The filmmaker mines these genres and formats in satirical ways, playing with their established high-stakes themes of romance, longing and lust, reinforced by a distinct visual style of female and feminine excess. Her protagonists with pleasure consume these media texts that are inexpensive in market cost and considered intellectually cheap because of their association with female audiences whose presumed tastes for devalued themes of romance and comedy are considered low-brow. In *Smithereens*, Wren and her co-worker read *Cosmopolitan* and *Those Who Died Young*, a fan magazine the cover of which features Jimi Hendrix, Marilyn Monroe and James Dean. In *Making Mr. Right*, Trish (Glenne Headly), Frankie's cousin, has taken refuge at her apartment after breaking up with an adulterous husband who is a daytime soap opera star. The two women gawk over the sensationalized headlines of a gossip magazine and watch *New Jersey*, Seidelman's camp mock soap opera, to track the dishonored spouse. Roberta, in *Desperately Seeking Susan*, moons over the newspaper personal ads where she follows star-crossed lovers, Susan and Jim, circling with a heart the couple's messages to each other. In *She-Devil*, Ruth devours donuts and Mary Fisher romance novels, together in bed. Her husband Robert is equally consumed by the romance novel fantasies as he falls fast for Mary seduced by her wealth and fame served to him with pink champagne. Lenore and Cookie's small, rented apartment is a working-class version of Mary's mansion, drenched in a feminized decorum of kitschy pink glitter and cream-puff-colored furniture and knickknacks. Through their enjoyment and purchase power (for Wren, as shoplifter), these characters use their knowledge as fans to critique, ridicule and reappropriate the styles and messages manufactured for them as women in acts of disorderly self-determination.

"The '80s are so conservative," observed Seidelman at the time of *She-Devil*'s release:

> I hope the '90s will bring back more liberal attitudes, more guts! These days, kids want to be stockbrokers; they don't rebel. But I believe rebellion is healthy. I hope my child will have a real healthy dose of that![28]

But it was within Hollywood's conservative approach to storytelling during the 1980s, so prevalent in popular genres, that Seidelman created a space to establish her style. Working within the steadfast conventions of comedy – romantic and buddy pictures – the filmmaker followed some rules as a way to break others. Historically, these kinds of genre films promise resolution by the movie's end with a proclivity towards the male hero or the male-female couple, and so often women characters have struggled under these patriarchal traditions to be the center of a film, let alone control the ending on their own shaky terms. In *Making Mr. Right*, Frankie rewrites cinematic love by choosing the android man, but even more reckless are the film's final images of Dr. Peters, the human man, disappearing into space's endless horizon, alone. In her four other films, Seidelman makes use of the freeze frame, holding the camera on the female protagonist in the film's final image. Wren, continuously on the go in *Smithereens*, is forced by the frame to stop and contemplate. Susan and Roberta, who are *Desperately Seeking Susan*'s true star-crossed lovers, are united, finally. At the end of *She-Devil*, Ruth, wearing a white power suit and having succeeded at revenge and self-actualization, struts down a busy Manhattan sidewalk absorbed into a sea of other professional women all wearing red. Cookie, attending a mob boss's funeral in the rain, is poised at the end of the film, on the brink of inheriting status; she stands out with a pink umbrella in a crowd of mourners in black when she turns and looks directly into the camera. By freezing in cinematic time these restless spirits, Susan Seidelman resists narrative closure and resolution to the women's antics, and in doing so, the filmmaker asserts her own independent and unruly tendencies in the production of 1980s woman's pictures.

NOTES

1. Susan Seidelman, interview by Maya Montañez Smukler, *Academy of Motion Picture Arts and Sciences: Visual History*, 22 September 2016.
2. Seidelman, interview by Montañez Smukler.
3. Ibid.
4. Ibid.
5. Richard Patterson, "An Interview with Susan Seidelman on the Making of *Smithereens*," *American Cinematographer*, 64, no. 5 (May 1983), 70.
6. Jimmy Weaver, "Making a Scene: The Female Punk Narrative in Lou Adler's *Ladies and Gentlemen, The Fabulous Stains* and Susan Seidelman's *Smithereens*," *Punk & Post-Punk*, 2, no. 2 (2013), 179–95.
7. As often happens, film theory and film practice are not in agreement. At the time of *Smithereen*'s release, Seidelman denied the film's punk sensibility. "It's not really a punk film. In fact, I think people who go expecting to see a "punk film" will be greatly disappointed. To me, it's a character study, a film about relationships, about people who are blinded by what glitters. She could have been a beatnik in the '50s or a hippie in the '60s, or she could have lived in Berlin in the '20s. Essentially it's about an outsider who's attracted to what she thinks is glamorous – her twisted version of the American Dream." Steven X. Rea, "Susan Seidelman's Not Punk," *Philadelphia Inquirer*, 8 May 1983.
8. Patterson, "An Interview with Susan Seidelman on the Making of *Smithereens*," 68.
9. For *Smithereen*'s acceptance to Cannes and distribution history, see Seidelman, interview with Montañez Smukler; Lewis Beale, "Film Maker Star in Her Own Dream," *Los Angeles Time*, 9 January 1983; *Smithereens*, DVD commentary.

10. Yannis Tzioumakis, *American Independent Cinema* (Edinburgh: Edinburgh University Press, 2006), 203–4.
11. Ibid. p. 205–6.
12. Deborah Caulfield, "Film Maker, Not a Deal Maker," *Los Angeles Times*, 2 April 1985.
13. Dan Yakir, "Celine and Julie Golightly," *Film Comment* 21, no. 3 (May/Jun 1985), 20.
14. Aljean Harmetz, "2 Women Succeed as Producers, but Easy Street is Down the Road," *The New York Times*, 14 September 1988.
15. Seidelman, interview with Montañez Smukler; Janis Cole and Holly Dale, *Calling the Shots: Profiles of Women Filmmakers* (Kingston: Quarry Press, 1993), 194.
16. Yannis Tzioumakis, "Major Status, Independent Spirit," *New Review of Film and Television Studies*, 2, no. 1 (2004), 89. For additional history of Orion, see Yannis Tzioumakis, *American Independent Cinema*.
17. For observations in the press on the 1980s career woman in film, see Aljean Harmetz, "Behind Five Top Films, Five Obsessions," *Los Angeles Times*, 10 April 1988; Constance Rosenblum, "Drop-Dead Clothes Make the Working Woman," *The New York Times*, 26 February 1989.
18. Seidelman, interview with Montañez Smukler.
19. Kathleen Rowe, *The Unruly Woman: Gender and the Genres of Laughter* (Austin: University of Texas, 1995), 19.
20. Rowe, *The Unruly Woman*, 96–97.
21. Dan Yakir, "Susan Seidelman Preaches Rebellion," *Boston Globe*, 3 December 1989.
22. Christina Lane, *Feminist Hollywood: From Born in Flames to Point Break* (Detroit: Wayne State University Press, 2000), 60.
23. Charles Champlin, "Critic at Large: Anything Wrong With 'Mr. Right'?" *Los Angeles Times*, 18 April 1987.
24. Julie Salamon, "On Film: Love and the Single Android," *Wall Street Journal*, 9 April 1987.
25. Myra Forsberg, "Susan Seidelman's Recipe for 'Cookie'," *The New York Times*, 29 May 1988.
26. Seidelman, interview with Montañez Smukler.
27. Forsberg, "Susan Seidelman's Recipe."
28. Yakir, "Susan Seidelman Preaches Rebellion."

CHAPTER 2

Susan Seidelman's *Sex and the City*: TV Authorship and Feminist Possibility

Elizabeth Alsop

A bored, suburban housewife makes a secret trip to New York City, where she adopts the persona of a downtown party girl. That, in a nutshell, describes the plot of Susan Seidelman's breakthrough film, *Desperately Seeking Susan* (1985). But it could just as accurately summarize events in "The Baby Shower," the tenth episode of *Sex and the City*, which, as it happens, was also directed by Seidelman, just over ten years later, one of three episodes she helmed for the HBO series' first season.

What, if anything, should be made of the apparent parallelism between these two Seidelman-directed media texts – the feature film and the half-hour television show? On the one hand, it might be easiest to frame the congruity as mere coincidence, a chance correspondence in a medium in which storyline is far more likely to be determined by writers and producers than by directors-for-hire, who may supervise discrete episodes but generally have little say in a series' ongoing development.[1] At the same time, cinephiles might be motivated to discern in these thematic continuities evidence of Seidelman's authorship, her capacity to "transcend" industrial constraints in the manner of canonical (male) auteurs and imbue this episode with her own distinct sensibility. Then again, even if one were disposed to see the episode as proof of Seidelman's agency, how would this conclusion square with feminist film criticism's long-standing opposition to auteurism as a theoretical framework, which derives from the conviction that auteurist approaches are "incorrigibly compromised," given their role in perpetuating a disproportionately male status quo?[2] Or, as Jessica Ford has succinctly described the problem, "[t]o absorb women directors into a discourse of autuerism is to ignore the embedded problems with this discourse."[3]

This chapter will explore the questions raised by this apparent instance of overlap within Seidelman's creative corpus, one of many resonances linking *Sex and the City* to the director's filmography. In the process, it will also reconsider inherited frameworks of moving-image authorship, which have not been optimized to recognize filmmaker's contributions across mediums and within production contexts, such as that of serial television, in which directors do not necessarily enjoy full (or even substantial) creative control. That female filmmakers – and particularly "commercially minded feminist media-makers" such as Seidelman[4] – have arguably been over-represented in such contexts makes the stakes of this interrogation into auteurism's limitations at once theoretical and political, in as much as it bears on the ways in which women's contributions to popular media have been counted – or not.[5]

This chapter, then, aims not only to provide a fuller account of Seidelman's contributions to *Sex and the City*, a series which, as Isabel Pinedo reminds us, was "as foundational to the template HBO set"[6] as more celebrated male-driven series like *The Sopranos*.[7] It will also consider the consequences of failing to recognize women directors' work across the distinct yet historically interrelated contexts of feature filmmaking and serial television production. Thus, even as I make the case for the singularity of Seidelman's achievements – in keeping with the aims of this volume, and the ambition of the *ReFocus* series generally – I will suggest that she is also representative, both in terms of her career trajectory and as the object of reflexive assumptions about commercial television that have served to minimize the visibility of women's achievements in moving-image media.[8] Seidelman, after all, is far from the only female filmmaker of her era to have also worked in TV, whether by choice or necessity. Directors including Amy Heckerling, Claudia Weil, Joan Tewkesbury, Nancy Savoca, Joan Micklin Silver and Julie Dash all share the experience of having made more or less temporary detours into directing television episodes, made-for-TV movies, or both, often after enjoying a degree of commercial and critical success as feature filmmakers, however brief. Some, including Seidelman and Heckerling, have recently been granted some benefits of auteur status – the release of their debut films by the Criterion Collection, for instance, or edited volumes devoted to their work. Yet, it remains the case that female directors committed to mainstream filmmaking have too often been subjected to a double bind: poorly served both by the inherited auteurist frameworks of film studies, which have disproportionately valorized women's contributions to art and experimental rather than commercial cinema,[9] and by television's understandable suspicion of authorship[10] and the industry's deprecation of directors as a creative force.[11]

In place of these polarized alternatives, then, I would like to propose a more flexible, inclusive and self-consciously feminist approach to television authorship and to recognizing where and how it has "shown up" in the production contexts in which commercially inclined female directors such as Seidelman have often found themselves. In such situations, it is reasonable to expect that creative agency may surface incompletely or intermittently, or through what Christina Lane calls "small practices" or "micro-strategies."[12] While Lane uses these phrases specifically to describe Seidelman's do-it-yourself tactics for navigating a rapidly changing digital landscape in the latter part of her career, the terms are also useful for conceptualizing methods employed by filmmakers working within the constraints of serial television. Similarly, if the more conventional auteurist paradigm presumes an agonistic relationship between a director's vision and generic structures – the conception of "genre as cramping auteurist style," to use Jane Gaines' phrase[13] – a more deliberately feminist approach might better attend to the ways in which female filmmakers have gone with the genre and acknowledge the extent to which individuals are already "contained within" it.[14] The issue, then, is not simply that certain directors, as Kaja Silverman implies, "may leave their signature only at random points within the diegesis"[15] – a practice that she does not explicitly gender, but that nonetheless seems more likely in scenarios where a director's creative control may be less assured or complete.[16] It may also be the case that scholars and critics need to recalibrate their theoretical assumptions: to reconsider default expectations of what counts *as* a signature, that is, what aesthetic, narrative, or ideological traces may be less detectable to an interpretive apparatus optimized for *big* practices – totalizing displays of authorship over a sustained body of work – or more conspicuously "subversive" interventions. Much as Patricia White has noted of Kathryn Bigelow, Seidelman has worked to "make her signature visible in commercial films, genre products."[17] But the need for such critical recalibration is particularly crucial in the case of a filmmaker like Seidelman, who, unlike Bigelow, has consistently gravitated towards topics strongly coded as feminine (friendship, sex, domesticity, fashion, aging) and is thus particularly vulnerable to what Lili Loufbourow calls "the male glance" – which is to say, the reflexive deprecation of women's art.[18]

It is with this pattern of reflexive marginalization in mind, then, that I follow film scholars such as Catherine Grant and Kataryzna Paszkiewicz in advocating for authorship in terms of agency and reclaiming for female filmmakers a degree of voluntarism disallowed by post-structuralist critiques of intentionality[19] – and, just as importantly, in embracing what Paszkiewicz calls the "turn to 'context' in the studies of female authorship."[20] This "contextual turn" allows for the kinds of critical sensitivity to the perhaps less legitimate ways in which female agency has manifested in the distinct production contexts of serial television. Similarly, I will draw on Jason Mittell's notion of the "inferred author function" to suggest that authorship might be not just implied but actively inferred by viewers, so as to allow for greater audience latitude in discerning an "authorial agency responsible for a text's storytelling."[21] In the case of *Sex and the City*, I will suggest that storytelling elements for which Seidelman is most actively responsible surface at the level of mise-en-scène – in the show's locations, production design and performances – and that a greater attention to these elements enriches both one's understanding of the series and Seidelman's sensibility.

At the same time, adopting a more context-aware and adaptive conception of authorship also offers feminist media scholars a means of indexing forms of creative activity not accounted for by an official filmography, or, to use philosopher Sara Ahmed's phrase, "putting a sponge" to women filmmakers' careers.[22] In short: What feminist possibilities are enabled by the assertion of authorship in contexts that might be less hospitable to it? How might feminist media scholars take from television's collaborative production model a license to think more capaciously about authorship? And how might thus generously erring on the side of authorship – even as a heuristic – help constitute a new archive of women's televisual work?

DESPERATELY SEEKING SUSAN . . . SEIDELMAN

Seidelman's career provides an instructive case-study in both the conditions that have led to the under-estimation of female authorship and the benefits of actively inferring it.[23] Specifically, by drawing on frameworks offered by Isabel Pinedo in her recent study of feminist television, I argue that Seidelman can be understood both as a direct author of *Sex and the City*, who would help shape the show's style and sensibility through her work on the pilot, in particular; *and* as one of its "indirect" authors, whose previous cinematic narratives of single and sexually liberated female life in New York helped to set the "larger cultural context in which the production [took] place."[24]

Seidelman directed three episodes during *Sex and the City*'s first season – *Sex and the City* (1:1), *The Power of Female Sex* (1:5) and *The Baby Shower* (1:10) – but the pilot is especially illustrative of her agency. Considering that the show would ultimately run for six seasons and air ninety-four episodes, Seidelman's contributions as an episodic director who did not write or produce the show might not appear, at first glance, to qualify as especially meaningful. As Mittell notes, however, pilots assume an outsized importance in setting a series' narrative coordinates and determining its fate, giving first episodes a correspondingly heavy lift. Among other things, he observes, they must "provid[e] the blueprint for the program going forward as well as assembling the cast, crew, and production routines that will be responsible for creating the ongoing series."[25] *Sex and the City* was no exception; by all accounts, Seidelman, through her involvement in the series' debut episode, exerted a considerable influence over everything from casting decisions, to production design, to the series' overall attitude and tone.

Indeed, it is important to note that producers Darren Star and Michael Patrick King actively sought out Seidelman's input. Star, in particular, was motivated to recruit not just a female director – to telegraph the show's feminist bona fides – but one who, like Seidelman, would bring a "filmic sensibility and unique visual style to the series."[26] Star was also reportedly drawn to the New York-centric nature of Seidelman's previous films, including *Desperately Seeking Susan*, "which topped Star's list of favorite movies."[27] Perhaps auspiciously, for a show centering on sex, Seidelman had also recently completed an Oscar-nominated short for a German TV series called *Tales of Erotica*.[28] It is clear, then, that Seidelman was recruited as an auteur with a recognizable signature, whose previous work had engaged with both the show's setting and its subject matter, and was encouraged to bring that expertise to the production.[29]

Given Star's interest in creating a "cinematic" series[30] ("as far from standard TV comedy as possible"[31]) as well as HBO's investment in branding itself as "not TV," it is perhaps unsurprising that Seidelman was afforded a degree of latitude, both financial and creative, that is unusual for commercial television directors. According to Jessica Armstrong's account, Seidelman enjoyed a "luxurious timeline for the shoot – nine days to make a half-hour show, plus several weeks of prep time," to the point that she felt "as if she were making a short indie film rather than a television series."[32] Along similar lines, Armstrong reports that Seidelman was invited to hire a "film-caliber staff," which included industry veterans such as cinematographer Stuart Dryburgh and production designer Mark Friedbergh.[33] In short, Star and HBO apparently delivered on the promise that Seidelman "would be able to invent the look and feel [of the show] from scratch."[34] As Seidelman herself noted, . . .

> Doing the pilot, you're creating the template. I wasn't following in someone else's path [. . .]. Being the director of the pilot gave me a certain amount of creative freedom because I was involved in the entire process, which included the casting of some of the major roles as well as the look and the feel of the show.[35]

Indeed, while there is some ambiguity about the scope of Seidelman's contributions to the casting effort, it is clear that she played an important role in recruiting Chris Noth, who would incarnate the series' deeply polarizing love interest, Mr. Big. As many commentators have noted, Seidelman gave Noth his feature-film debut in *Smithereens* (1982), in which he appears, briefly, as a trans sex worker, hanging out in a van on the West Side Highway.[36] While several critics have remarked on their affiliation – noting that Seidelman would "reteam" with Noth,[37] or that she had cast him in a "bit part" in her earlier film, "so [she] knew from the start he had range"[38] – most present his appearance in *Sex and the City* as a "coincidence."[39] Film critic Marya Gates, by contrast, has suggested that the reunion was not an accident, but rather a casting decision on Seidelman's part,[40] which Seidelman herself has confirmed: "I was involved in the N.Y. casting – which included Miranda and Mr. Big, as well as the secondary roles on those episodes I directed."[41]

Seidelman may also have influenced casting in even more subtle ways. In a recent interview with episode one's "toxic bachelors," for example, several actors highlighted Seidelman's involvement with the series as the determining factor in their own decision to sign on.[42] One, Bruce McCarty, noted that "Susan Seidelman directed the pilot [. . .] and I was most excited about it because I liked her so much, and I liked her work so much. I thought she was so smart."[43] Bill Sage – who played the womanizer Kurt Harrington – similarly described Seidelman's attachment to the series as a major incentive:

> It was great to work with Susan Seidelman [. . .] Susan and Darren explained what they were doing a little bit, just that women were going to be allowed to be promiscuous and unscripted about relationships, and they were going to be flawed and exciting. And I gotta tell you, I was honored to be part of it.[44]

It is not an overstatement, then, to say that Seidelman's reputation as a filmmaker served as a selling point for actors and vouchsafed the "quality" of a series with a risqué name, which debuted at a moment when neither HBO nor television as a medium enjoyed their current levels of prestige.

Seidelman's influence, notably, extended beyond casting and into the realm of performance. McCarty, for instance, describes Seidelman's direction as definitive:

> She gave me the best direction, she said to me: "Do it like a guy who had been really overweight in high school" . . . I got on set and I asked and she said, "No, we'll do it this way," which I thought was very funny – a very funny way to look at male pomposity.[45]

It is one indication of Seidelman's role in shaping the show's portrayal of toxic masculinity – a theme, if not a term, that had been present in her previous films, from *Smithereens* and *She-Devil* (1989) to *Making Mr. Right* (1987). Indeed, based on the insouciance that Noth brings to his performance in the pilot, Seidelman seems to have helped influence his interpretation of the caddish Mr. Big. After all, Noth's line-reading in *Smithereens* ("Say 'hi,' bitch") is not so far removed from the one he offers near the end of *Sex and the City*'s first episode, when Carrie asks Mr. Big if he has ever been in love: "Abso-fucking-lutely," he replies, smirking.[46] Such examples attest more broadly to Seidelman's aptitude for working with actors, one she evidently brought to her work with the *Sex and the City* cast and which has remained a constant across her filmmaking, even with her smaller or less successful efforts featuring stand-out performances by acclaimed actors such as Peter Falk, Brenda Vaccaro, Dyan Cannon, John Malkovich and Meryl Streep. When asked to describe the experience of working on *The Hot Flashes* (2013), for instance,

Virginia Madsen reported that "Seidelman created an environment on the set that allowed that sense of sisterhood to flourish."[47] Significantly, however, it is a skill that seems too readily overlooked in appraisals of authorial talent. In a discussion specifically about female directors' side-lining in American cinema, for instance, Robin Wood includes the offhanded observation that Amy Heckerling is "obviously marvelous with actors," based on the evidence of *Fast Times at Ridgemont High* (1982).[48] The fact that this assessment is confined to an aside, however, suggests both that there is comparatively little value placed on such gifts and that they may be understood as the "obvious" purview of women, and thus, not worth discussing. It does not seem a stretch to suggest that Seidelman, too, is "marvelous with actors" and that she contributed these talents to the show in its first season.

Just as instrumental in terms of Seidelman's influence on *Sex and the City* was her role in establishing its look, through production design and choice of locations. In an interview with Armstrong, Seidelman describes "shooting in downtown Manhattan neighborhoods where she'd lived for decades" and evoking a New York "audiences rarely got to see [. . .] on screen":

> She loved being able to explore SoHo's hidden clubs and streets. She filmed one scene at the East Village restaurant Lucky Cheng's, known for its drag queen waiters. She couldn't believe she got to put that in a television show; this was not *Friends* New York or *Seinfeld* New York [. . .] HBO placed no limits or demands on what should be shown. The network trusted the creative team to do as it pleased.[49]

Indeed, commentators have noted the exceptionalism of the pilot's mise-en-scène: the fact that it is, comparably speaking, grittier and darker, both literally and figuratively, reflecting a world closer to the one inhabited by downtown denizens like Madonna's Susan in *Desperately Seeking Susan* or Wren from *Smithereens*. In one of the many appreciations published to commemorate the twentieth anniversary of the show's debut, Jocelyn Silver catalogues some of the features differentiating the first episode from the series as a whole:

> In Seidelman's pilot, Carrie lives in a dark apartment on Third Avenue with a plastic blue chandelier, hair shorter and the color of burnt honey as opposed to what's in the jar. Characters are introduced with cruel chyrons like "toxic bachelor" and "unmarried woman." It's no *Smithereens*, in which people reach for unboxed slices of pizza in dirty fridges with hands covered in unexplained bloody bandages, and women on the highway share chicken salad sandwiches their mothers made, offering to show you their scars for $5, and you can get in a physical fight at Café Orlin while a rock star eats a rare burger. But it's a bit more raw than the rest of the series.[50]

Silver's attribution of the episode *to* Seidelman is one indication of both the increased centrality of authorship to viewers' reception and interpretation of serial television,[51] generally, and, perhaps, Seidelman's own growing prominence among a newer generation of fans. In keeping with this auteurist reading of the show, Silver suggests that Seidelman's imprint lingered well beyond the pilot and remained especially visible over the show's first two seasons, which are "less gauzy and glitzy than the rest" and in which "the clubs are dark and steamy and more men have greasy hair and tongue rings."[52] Indeed, the pilot's

Figures 2.1 and 2.2 Wren (*Smithereens*, 1982) and Carrie Bradshaw (*Sex and the City*, 1998), wearing leopard print dresses, consider their options.

visuals are at times almost directly evocative of Seidelman's earlier work, with the freeze frame that ends the episode calling back to the final shot of *Smithereens*, or the sequences of Carrie and Big in the backseat of a limo echoing images from *Cookie*, Seidelman's comic take on the New York gangster film (1989).

Cumulatively, then, the evidence suggests that Seidelman enjoyed a degree of creative agency atypical for episodic directors of scripted television. If usually it is the "ongoing writing and production teams [rather] than [. . .] the rotating crew of directors" who are likely to determine a show's "distinctive visual sensibility, performance style, and pacing," several factors – including Seidelman's presence at the show's inception, which left her less constrained by precedent; the producers' investment in a "cinematic" model; and Seidelman's New York bona fides and filmic credentials – granted her, even as a for-hire director, a surprising degree of input into the discrete episodes she directed, which in turn shaped the series' style and sensibility more broadly.[53]

AUTHORSHIP AT A DISTANCE

Having examined the ways in which Seidelman's authorship manifests in the series – in its casting, performances and production design – it is worth considering the ways in which Seidelman, as a romantic-comic chronicler of the single, striving urban woman, may have helped set the sociocultural conditions for a show like *Sex and the City* to emerge. Like Carrie Bradshaw, sitting in front of her laptop and staring at the blinking cursor, one could ask: Could *Sex and the City* have existed in the form it did without the films of Susan Seidelman?

Here, it is helpful to consider Isabel Pinedo's concept of indirect authorship, the term she uses to designate the role of external forces – including "the creative influence of network imperatives" and the "larger cultural milieu" – in shaping both the production and reception of (feminist) media.[54] It is a framework that usefully positions authoring as a social, contextual and intertextual phenomenon, as well as a voluntaristic one. As an approach, it also licenses a broader range of authorial inferencing and allows for the possibility that Seidelman's films, although released a decade prior to the show's premiere, may have nonetheless influenced it. Well before *Sex and the City*, after all, Seidelman had been crafting narratives about smart, single women pursuing their professional and romantic ambitions in the big city and developing a visual lexicon to express them. While Amanda D. Lotz traces *Sex and the City*'s 1990s rebooting of the "new woman character type" back to its origins in the "single-woman stories" of 1970s television, it is worth noting that the specific "type" explored in *Sex and the City* – the savvy, sexually liberated New York woman who has priorities other than monogamous coupling – also had an important precedent in Seidelman's films, from *Smithereens* (1982) and

Desperately Seeking Susan (1985), to, in a different sense, *She-Devil* (1989) and *Cookie* (1989).[55] While there may not be a perfect "match" between Seidelman's protagonists and their *Sex and the City* counterparts, I would argue that characters such as Samantha and Miranda owe more than a little of their chutzpah to self-possessed rebels such as Wren, Susan and their Miami peer, *Making Mr. Right*'s Frankie, a tough-talking executive who enters a corporate boardroom with a line straight from the Samantha Jones playbook: "I'm always late, but I'm worth it. Come on boys, let's see what you got." In fact, any number of Seidelman one-liners would be right at home in *Sex and the City*, and vice versa: "Susan, we all thought you were dead!" "No, just in New Jersey" (*Desperately Seeking Susan*); "A stimulated accountant sounds very exciting" (*She-Devil*); "It was hard enough to get him alone. And then it still wasn't hard enough" (*Making Mr. Right*). In short, Seidelman's characters laid important groundwork for the creation of urban anti-heroines wisecracking about sex *and* the city.

Sex and the City's greatest debts to Seidelman, however, may be most evident in its tone, which swerves between effervescence and cynicism, much in the manner of Seidelman's own films. Critic Emily Nussbaum, for one, suggests that the first season is distinguished precisely by this tonal balancing act, the way in which the show "swiftly establishes a bold mixture of moods – fizzy and sour, blunt and arch – and shifts between satirical and sincere modes of storytelling,"[56] a description that could just as easily be applied to Seidelman's films. Indeed, her cinema generally shares the show's commitment to what Seidelman describes as "pushed realism," a way of combining select reality effects (New York accents, household clutter, Jewish humor) with heightened elements – candy colors, propulsive pop music, snappy editing and improbably happy endings for some (if not all) of most of her striving characters, who, regardless of prior transgressions, viewers are never encouraged to judge.[57]

The kind of compassion with which *Sex and the City* regards its own characters' worst conduct – cheating on partners, lying to friends, mishandling money – thus likewise finds a precedent in Seidelman's films, in which even "bad" behaviors or impermissible desires are treated matter-of-factly. *Smithereens*, after all, opens on a scene of its protagonist committing petty larceny; in *Desperately Seeking Susan,* the eponymous Susan, played by Madonna, is a thief and opportunist, unapologetically and joyfully promiscuous. Decoupling sex from shame is a consistent theme in Seidelman's films, perhaps reaching its apex in the made-for-TV movies, *Power and Beauty* (2002) and *The Ranch* (2004): the former, a sex-positive portrayal of JFK's affair with his mistress, Judith Campbell; the latter, a surprisingly clear-eyed look at the day-to-day lives of sex workers in a Nevada brothel. (When the madam is questioned about her career choice, she responds, simply: "The truth? It was the best-paying job I could find.") When, in *Making Mr. Right*, the protagonist's sister counsels her after a break-up, her advice seems to anticipate the ethos of Samantha, or perhaps Miranda or Carrie: "You know . . . being single again could be really great. Go wherever you want, sleep with whoever you want, have absolutely incredible sex with a stranger." That the two female leads of *Desperately Seeking Susan* follow this playbook – with successful results! – signals Seidelman's films' refusal to moralize about female sexuality and helps explain why Seidelman was so interested in taking on a television project that might even help to normalize some degree of sex positivity. As she put it in one interview, . . .

> When I was sent the script for the pilot episode, instantly I knew: *I can do this. I see this in my head* . . . It was just so refreshing and bold. Now TV has gotten much bolder, but back then the things that the women would talk about on *Sex and the City*, we hadn't heard women saying on TV before.[58]

This kind of radical transparency characterizes her films' mise-en-scène, which – like *Sex and the City* – devotes close attention to the rituals of female adornment. Starting with *Smithereens*, her films evince a clear fascination with clothing, hair and cosmetics as vehicles of self-transformation, since persona in her films is something frequently, and playfully, in flux. Nearly all of her films include at least one scene showing a character in the midst of beautification – from Cookie primping in front of her bedroom mirror, to Frankie in *Making Mr. Right* dry-shaving her legs in the car.[59] Some of these sequences – the depressing makeover montage of *She-Devil*, or the hair salon sequence that opens *Desperately Seeking Susan*, which finds Roberta trapped beneath a hair-dryer – make it clear that the heroines, in such moments, are attempting to satisfy normative ideals of female beauty. Just as often, however, these grooming displays are portrayed more positively, as powerful and pleasurable forms of self-expression. One could think of the obvious satisfaction that Madonna takes in her own appearance as she slips into a black mesh shirt, admiring herself in a Penn Station bathroom mirror in *Desperately Seeking Susan*. Fashion in Seidelman's films, as in *Sex and the City*, is clearly linked both to the space of New York and to the act of self-fashioning, or what she herself calls that "whole theme of reinvention."[60]

One could even go so far as to suggest that Seidelman indirectly shaped the iconography of *Sex and the City*'s opening credit sequence, in which Sarah Jessica Parker, dressed in a pale-pink tutu, sashays down Fifth Avenue, before getting sprayed by a city bus bearing her likeness. While costume designer Patricia Field has taken credit for Carrie's outfit, it also clearly calls back to *Desperately Seeking Susan*, in which another petite, curly-haired blonde bombshell, played by Rosanna Arquette, traverses downtown Manhattan in a pink tutu and high heels, fending off various urban assaults.[61] (At one point, after her character, Roberta, has been arrested, a jail guard explicitly underscores the incongruity of her ensemble, yelling "you, in the pink tutu!") Seidelman's film, in short, develops a set of visual and thematic contrasts that *Sex and the City* would similarly evoke and which is readily distilled in the image of a whimsically dressed blonde screwball heroine, comically buffeted by New York's mean streets.

Perhaps most significant, however, in terms of assessing Seidelman's ambient influence on *Sex and the City*, is the extent to which her films dramatize the importance of female friendship, which is continually presented as either a satisfying complement or potential antidote to heterosexual coupling. Starting with *Desperately Seeking Susan* and *She-Devil* and continuing in more recent films such as *The Hot Flashes* (2013) and *The Boynton Beach Club* (2005), Seidelman has continually made relations between women her films' narrative fulcrum. Even *Desperately Seeking Susan*, which more clearly centers on a romantic plot, nonetheless makes a point to spotlight women's intimacies. It is Susan and Roberta's long-delayed and much-desired meeting, after all, that provides the plot's impetus, while Susan's scenes with her long-suffering pal Crystal model both intimacy and reciprocity ("I'll pay for the movies if you pay for the popcorn"). That is not to say, of course, that there is not a long tradition of network television built around the theme of female friendship, featuring "new women" characters – like their *Sex and the City* successors – "liberat[ed] from the marriages that [. . .] limited the available stories about women."[62] But Seidelman's cinema also represents an important and often explicitly feminist contribution to this tradition.

Ultimately, *Sex and the City*'s post-feminism would ensure its ideological divergence from Seidelman's films,[63] which, by contrast, reflect their director's second-wave politics and a sustained interest in the social forces circumscribing her charismatic heroines. Yet there remains a shared iconography and set of themes, along with an irreverent energy, that link her cinema to the series. Even as audiences await the series revival on HBO Max,[64] the wave of twentieth-anniversary appraisals in 2018 revealed a new level of auteurist appreciation for the ways in which Seidelman directly shaped the first season and indirectly set the conditions for this series to emerge.

CONCLUSION: AUTHORSHIP AND FEMINIST INTERVENTION

If the latter portion of Seidelman's career, as Christina Lane suggests, has "shin[ed] a light on new paths for women in the age of digital film and media" (83), it is fair to say, based on the above analysis, that her work on *Sex and the City* also "shines a light" on an older, more established path – one that winds through television and has been among the most commonly walked by women filmmakers, albeit one of the least closely examined.

That it also remains among the least respected says much about the persistence of the industrial double standards with which female filmmakers have long contended. As one critic writing for the online site *Film Reference* candidly notes, . . .

> If you are, say, Steven Spielberg or Barry Levinson and you choose to latch onto a television series, that involvement will be viewed as slumming. Or if you are Martin Scorsese or Woody Allen and you direct a short, that work will be considered an exercise in creativity. But if you are Susan Seidelman, and you haven't had a critical or commercial hit in well over a decade, your TV work and short film, however fine, will be viewed as a comedown.[65]

The problem, in short, exists not only in the realm of production, but at the point of reception. Whether women directors of Seidelman's era were forced into televisual byways or chose to take them – often as an off-ramp from the punishing demands of Hollywood – viewers have been passively and at times actively encouraged to devalue the results. It is usual, after all, not to reference directors' television work in their filmography, or not to find episodes "attributed" to them in any meaningful way in reviews or criticism. Happily, circumstances continue to change with the advent of TV's cultural ascendency and the relative degree of opportunity it presents to female showrunners. Yet, I would argue that viewers still need a more robust feminist framework to counter the reflexive devaluation of female-driven work or genres coded as feminine, such that "the show about boys [gets] way too much credit, and the show about girls [. . .] way too little."[66] As Loufbourow writes, "the effects are poisonous and cumulative, and have resulted in an absolutely massive talent drain. We've been hemorrhaging great work for decades, partly because we were so bad at seeing it."[67]

The advantages of a more capacious and contextual understanding of authorship, then, is precisely that it helps license the strategic assertion of women's agency where it has not previously been recognized – which is to say, it may allow us to better "see" the work and the women who make it. The growing awareness of just how often women have had to author by proxy – one could think of producer Polly Platt, unofficially ghost-directing *The Last Picture Show* (1971),[68] or Elaine May, anonymously or pseudonymously authoring scripts – means it is only more imperative that the extension of auteur credentials not be contingent on the exercise of complete and totalizing control over production. As Nicholas Godfrey suggests in his study of authorship in New Hollywood, women's continued exclusion from its canon highlights both the "limits of auteurism" and the need for "alternative configurations of film authorship that move beyond reductive, director-centric approaches."[69] To recuperate this lost archive, in other words, it is not enough simply to bolster the auteurist credentials of specific directors, like Seidelman, however important that effort also is. At the same time, media scholars also need to reckon with theoretical models and legacies – including those of auteurism – that continue to militate against women's full representation in film and television history. Seidelman's work on a seminal series such as *Sex and the City*, then, offers an important opportunity to move away from the auteur debates that have ensnared film studies and to adapt a more pluralistic and less romantic concept of authorship that is at once endorsed by the television industry and necessitated by its production model. It is this hybrid model, which recognizes authorial agency, however intermittent or dependent on context, that might be most productively bent to feminist purposes.

NOTES

1. See Jason Mittell, *Complex TV: The Poetics of Contemporary Television Storytelling* (New York: New York University Press, 2015), for a more detailed account of television as a writer's or "producers' medium" (88): 'Since most programs' managerial oversight typically comes from a writer, the writing process is seen as more central to a series' creative vision than is the contribution of directors, who are often hired as rotating freelancers rather than permanent members of the production team' (90).
2. Katarzyna Paszkiewicz, *Genre, Authorship, and Contemporary Genres* (Edinburgh: Edinburgh University Press, 2019), 5.
3. Jessica Ford, "Feminist Cinematic Television: Authorship, Aesthetics, and Gender in Pamela Adlon's *Better Things*," *Fusion Journal*, 14 (2018), 22.
4. Christina Lane, "Susan Seidelman's Contemporary Films: The Feminist Art of Self-Reinvention in a Changing Technological Landscape," in *Indie Reframed: Women's Filmmaking and Contemporary American Independent Cinema*, edited by Linda Badley, Claire Perkins and Michele Schreiber (Edinburgh: Edinburgh University Press, 2016), 72.
5. See, for instance, Nicholas Godfrey's examination of auteurism's role in shaping "the typical New Hollywood canon," which "privileges a limited brand of white, male, heterosexual orthodoxy that closely mirrors the makeup of the studios' boardroom at the time" (8). Nicholas Godfrey, *The Limits of Auteurism: Case Studies in the Critically Constructed New Hollywood* (New Brunswick: Rutgers University Press, 2018).
6. Isabel Pinedo, *Difficult Women on Television Drama: The Gender Politics of Complex Women in Serial Narratives* (New York: Routledge, 2021), 11.
7. Emily Nussbaum in "Difficult Women: How *Sex and the City* Lost Its Good Name," *The New Yorker*, 22 July 2013, argues similarly that *Sex and the City*, despite being one of "HBO's flagship shows," saw its reputation plummet even as contemporary series like *The Sopranos* centring on "difficult men" became canon.
8. As scholar Stefan Solomon commented in a recent talk, there is an implicit message that, for filmmakers, "work in television or other media is not as important, because you're not performing the work you imagined you would or [would] want to, so it's another sign of failure." Stefan Solomon, "The Feminist Possibilities of Unfinished Film," *Society for Cinema and Media Studies Conference*, Roundtable Discussion, 20 March, 2021.

9. As Kataryzna Paszkiewicz in *Genre, Authorship, and Contemporary Women Filmmakers* points out, even "feminist analyses of films made by women tended to centre on experimental or art-house cinema, in the wake of early feminist cine-psychoanalysis and its indictment of classical Hollywood cinema" (11).
10. See Mittell's chapter on "Authorship" in *Complex TV*, which notes that television has long been perceived "as something that is *produced* rather than *authored*" (95).
11. It is a problem that persists despite women's increased prominence within television and the medium's growing prestige. Thus, as Jessica Ford points out in "Feminist Cinematic Television," even as we have witnessed the rise of "feminist cinematic television," we are still "lacking the adequate interpretive and evaluative frameworks" to respond to it (18).
12. Lane, "Susan Seidelman's Contemporary Films," 83.
13. Jane Gaines, "The Genius of Genre and Ingenuity of Women," in *Gender Meets Genre in Postwar Cinema*, edited by Christine Gledhill (Chicago: University of Illinois Press, 2012), 26.
14. Paszkiewicz, *Genre, Authorship, and Contemporary Women Filmmakers*, 19. Gaines' "The Genius of Genre and Ingenuity of Women" effectively challenges "the Romantic notion of the individual by reaffirming the interchangeability of the critical categories 'women' and 'genre'" (17–18). Paszkiewicz has helpfully glossed her argument, noting that "instead of 'violating,' 'transgressing,' or 'subverting' the formal dictates of the industrial genre (that is, instead of 'going against genre'), some women filmmakers 'go with genre'" (19).
15. Kaja Silverman, *The Acoustic Mirror* (Indianapolis: Indiana University Press, 1988), 68.
16. For instance, as a director who works with other peoples' screenplays, Seidelman has had to master the art of "selecting [her] material and maintaining authorship over a project while bringing it to the screen," balancing her directorial vision against these various inputs (Maya Montañez-Smukler, *Liberating Hollywood: Women Directors and the Feminist Reform of 1970s American Cinema* [New Brunswick: Rutgers University Press, 2018], 284).
17. Patricia White, *Women's Cinema, World Cinema: Projecting Contemporary Feminisms* (Durham: Duke University Press, 2015), 3.
18. When Dyan Cannon, a star of Seidelman's *Boynton Beach Club* (2005), was asked why the filmmaker "isn't a better-known name among female directors, such as Kathryn Bigelow," her response was revealing of the perceived monopoly of the "male gaze": "Well, I think she is a big name. Why she isn't bigger, I have no idea. I don't think she wants to make movies about war and killing and fatalities" (Christine Lemire, "Susan Seidelman: Survivor," *Rogerebert.com*, 12 July 2013).
19. Silverman deftly summarizes the position of post-structuralist theorists such as Peter Wollen, for whom "the film is not a communication, but an artifact which is unconsciously structured in a certain way" (57). As Paszkiewicz observes, some scholars "have more recently begun to reclaim women's agency in the realm of filmmaking; yet, this reclaiming seems to have affected only some practitioners" (5). See also Catherine Grant, "Secret Agents: Feminist Theories of Women's Film Authorship," *Feminist Theory*, 2, no. 1 (2001), 113–30.
20. Paskiewicz, *Genre, Authorship, and Contemporary Women Filmmakers*, 10.
21. Mittell, *Complex TV*, 107.
22. Sarah Ahmed, *Living a Feminist Life* (Durham: Duke University Press, 2017), 22. Ahmed invokes the metaphor of the sponge – "a material that can absorb things" – to describe feminist acts of recuperation: "We hold it out and wait to see what gets mopped up" (22).
23. Here, I am indebted to Mittell's notion of the "inferred author function," although I go further in suggesting that authorial inferencing might constitute not only a helpful viewing practice but a political tactic (107).
24. Pinedo, *Difficult Women on Television Drama*, 24.

25. Mittell, *Complex TV*, 56.
26. Jessica Keishin Armstrong, *Sex and the City and Us* (New York: Simon & Schuster, 2018), 40. As she notes in her cultural history of the show and its legacy, "[Seidelman] hadn't done much television, and that was the point" (40).
27. Armstrong, *Sex and the City*, 40.
28. Lemire, "Susan Seidelman: Survivor."
29. Armstrong, *Sex and the City*, 40.
30. Yohana Desta, "Meet the Women Who Molded *Sex and the City*'s Very First Season," *Vanity Fair*, 6 June 2018.
31. Armstrong, *Sex and the City*, 40.
32. Ibid. p. 41.
33. Ibid. p. 40–41.
34. Ibid. p. 41.
35. Simon Hardy Butler, "Interviewing Susan Seidelman: From Madonna to Menopause," *Curnblog*, 7 March 2014.
36. It is also worth noting that *Smithereens* had brought Seidelman into contact with another *SATC* contributor, Patricia Field – owner of the punk clothing store on St Marks that Seidelman had used to source clothing for Susan Berman, the star of her debut film, and, eventually, the high-profile costume designer for *Sex and the City*.
37. Melissa Anderson, "Wrecks and the City: A Downtown-NYC Classic Surveys the Damage," *The Village Voice*, 26 July 2016.
38. Desta, "Meet the Women Who Molded *Sex and the City*'s Very First Season."
39. Armstrong, *Sex and the City*, 40.
40. Marya Gates in "Female Filmmaker Friday: *Smithereens* (Dir. by Susan Seidelman)," *Cinema-fanatic.com*, 31 January 2014, writes that "[y]ears later the actor and director reunited briefly on the set of *Law and Order*, and when Seidelman was casting for the pilot episode of *Sex and the City*, which she directed, she was the one that suggested Noth for the role of Mr Big. The rest, as they say, is history."
41. Pat Sapirstein, "*Desperately Seeking Susan* Director Susan Seidelman on Casting Madonna and Shooting the *Sex and the City* Pilot," *Vanity Fair*, 16 March 2021.
42. Kelly Conaboy, "Being a Male Jerk in the *Sex and the City* Pilot: An Oral History," *The Cut*, 7 June 2018.
43. Ibid.
44. Ibid.
45. Ibid.
46. Meanwhile, at least one critic has seen Noth's *Smithereens* cameo as an anticipatory echo of *Sex and the City*'s irreverent approach to style, noting that he appears in Seidelman's film "dressed like a mid-season three Carrie Bradshaw with an ice-blue scarf tied around his head and a low-cut red dress [. . .] a cigarette dangl[ing] from his pink lips" (Jocelyn Silver, "Mr. Big Did Drag, and It Is Glorious," *InStyle.com*, 7 May 2020).
47. Lemire, "Susan Seidelman: Survivor."
48. Robin Wood, *Hollywood from Vietnam to Reagan. . . and Beyond* (New York: Columbia University Press, 2003), 197.
49. Armstrong, *Sex and the City*, 41.
50. Silver, "Mr Big Did Drag, and It Is Glorious."
51. Mittell makes a strong case for the "central importance that authorship plays in framing our engagement with serial television," particularly in the case of narratively complex TV (87).
52. Silver, "Mr Big Did Drag, and It is Glorious."
53. Mittell, *Complex TV*, 90.
54. Pinedo, *Difficult Women on Television Drama*, 19–21.

55. Amanda D. Lotz, *Redesigning Women: Television After the Network Era* (Chicago: University of Illinois Press, 2006), 91, 89.
56. Putting aside the implications of Nussbaum's suggestion that this first season – the only one overseen largely by women directors, including Alison MacLean and Nicole Holofcener, as well as Seidelman – is also its "slightest," it is worth noting that she nonetheless credits these early episodes with establishing the series' narrative architecture.
57. Desta, "Meet the Women Who Molded *Sex and the City*'s Very First Season."
58. Laia Garcia, "The Lenny Interview: Susan Seidelman," *Lenny Letter*, 9 September 2016.
59. Critic Marya Gates in "Female Filmmaker Friday: *Cookie*, 1989 (Dir. by Susan Seidelman)," *Cinema-Fanatic.com*, 21 February 2014, has also noted this parallelism, observing the recurrence in Seidelman's films of images of "women applying makeup, or grooming of some sort. Usually, it's the 'unpretty' moments in the process of becoming 'pretty'."
60. Garcia, "The Lenny Interview."
61. Harling Ross, "Patricia Field on What It Was Like to Style Carrie Bradshaw," *Repeller.com*, 4 May 2018.
62. Lotz, *Redesigning Women*, 89.
63. For a discussion of the show's long-standing if somewhat contested relationship to post-feminism, especially in academic publications, see Fine Adriaens and Sofie Van Bauwel, "*Sex and the City*: A Postfeminist Point of View? Or How Popular Culture Functions as a Channel for Feminist Discourse," *The Journal of Popular Culture*, 47, no. 1 (September 2011), 174–95.
64. John Koblin, "HBO Max Orders a Sex and the City Revival," *The New York Times*, 10 January 2021.
65. Rob Edelman, "Susan Seidelman: Director," *Filmreference.com*, [n. d.].
66. Lili Loufbourow, "The Male Glance," *Virginia Quarterly Review*, March 2018.
67. Ibid.
68. See Karina Longworth's podcast series examining Polly Platt's career for *You Must Remember This*, which documents her extensive and often un- or under-credited work on many of then-husband Peter Bogdonovich's early films (Karina Longworth, "Polly Platt: The Invisible Woman," *You Must Remember This*, 25 May–27 July 2020).
69. Godfrey, *The Limits of Auteurism*, 9. Kyle Stevens, in *Mike Nichols: Sex, Language, and the Reinvention of Psychological Realism* (New York: Oxford University Press, 2015), has argued similarly for a "notion of auteurism that can accommodate filmmakers who develop mutable signatures (especially humorous ones) in order to intervene into urgent social and political issues over time" (26).

CHAPTER 3

"I've Always Been a Voyeur": An Interview with Susan Seidelman

Susan Santha Kerns

This interview was conducted over two zoom discussions and multiple email exchanges from 2020 to 2022. It has been edited for clarity and length.

Susan Kerns: Let's start with how you became interested in filmmaking.

Susan Seidelman: I'm originally from Philadelphia and went to Drexel University in the early 1970s. I thought I wanted to be a fashion designer, but I soon grew impatient with the program because it involved hours sitting behind a sewing machine. As a kid, I loved watching movies but never thought about making one until I took a film appreciation class. That opened my eyes up to watching movies in a different way. I realized movies contain a mix of all the creative elements I love: storytelling, characters, design, music, costumes. In the mid-1970s, film schools weren't nearly as popular or competitive as they would eventually become. I applied to New York University graduate film school and somehow got accepted. There were about thirty-five people in my class: thirty men and five women. As soon as I started to make student films, I was hooked. NYU gave me the tools, the camera equipment and editing facilities, as well as the means – a crew of other students – to start making short films.

SK: *Deficit* is sometimes listed as your first short, though not on IMDb. Can you clarify?

SS: *Deficit* was a student film I made during my second year at NYU, in 1975–76, and my first film shot in color. It was based on a stage play about a young man who wanted to get revenge on a married couple who had cheated his father out of money, so he has an affair with the wife and then tries to blackmail her. Except for a few NYU screenings, it basically stayed in a can in my closet. When I started my third and final year at NYU, I got busy working on my thesis film – something I wrote, with subject-matter I felt more personally connected to, *Yours Truly, Andrea G. Stern*. Unfortunately, *Deficit* was made before VHS or DVD, so I don't have a video copy of it and don't know what happened to the 16mm print or the negative.

SK: Knowing your career and focus on women, I found it interesting that your next short, *And You Act Like One Too*, sees a man opening the world for the female main character, though it's ultimately about her desires and dreams. That changes quickly in your oeuvre, but is that something you consciously considered?

SS: I wasn't, but in *Smithereens,* it's also a relationship with a man that leads Wren on an adventure. I wanted to focus on stepping out of your comfort zone. People talk about feminism, but I had never heard about it until I went to college. Feminism was a 1970s, not a 1960s experience for me. The idea that women are empowered to make choices, whether they're good or bad choices, was something that informed my personal life and the reason I wanted to make *And You Act Like One Too*. Ideas about women's place in society and within their families, and about women actively having adventures, good or bad, permeated my early films.

SK: The opening of that film is so interesting because the daughter interrupts the parents having sex, and it becomes this lovely moment of family bonding – yet is a scene that might now be considered controversial.

SS: I hadn't seen the film in about twenty-five years, and when they asked me if I wanted to include it in The Criterion Collection, I watched it again. I was pleased the opening felt so natural and didn't make a big deal about the parents having sex: the kid walks in, they bring her into their bed, and they talk about dreams. The film was shot in my childhood house, my parents' house, with friends of mine.

SK: It's a great moment to start a career.

SS: Making that film gave me confidence in being a storyteller and knowing I had something to say, because of the response it got. It was accepted into a bunch of film festivals and nominated for the Student Academy Awards. It was validation. Before that point, there must have been part of me saying: "What are you doing in film school? If you wanted to live in New York, you could have just moved to New York."

SK: Your next short, *Yours Truly, Andrea G. Stern*, grounds how you use voiceover in many of your films and TV shows. Andrea reminds me of Carrie Bradshaw also with how she utilizes her diary.

SS: Voiceover allows you to literally get inside the character's head to hear their thoughts. I find it intimate when somebody can tell me, on camera or through voiceover, what they're thinking. *Andrea* was the second sound film I made using some of the same actors. The little girl, Jillian Frank, was now two years older and more articulate. I don't remember much about making it except that I enjoyed working with a child actor, it went smoothly, and it was again shot in my suburban hometown outside of Philadelphia.

SK: Can you tell me about making *Smithereens*?

SS: After film school, I stayed in touch with many people I met at NYU who had worked with me on my short films. I told them I wanted to make a low-budget indie film. This was around 1979. I had been living in the East Village since 1974 and knew that neighborhood pretty well. It was clear by the end of the 1970s, especially in Lower Manhattan, that things were changing. The older hippie counterculture was giving way to something different, and a few interesting punk music venues started popping up downtown that attracted various types of artists, musicians, painters as well as groupies and hangers-on. Clubs like Max's Kansas City, CBGB and the Mudd Club.

Also, New York was in the midst of a financial crisis. The city was bankrupt, and there wasn't much of a police presence. Housing was cheap. Buildings were abandoned, which became squats or sometimes shooting galleries. There was a general atmosphere of a free-for-all and a feeling that anything was

Figure 3.1 Susan Seidelman directing *Yours Truly, Andrea G. Stern*, 1979. (Courtesy of Susan Seidelman.)

possible. This turned out to be a good time for artists because they could afford to live and work in Lower Manhattan. There was a vibrant street culture and an eclectic mix of people. Old bars and storefronts turned into funky galleries and music venues. The walls of the neighborhood became large canvases for graffiti artists and flyposting. It was cinematic.

I wanted to make a film set in the East Village about the types of characters I encountered. I also wanted to tell a story with a strong female protagonist: someone I hadn't seen portrayed on film before. I didn't set out to make her "likeable." I wanted her to be compelling. Although the film wasn't autobiographical, I certainly identified with Wren, a determined young woman who left the boring suburbs for the excitement of Lower Manhattan. A young woman who was running after something, even if she didn't know exactly what that was. I liked her energy and determination, even if she is at times obnoxious and manipulative. I also wanted Wren to be vulnerable. Trying to capture this type of female character on film was my motivation for making *Smithereens*.

SK: Your interest in fashion is evident in the film, like your interest in unruly urban women.

SS: Because film is a visual medium, I like to put characters in specific clothing and settings as a way of defining the character right from the start. As soon as you see that vinyl black-and-white checkered miniskirt enter the frame at the opening of *Smithereens* – and you don't even know who Wren is yet – you just see her skirt and another woman on a subway platform holding a pair of black and white checkered sunglasses, and you just know Wren is going to grab those sunglasses. If there's ever a way to say something about characters using images rather than dialogue or exposition, you do it.

As a kid, I used fashion as a way to rebel. I dressed outrageously as a teenager because I think that was my way of saying, "I feel different, I don't want to fit in." You can see the influence of my interest in fashion in many of my movies.

SK: Wren is increasingly becoming an iconic character, too. People talk about her use of photocopies as an early kind of Instagram.

SS: Posting her image all over the walls and putting it under windshield wipers is sending out the message, "I am here," which is, I guess, what we do on Instagram or Facebook or whatever – a way of just saying "I exist." The same with the character played by Madonna in *Desperately Seeking Susan*: the first time we see Madonna in the film, she's taking a selfie with a Polaroid camera, and then that selfie ends up in Rosanna Arquette's possession.

SK: The opening of *Smithereens* is also so propelled by the music.

SS: That driving music by The Feelies feels so integral to the film, but it was actually put in later, after the film was edited. At the time, I didn't know much about the process of film scoring, and I had no money to hire a composer. A friend of mine, the screenwriter Ron Nyswaner, put me in touch with a director, Jonathan Demme, who was in the early stages of what would become a very successful film career. Jonathan loved music and had a great and varied musical knowledge. He was also a very nice person and willing to help a first-time director. I showed him a cut of *Smithereens*, and he suggested some music that I should listen to. I met with a couple of his suggestions, and one of them was the band The Feelies, who hadn't released their first album yet. Something about the throbbing energy, the jittery anxiety of their music, and the feeling of impatience just felt so right for the character Wren. I thought, "This is what the main character sounds like." They agreed to let me use their music in the film, and I then went back and re-edited sections of the film to fit the music. Usually, you do it the other way around, but I actually recut the opening sequence and some of the scenes with Wren wandering around on the streets to fit the rhythm of their music.

SK: What a great person to accidentally get connected with.

SS: Yes, Jonathan Demme was very supportive of a lot of filmmakers when they were just starting out.

SK: Were you surprised by *Smithereens*' reception?

SS: The reception was pretty strong when it was released in 1982 after it premiered at the Cannes Film Festival. The film's acceptance into Cannes came as a big surprise, since I had never been to a film festival before, and to be in the Official Selection at Cannes with my first feature film was a bit surreal. Cannes turned out to be a big boost to my future as a film director. As a result, I got an agent and started reading scripts that were now being submitted to me. Most of them weren't very interesting.

I knew I didn't want to make a traditional "Hollywood" movie, since my heart was in the New York indie film world, so I read a lot of mediocre scripts and just waited until I found a story I felt I could put my own stamp on. After a year and a half, I was sent *Desperately Seeking Susan*.

SK: Let's talk about *Desperately Seeking Susan*.

SS: *Desperately Seeking Susan* was written in 1979 by Leora Barish. It had drifted around the Hollywood studios for a few years without getting much traction. Some studio executives liked it, but no one wanted to make it. Then in 1983, it was sent to me by producers Midge Sanford and Sarah Pillsbury after they saw *Smithereens*. I read the script, loved it and connected with both main characters. Ironically, the script already had my name in the title and, being a superstitious person, I took this as a sign it was the movie I should direct next. But more importantly, it had a theme I personally related to – a woman who wanted to reinvent herself.

Desperately Seeking Susan never would have gotten made if it wasn't for a woman executive, Barbara Boyle, who was the Senior VP of Production at Orion Pictures under Mike Medavoy at the time. She wanted to make films with, by and about women. She was given permission to greenlight *Desperately Seeking Susan* if we could make it for under $5 million, which was a relatively modest budget for a studio movie, but a huge budget compared to the $60,000 cost of *Smithereens*. Barbara was a fan of *Smithereens*, and she liked that *Desperately Seeking Susan* had two women producers, a woman writer, two women stars and could be made cheaply on location in New York. But it was really this one woman, along with my tenacious women producers, who pushed to get the film financed. It wasn't a committee decision, as so many things are these days.

Rosanna Arquette was already attached in the role of Roberta when I came onboard, but I was actively involved in the search for the actress to play Susan. I knew about Madonna who happened to be living a block away from my apartment in SoHo and performing at some local clubs. This was the very early days of MTV, and I had seen her music videos for *Borderline* and *Holiday* and thought she had a natural quality that might be right for the role. Despite her limited film-acting experience, she was cinematic. The camera liked her. I always loved those 1930s actresses like Carole Lombard, Barbara Stanwyck, or Rosalind Russell because they were bold, sassy and strong. We were looking to find someone who could embody that kind of sexy, mysterious but slightly naughty, free spirit. I auditioned Madonna, and we shot some footage of her outdoors in a park. I was able to use that screen test to convince the studio that she would be perfect for the role. It was a risk on Orion's part because she was still relatively unknown at the time, but that risk definitely paid off.

Once the budget and cast were approved, the studio pretty much gave us the freedom to make the movie the way we wanted to. Orion had a reputation of giving directors freedom. Even though I had never directed a studio movie before, I felt relatively confident, because I had a clear sense of what the film should look and feel like. I also had great collaborators, and we were all creatively on the same page.

The look and tone of *Desperately Seeking Susan* wasn't intended as realism. We wanted to capture a magical, but gritty, fairy-tale version of New York. It's a story about a young woman who gets banged in the head, has amnesia and lives out her fantasy of a new and more exciting life. It's *Alice in Wonderland*, and to create New York as Wonderland was a fun part of the process. Cinematographer Ed Lachman was trying to use the grittiness in a hyper-realistic way by using a lot of color gels outside, which hadn't been done before. So, the streets and alleyways looked not quite real. By the end of the 1980s and early 1990s, many music videos began using colored gels, but it really hadn't been done when we started filming in 1984.

Santo Loquasto was both the Costume Designer and the Production Designer, which allowed him to create a total world, because he knew both what the characters would be wearing and the color palette of the room they would be standing in. That coordination of set and costume added to the fantasy of New York we were going for. And I never expected the pyramid jacket to become iconic. I think you could also buy Susan's sequin-studded boots at one point, and you can still buy a reproduction of the jacket online.

Casting Directors Billy Hopkins and Risa Bramon introduced me to some great up-and-coming actors like John Turturro and Laurie Metcalf. I sprinkled in some downtown character actors I had known from other NY indie films, performers like Rockets Redglare, Richard Edson, John Lurie, Arto Lindsey and Ann Carlisle. I think the film's success was all about the right combination of people, the right story and the right timing. One can never under-estimate the importance of timing.

SK: In the film, Roberta seems to desire Susan, not necessarily physically, but also not necessarily not physically.

SS: I think a lot of women have girl crushes. When I think back to my childhood, and maybe it comes through in *Confessions of a Suburban Girl*, relationships with girlfriends are not necessarily romantic, but can be really intense and even possessive. "Am I still your best friend? Do you still like me? Is she your best friend now?" I think the Rosanna Arquette character has a major girl crush on the Madonna character. And as it turned out, an entire generation of young women, and some men, would soon develop the same sort of infatuation with the real Madonna.

I always say *Desperately Seeking Susan* is a love story, though not a sexual love story. It's about something else between the two women, because the relationships with the men in the film are secondary to the two women's relationship. And what's interesting is that they only meet at the end of the movie. Roberta follows Susan around the streets spying on her, but that's just a voyeuristic thing. She's curious about how Susan lives her life, where she goes, what she does. Interestingly, they never actually talk. They only speak to each other at the very end of the film. And I think their only line of scripted dialogue is "Good going, Stranger."

SK: After this you made *Making Mr. Right*.

SS: *Making Mr. Right* interested me because I, and many women I knew in the mid- to late-1980s, were out in the workforce, independent, making our own living and not depending on a man to define or take care of us. Yet, trying to find a balance between work, independence and personal fulfillment was not easy. The fantasy of being able to create your perfect lover – in some ways it was like a *Frankenstein* story, and obviously the leading lady's name, Frankie

Stone, was intentional – was a playful premise to hang the narrative on. It also allowed me to say some things about contemporary relationships between men and women.

When I read a script, I also think about the world it's set in. In the case of *Making Mr. Right*, the inspiration came from those colorful, but optimistic, futuristic cartoons of the 1960s I watched as a kid. For example, *The Jetsons*. It was also inspired by the look and feel of the 1964 New York World's Fair and the modern designs of Raymond Loewy. Since the movie involved an android going into outer space, we decided, rather than give it a dark, ominous look, like *2001: A Space Odyssey* or *Alien*, to give it an optimistic, colorful, retro feeling. After all, this was essentially a romantic comedy with a twist. Instead of girl-meets-boy, it was girl-meets-robot. The original script for *Making Mr. Right* was set in New York, but we changed the location to Florida. NASA is based in Florida, and Miami had a very distinctive color palette and design, especially with all its pastel Art Deco architecture.

SK: I love the film's color scheme. You have the pink of her office with the blue of Chemtech, but then Frankie is associated with primary colors. The whole world feels like that modern futurism you're describing. Also, John Malkovich's performance is criminally underrated.

SS: He was very good. There are certain movies that were just fun to make. Part of the reason was because we were filming in Miami Beach, which is such a quirky and unique place that everything felt slightly unreal. And the actors were so generous and collaborative. Ann Magnuson had the kind of cool, no-nonsense intelligence of the "tough" actresses I love in 1940s comedies. And I think Laurie Metcalf is an underrated comic genius. Metcalf, Malkovich and Glenne Headly, his wife at the time, all came out of the Steppenwolf Theatre Company and were just so versatile.

If you look at those first four films, *Cookie* aside for a moment, Wren is the youngest protagonist, a twenty-year-old girl. In *Desperately Seeking Susan*, Madonna is in her mid-twenties, and Roseanna Arquette has just celebrated her thirtieth birthday. *Making Mr. Right*, which came next, is starting to deal with women in their mid-thirties. They are out on their own. They are independent. They are working. They are successful, and yet there's part of their life that isn't quite gelling. That age progression sort of reflects my own aging process. As I was getting older, so were my female characters.

SK: Speaking of *Cookie*, the title character functions like Roberta, Susan and Wren trying to find her place in urban America, and Cookie takes pictures with her Le Clic camera, like Wren and Susan. The film also centers women breaking into an industry and trying to change it.

SS: That theme attracted me to the script. Also, I love taking genres and twisting them – viewing them through a female lens. It gives me the opportunity to make observations about contemporary life. *Desperately Seeking Susan* is a twist on a 1940s screwball comedy, using old-fashioned plot devices like amnesia, but reinterpreted to say something about a contemporary woman – or anyone, for that matter – who wants to reinvent herself to live a more interesting and fulfilling life. *Making Mr. Right* reimagines a 1950s science fiction movie, or a Pygmalion-type story, but from a female point of view to talk about the complicated relationship dynamic between men and women. *Cookie* turns a typically male genre mafia/gangster movie into a father-daughter relationship story about a young woman who wants to prove to her father she's as smart, tough and capable as any son.

SK: Can you say more about the production?

SS: *Cookie* was a difficult movie to make. It was freezing cold in New York the winter we filmed it. There were a lot of technical challenges, car chases, explosions and action sequences I had never directed before. My earlier films had been more intimate and personal, but on a technical level I learned a lot while making it.

I rewatched the film in preparation for our conversation and liked the first half. Much of Nora Ephron and Alice Arlen's dialogue is sharp and clever, and I love the characters. But I felt in the second half of the story, there were some convoluted plotlines that needed to be tied up and that took time away from what I liked most, the characters. Especially the relationships between the older characters. Peter Falk as a mob boss recently released from jail. Dianne Wiest as his long-suffering mistress. Brenda Vaccaro as his tough and brassy wife. If I had the chance to reshoot *Cookie*, I would do some things differently. But again, every time you direct a movie, you learn something.

SK: Next up is *She-Devil*.

SS: *She-Devil* is based on a book by Fay Weldon, and like *Desperately Seeking Susan*, it revolves around two women who are polar opposites and the impact they have on each other's lives. Unlike *Desperately Seeking Susan*, which is a romantic comedy, *She-Devil* is a revenge-comedy. It deals with a theme that is even more relevant today: our national obsession with wealth, glamor and celebrity. The two protagonists are totally different. One is an under-appreciated, powerless housewife, played by Roseanne Barr. The other is a rich, vain and glamorous romance novelist, played by Meryl Streep.

Just as the fictional characters are opposites, I wanted that to be reflected in the casting as well. And I couldn't think of two more seemingly opposite actresses than Roseanne and Meryl. The idea of casting the most acclaimed

Academy Award-nominated film actress of her time, Meryl Streep, and then having her play opposite Roseanne Barr, a popular, overweight TV actress and comedian who had never appeared in a movie before, felt like an interesting contrast both on screen and off. Both had such strong and distinctive personas.

I also believe actors can't help but bring their personas to the characters they play. With Madonna, I knew she was coming with her Madonna persona, as was Meryl Streep. I wanted that baggage. The same with Roseanne Barr. Meryl had never done a film comedy before, but I knew she was extremely intelligent and skilled, and it takes a lot of intelligence to pull off comedy. In a drama, the dramatic situation gives the actor something to fall back on, but in a comedy, it's all about skill and good timing. Meryl was game to give it a shot, and she's terrific in the role.

SK: Looking back, it seems like critics and audiences didn't know what to make of *She-Devil* when it was released.

SS: Women, I think, liked it. But, at that time, many of the powerful film critics were men. This was before the Internet, so there were only a few major critics, and they wielded a lot of power. Thankfully, the Internet has now given many more and diverse people a voice and platform to express their opinions, but thirty years ago, what the *New York Times*, *LA Times*, *The Hollywood Reporter* or *Variety* critics said set the tone for how the lesser-known, local critics would respond to a film. Gene Siskel and Roger Ebert were very influential. Their show was interesting because their opinions balanced each other, and they often disagreed. *She-Devil* got mixed reviews from them. Ebert gave it a "thumbs up." Siskel gave a "thumbs down." But if you look back at many of the films Ebert liked, he seemed to appreciate underdog characters and outsiders, so maybe he responded to the theme and understood the intended social satire about our culture's obsession with fame, money and beauty.

In some reviews, it was accused of being man-hating, which is not true. The plot revolves around an ordinary, powerless housewife who gradually turns into a powerful avenger. It's not just about gender, it's about power. But interestingly, as times have changed and women's voices have become stronger, bolder, the response to *She-Devil* has changed. Today's young audiences get the intended satirical, feminist tone, and they root for Ruth Patchett when she transforms herself into a 'She Devil'.

SK: I also think about *She-Devil* in terms of 1980s women's labor films with how Ruth Patchett acknowledges the value of women's labor and uplifts it.

SS: The character Ruth Patchett starts the Vesta Rose employment agency to help unemployed and under-appreciated women. She empowers them and is then able to harness their power for her own purposes. She's doing a positive thing but using it to her personal advantage, to get revenge on her abusive husband.

SK: Why did you change the ending of the novel for the film?

SS: There was so much I liked about the Fay Weldon novel, obviously, or else I wouldn't have made the film. You can do different things in novels because you're often inside the character's head. In film, you have to physicalize the emotions, turn the emotions into actions or dialogue. In the novel, at the very end, Ruth Patchett ends up becoming very rich, getting massive plastic surgery and physically turning herself into Mary Fisher. I believe she also goes back to her now beaten-down, repentant husband.

I wasn't sure that was the message I wanted to end with. It's quite cynical. It was as if Ruth Patchett went through this enormous metamorphosis, changed her entire life, found her power and then ended up as the person she most detested, Mary Fisher. It was an intellectually interesting concept, and even though I like a twisted dark ending, I still want to believe in someone's ability to empower themselves and change their life for the better. I didn't want Ruth to become powerful only to end up as Mary, living Mary's superficial lifestyle in a big pink mansion. I wanted Ruth to end up a better version of Ruth, only stronger, smarter and more attractive, but still herself. That's why I made the ending more optimistic. At the end of the film, we see Ruth walking down the street leading her army of strong, confident women, and they are all wearing Vesta Rose pins. Then her eyes glow red.

SK: I love the song *The Devil in Disguise* playing over that final image. Obviously, it plays with the title *She-Devil*, but it also speaks to how Ruth was under-valued and totally under-estimated because of her looks. The "she devil," then, is a woman who isn't conventionally attractive and who assembles a legion of other under-estimated women, which I think is great.

SS: Women doing work, no matter what that work may be – a mafia driver, a prostitute, an Image Consultant hired to program an Android, a Spanish book translator, a housewife-turned-entrepreneur – is an important factor in almost all of my films. Even at the end of *Desperately Seeking Susan*, the women succeed in finding the stolen Egyptian earrings and putting the bad guys in jail. In *Cookie*, the young woman outwits the Mafia big shots and helps her father start a new life. Judy Davis in *Gaudi Afternoon* succeeds in playing detective and finding a missing child. The prostitutes in *The Ranch* are professional and non-judgmental about their work. Even in the films that contain a romantic subplot, that's often in second position to the protagonist's "work" or personal accomplishment. Obviously, this is most blatant at the end of *She-Devil*.

SK: Next you made *Confessions of a Suburban Girl*, which is such a unique opportunity for a filmmaker – not just to reflect on your films in a film, but also to return with your girlfriends to where you grew up. How did that documentary come about?

SS: BBC Scotland was making a series of documentaries with international film directors and asked if I wanted to make a film about something that influenced my work. I started to think about growing up in a rather homogenous, middle-class suburb of Philadelphia in the 1960s, and how that had an impact on my work. There were things about my childhood that felt comforting, but there were also many things I wanted to escape. And I think my fantasy of escaping, of being able to recreate yourself, absolutely informs *Smithereens, Desperately Seeking Susan* and *She-Devil*. Had my life gone down a different path, had I not chosen to escape my suburban roots, I might have been the Rosanna Arquette character in *Desperately Seeking Susan*. Or could I have been Ruth Patchett in *She-Devil*? But like *Alice in Wonderland*, I decided to follow a White Rabbit down the rabbit hole, and I ended up in New York City, where I had always fantasized about living.

I was in high school at the end of the 1960s, and in college during the 1970s, and the world was changing rapidly. People talk about the 1960s counterculture revolution; well, it didn't really hit the American suburbs until the early- to mid-1970s. By the time my friends and I graduated from college, the world had become dramatically different. I think second-wave Feminism had the biggest personal impact on me. The "program" most of us had grown up with was: go to college, maybe work a little until you find a husband who can support you, have some kids, buy a nice house. But then suddenly the "program" changed, and women's roles within it also changed. That's what *Confessions of a Suburban Girl* is about – how this mindset influenced my films.

I've always been a voyeur, because that's what a director is, right? We observe. What I found out in talking to all my friends at age forty – I made the film when I had just turned forty – was the world had changed so much that none of them followed the path they thought they were going down.

SK: Girl bonding is so central to that film, and it marks a point where your work starts reflecting girl groups, whether it's *The Dutch Master*, *Sex and the City*, *Gaudi Afternoon*, *The Ranch*, *The Hot Flashes*, or *Boynton Beach Club*.

SS: That's true. It's funny, because if I look at the films I made earlier in my career, there's usually two main female characters whose lives impact each other, often from afar. And in *Smithereens*, Wren is a loner without connections to anyone. I never thought of it that way, but many of my later films do deal with groups of women, and female friendship becomes more important.

SK: *Sex and the City* obviously became a massive female-bonding phenomenon. You directed the pilot and a couple of episodes in the first season. How did you get involved with that project, and how did your vision help shape it?

SS: Every once in a while, a piece of material comes your way and you just say, "I see this. I know how to do this. This script was written for me to direct." And that's what happened when I read the pilot script. I had my agent put me in touch with Darren Star that day, and I said: "I'm on board." And it was all because I liked the script. I liked the tone of it. This was 1996 or 1997, and there really hadn't been another show with a group of women speaking so candidly and honestly with each other about such intimate topics. It had the kind of unfiltered conversations you might overhear in a ladies' room at a restaurant, or at a drunken night out with your girlfriends, but not in a TV series.

When I came onboard, I felt my job was to figure out how to put the energy and boldness of the script into something visually interesting and authentically "New York." Also, how to make the characters as specific and vibrant as possible. But the words and the relationships were already on the page, as written by Darren Star and Candace Bushnell. I just needed to figure out a way to translate that onto film.

One technique used in the pilot was to have the lead character Carrie Bradshaw, Sarah Jessica Parker, speak directly to the camera. I decided to do that to engage the viewer in a personal relationship with the main character, as if Carrie were telling you a secret, because you were her best friend, and she is going to tell you something she didn't tell other people in the scene. I played around with this same technique in my short film *The Dutch Master*.

SK: When you moved into television, was that deliberate? Was that just where opportunities arose, or did you prefer it?

SS: That's where the opportunities were. At that time, the 1990s, cable TV was getting much bolder and more inventive in its content. It was no longer a stigma to work in cable TV, particularly HBO and SHOWTIME.

If I look at my life and work, there was a clear break after *She-Devil* came out. It was released the exact week, actually the exact day, I gave birth to my son. I was literally in the hospital, in labor, watching Siskel and Ebert reviewing the movie on the hospital TV, staring up at the screen in between contractions. For the next year, I enjoyed being a mother and having a personal life with my partner, Jonathan Brett. Also, because *She-Devil* had not been successful at the box office, it wasn't as if I was being hounded with offers to direct lots of great scripts. I had worked straight through the 1980s, I was tired, and I was not unhappy to take a break. So, I took this time to spend with my family and work on smaller, less time-consuming projects, such as *Confessions of a Suburban Girl* and *The Dutch Master*, which surprisingly ended up being nominated for an Oscar.

During this time, I directed a few episodes of already-established TV series to stay active, but it wasn't creatively satisfying to work on episodic TV shows that already had a specific look and pretty rigid template. I approached it like doing exercise. I got to practice working on a set, meeting deadlines, figuring out how to translate script pages to images on a screen, and I got to work with actors, which I enjoyed.

I also tried to get a feature going in France in 1993, called *Yesterday*. The script was written by my partner, Jonathan, and inspired by a found diary written by his Welsh mother who at sixteen had gone to Paris as an exchange student and fallen in love with a Frenchman. This was shortly before the outbreak of World War II. Loosely based on the true story, years later the woman, now married with grown kids, is diagnosed with cancer and goes back to Paris to track the man down. It's about the "what ifs" in life. The path not taken. We were able to put together a nice cast – Dianne Wiest, Juliette Lewis, Samantha Mathis – and went to Paris to begin preproduction. Unfortunately, the financing fell apart only a few weeks before the start of shooting. Polygram, the company our French producer was working for at the time, changed their Head of Production, and he backed out, wanting to develop his own slate of movies.

It had been several years since I made a feature-length film, and I was getting itchy. After returning to New York, I was sent the script for *The Barefoot Executive*. It was part of Disney's mid-1990s package of remakes of their old films from the 1970s – *Freaky Friday*, *Escape to Witch Mountain*, et cetera. It was an offer with a greenlight, so I knew it would get made. And after the disappointment of Paris, I wanted to get back to work on a film set. *The Barefoot Executive* script was a satire about the TV business and the sometimes idiotic decision-making process involved in selecting what TV shows get made. How content is often selected by market research, focus groups and internal corporate politics. So, I signed on to do it. Also, I had never shot a film in LA before, so I thought that might be an interesting experience. I haven't a clue why it is unavailable for viewing since it got nice reviews, but somehow, it got lost in the streaming shuffle.

Then I started getting offers to direct feature-length cable movies. Working for SHOWTIME gave me the opportunity to make *A Cooler Climate*, *Power and Beauty*, about JFK's clandestine relationship with party girl Judith Exner, and *The Ranch*, about a brothel in Nevada. Since they were one-off movies, it felt the same as making a feature film.

SK: When you speak about *A Cooler Climate*, it's clear you have a genuine affection for the film.

SS: Yes. The premium cable TV companies, like HBO and SHOWTIME, were trying to be a little edgier and make the kind of character-driven movies Hollywood studios were no longer making. *A Cooler Climate* was one of those. It was based on a book by Zena Collier, and I got to work with a wonderful playwright named Marsha Norman on the screenplay. What I loved about it was it fit right into the stories I am fascinated with: two very different women whose lives intersect and impact one another. Being an optimist, I'd like to think they both end up a little better as a result of that collision. And I liked the idea of working with these two very good, strong but different actresses. Sally Field had won two Academy Awards and was onboard already, and I suggested Judy Davis, who is just such an interesting actress.

SK: *Power and Beauty* is the second film you made with SHOWTIME, and your only historical biopic. What resonated for audiences about Judith Exner at the time of the film's release?
SS: Her autobiography had just come out, so that's what the movie was based on. She was a beautiful woman who was used and manipulated by three of the most powerful men of that time: John F. Kennedy, Sam Giancana and Frank Sinatra. She was passed around like a pawn. The idea of being a mistress, of being the one people whisper about, is fascinating.

It was a project SHOWTIME wanted to make and brought to me. I liked the idea of that character, and I also loved that glamorous 1962–63 world. The idea of nightclubs, hotels, mobsters, politics and the fashion and style of that time-period was very much part of the appeal. My biggest concern before we made it was that I'd seen people play JFK on screen before, and I always cringed a little bit. I think Kevin Anderson gave an amazing performance.

SK: The style of *Power and Beauty* took me back to *Making Mr. Right*, but this is the glam version of that period. I love how Judy is defined by pink.
SS: It's the things from your childhood. When you're just about to become a teenager but still a little girl – eleven, twelve – you're especially impressionable. I have very strong impressions about the early 1960s: the feel of it, the clothes I wore, the music I listened to, the TV shows I watched. In my head, it's probably a little bit glamorized or romanticized, but I see the images in Technicolor.

SK: The third of your SHOWTIME films was *The Ranch*.
SS: I hadn't watched *The Ranch* in probably seventeen years and was a little nervous to watch it again. I had forgotten almost everything about it, but rewatching it, I was surprised by how important female bonding is in that film. The friendships between the women are a big part of the story and the reason I was attracted to directing it. I also hadn't remembered the boldness and casual-

ness of the sexuality. In several scenes, the women walk around almost naked in front of each other, and it's no big deal. They make crude jokes, say nasty and funny things, but it's all done in a casual, very matter-of-fact manner. I was pleased to see it treated prostitution as work in a non-exploitative way. It's just work.

SK: I agree, and the film holds up. With *Hustlers* and *Zola* out, and people talking more about representations of sex work, I'm hoping for a resurgence for *The Ranch*. Can you talk about the development process?

SS: I wasn't involved in the early development of the script. Lisa Melamed wrote it. The project had gotten a greenlight from SHOWTIME to make as the feature-length "pilot" for a TV series. SHOWTIME originally hired Garry Marshall to direct it. For whatever reasons, it didn't work out with Garry, and then SHOWTIME asked me to come on board. I liked the concept very much and worked with Lisa on some minor revisions. There are always little changes to be made, but the essential script was pretty much there.

I don't remember why SHOWTIME made the decision not to continue the series. I'm sure the ending would have been different if we had known it was going to be released as a one-off feature-length film.

SK: To contextualize the film, I looked at what else SHOWTIME was doing then, and they seemed invested in representations of sexuality.

SS: They had *The L Word*.

SK: Right, and *Queer as Folk* came out around the same time as *The Ranch*.

SS: I think they were trying to provide an adult alternative to network television. Network television was so watered down, because it had to appeal to all of America for free. When doing *The Ranch*, I kept thinking, "This is bold." There are some pretty raw and graphic scenes in the script, and I was encouraged to go for it. They probably pushed me beyond where I might have gone without their nudge. But I think it was to provide an alternative to the tame choices of what was showing on network TV in those days.

SK: *Gaudi Afternoon* came out while you were making movies with SHOWTIME. You mentioned via email that the film was embraced by the LGBTQIA+ film festival circuit yet received a limited theatrical release in the US.

SS: *Gaudi Afternoon* was shot in 2000, and I think the subject-matter was a few years ahead of its time. That's why we had to go to Barcelona to get the financing. The story was about an alternative kind of family and asked the question: what defines a mother? I could sense the conversation about gender changing, and that appealed to me. But this was years before the Amazon series *Transparent* would find its way onto TV. *Gaudi Afternoon* did eventually get a small art house American release and a wider release in Europe.

SK: Your next independent film was *Boynton Beach Club*. Can you talk about collaborating with your mother?

SS: For many years my mother had been sending me newspaper clippings with post-it notes attached, saying: "Wouldn't this make a good movie?" Some of them were nice ideas, but not stories I was interested in working on. And then one day she said: "Well, I have another idea." She was living in a retirement community in South Florida and started telling me stories about her friends, people her age or older, who had recently lost a spouse or had gotten divorced and found themselves single again and looking for love, companionship, romance and sex! She told me about a bereavement club a friend of hers was going to after the loss of his wife. I was working on another project at the time, so I said, "If you like that idea, mom, go to Barnes and Noble and buy a book on how to write a screenplay." She said "Okay," and we didn't talk about it again for several months. Then one day, I got a manila envelope in the mail with her completed 110-page script inside.

My mother had never written a screenplay before, so structurally it was messy, but there were wonderful, authentic moments sprinkled throughout that could only be written by somebody who intimately knew these people and that world. I said, "Is it okay if we collaborate, if I take your script as source material? But I'd like to rewrite it and give it a different shape." She agreed, so working with a collaborator from Florida named Shelly Gitlow, we revised the dialogue and the structure. But most of the story beats and characters came directly from my mother.

It was a story I hadn't seen on film before. Unlike some Hollywood movies where cute and neutered old people are portrayed sitting on rocking chairs, reminiscing about their past, or having silly "senior moments," I wanted to make a film about the aging Baby Boomer generation who are redefining what it means to grow old. Who are still interested in having a future with new experiences. Who still want romance in their lives, or maybe just companionship, or maybe just sex. At that time – 2004, 2005 – I hadn't seen any other films that treated older characters in this way.

What was weird, and I'm jumping ahead here, is that after the film had its premiere at the Hamptons Film Festival and Palm Beach International Film Festival, where it got a great review in *Variety*, we started to look for a distributor. All the major indie distributors who saw it said, "Nice movie. But no one's going to want to see this. There's no market for this kind of story, whatsoever."

They all turned it down, but my producer-partners and I had this strong belief there was an audience out there who would find this story interesting. We just needed to figure out how to reach them.

We started by self-distributing the film in about ten theaters in Florida, where it did phenomenally well at the box office. We knew there were other large, concentrated older audiences in cities around the country, like Arizona, Palm Springs, Las Vegas, Southern California. After seeing the strong Florida box office results, some of the distributors who originally rejected the film came back with an offer to distribute it nationally. That's how Roadside Attractions and Samuel Goldwyn Company came onboard. But that never would have happened if we, the producers, hadn't believed in the film and been proactive about self-distribution at the start.

SK: I appreciate *Boynton Beach Club*'s spotlight on its actresses. There's even a nude scene with Sally Kellerman, and she's obviously incredibly beautiful – was her entire life – but did that feel like a bold moment?

SS: I wanted it to be bold, to be a statement. Sally Kellerman happened to have a terrific body, but even if she didn't, I wanted to say, "Aging is okay, and it's okay to be sexual and not be embarrassed by who you are, at any age." It was also wonderful to see actor Len Cariou's reaction. His character hadn't seen a naked woman, aside from his wife, in thirty years, so his reaction is also very important. This is all brand-new territory for him, and he is both excited and nervous, like a teenager on his first date.

SK: Scenes like that, as you're saying, expand representations of sexuality. Your next film, *Musical Chairs*, also expands representations, though in different ways.

SS: *Musical Chairs* is about a wheelchair ballroom dance competition. Before making the film, I was not aware that there were wheelchair ballroom dance competitions all around the world and was surprised by the beauty and creativity of the dancing. When we were filming the dance sequences, there was a mix of disabled and non-disabled dancers. We took every opportunity we could to cast disabled performers as long as it worked within the context of the story. It was an amazing experience on a personal level and made me look at disability through different eyes.

SK: In interviews, Laverne Cox discusses how excited she was to play her character, Chantelle, one of the first Black, transgender, disabled characters in American film.

SS: Back in 2010, casting a transgender actress to play a transgender character in a serious dramatic role – someone who was just saying, "This is who I am," and dealing with what happens to her character in the story – was important to me. Authenticity in terms of casting as well as location is so important because the location is the world that you're setting your story in. This also was the first time I'd worked with a predominantly Hispanic and Black cast, which was reflecting a truer representation of the diversity in New York. I lived in New York for years, but I had never filmed all the way uptown before. I had one of the best production experiences working on *Musical Chairs*.

There is one film where I feel like I didn't take full advantage of the location – my next film, *The Hot Flashes*. The script was set in Texas, so when I first read it, I was imagining big sky and a dusty Texas small town, because that's what was on the page. While the producers were putting the financing together, I was busy filming *Musical Chairs*, so I was not involved in the decision to change location. At that time, New Orleans had a very advantageous tax incentive that was attracting a lot of film production, so suddenly it became a fait accompli that we would be filming in New Orleans. And while New Orleans is a great city to spend three months in, it wasn't the look I imagined when reading the script. I remember discussing the idea of revising the script to set the story in New Orleans so we could take advantage of all the great, authentic locations NOLA had to offer, but it was too late. All the production wheels were already in motion.

It was a joy working with *The Hot Flashes* ensemble cast. Several had been young "leading ladies" in the 1980s and were now in their late forties, early fifties. That aligned perfectly with the theme of the story about a group of middle-aged women, who had been the girl's championship basketball team in high school and are reunited twenty-five years later to raise money for breast cancer and prove they can still strut their stuff.

SK: And you had them go to basketball camp together?

SS: That's what helped them bond. No matter how good or bad they played basketball, and Wanda Sykes and Camryn Manheim happened to be very good, just having to learn and practice a new skill helped make them feel comfortable with each other and physically get in touch with the characters they were playing.

SK: You can see that in the film. There's genuine joy on the court.

SS: They were absolutely having fun. I wanted to use the basketball game as a way to say something about this group of women who felt under-appreciated because of their age – who wanted to prove to the world, and to themselves, most of all, that they still had what it takes to succeed. To feel valued. Like the other twists on genres I'd made in the past, the sports genre was intended as a vehicle to say something about being a woman, no matter the age.

SK: Your most recent film is *Cut in Half*. What brought you back to shorts?

SS: That was an interesting experience. *Cut in Half* was made through a non-profit organization to give city kids a chance to tell their own stories on film. They were then partnered with a professional film director to direct their story. The DP was a professional, but much of the crew were kids or film students.

It was interesting to see how many women were now on the set. I'd have to look through the credits again, but thinking back to *Yours Truly, Andrea G. Stern* or *And You Act Like One Too*, my guess is there were very, very few women working on either of those films. Seeing that change and how casually and easily women fit into a set environment was wonderful.

SK: That's a great segue for asking about #TimesUp. Are you optimistic about women's opportunities in the film industry?

SS: Lately I've noticed so many more wonderful women writing, directing and producing movies, particularly for the new streaming services – especially now that TV has, in many ways, become more exciting in its programming than the theatrical feature film business. The industry is still in a state of flux, so it's unclear how things will be in the future, or when film production will return to some kind of "new normal." I think the pandemic may have changed the way we watch movies for a very long time, and the kinds of movies that will be made, but I'm guardedly optimistic since there now seem to be many more opportunities for women, POC filmmakers, as well as the LGBTQ community, and it's about time for alternative stories to be told from different points of view.

SK: As streaming studios expand, are you concerned about theatrical? I envision people still going to theatres for Disney and Marvel films, but I'm concerned smaller movies are losing their footing.

SS: We've been in that space for quite a while, though. The movies I directed in the 1980s would probably not have been made in the 2000s. Movies that won Academy Awards, like *Terms of Endearment* or *The Graduate* or *Midnight Cowboy*, would not be made by studios today. They would now be TV movies. But let's keep in mind that this year, 2022, the industry is in the process of being redefined, and everyone is still walking on shaky ground. Most successful big-screen films now involve comic book characters.

Also, what's considered successful has changed. Studios would rather spend $200 million on one movie to potentially generate a billion dollars of worldwide revenue than $10 million on a more intimate movie and only get back $40 million. It's a different business model that impacts the kinds of movies getting made, which is very unfortunate.

SK: Can you tell me what you're currently working on?

SS: There's a great quote from John Waters when he was once asked this question. "Haven't I already done enough?" I'll steal his answer.

SK: Any parting words on your career thus far?

SS: I look back on all my films, and I say, "I'm happy. I tried." Maybe I would have done some things differently, maybe I could have made this or that part better, but they are what they are: a reflection of the times I've lived in. And I'm fortunate to have gotten the opportunity to make them. It's a privilege to be able to share your imagination with an audience, and I don't take that at all for granted.

PART 2

Embodied Spaces

CHAPTER 4

"Who is This?" *Smithereens*, Susan Seidelman's Auspicious Debut Feature

Susan Santha Kerns

Arguably Susan Seidelman's most critically acclaimed film, *Smithereens* put Seidelman on the map when the film was released in 1982 and broke independent American filmmakers into the Cannes Film Festival. *Smithereens* also bridged Seidelman's career from New York University student to independent feature filmmaker and finally to Hollywood director while showcasing her budding authorial sensibilities. Emerging at a moment of invention, if not intervention, for women in American popular culture, *Smithereens* nevertheless remained something of a vagabond in film history – a success story only recently securing its foothold in academic study as scholars, film festivals, distributors and streaming services revisit women directors. Despite the film's acclaim and a profitable, months-long art-house theatrical run,[1] *Smithereens* has not been wholly incorporated into histories of New York filmmaking during the late 1970s and early 1980s. Seidelman's contemporaries – filmmakers such as Jim Jarmusch, Lizzie Borden, Scott and Beth B, Vivienne Dick, Richard Kern, Jamie Nares, Amos Poe, Eric Mitchell and Nick Zedd, among others – have been codified as the Cinema of Transgression, No Wave, punk cinema and Downtown Cinema, for example.[2] While *Smithereens* and Seidelman share a partial lineage with these directors and cinematic movements, or moments, they also defy these categorizations, in part due to Seidelman's quick move into Hollywood filmmaking. Like her *Smithereens* character Wren, Seidelman had her finger on a pulse that resonated with audiences. The film also anticipates interests that Seidelman picks up later: driven but overlooked women pursuing their desires in urban environments, traditional expectations be damned. Through a mix of punk and neo-realist aesthetics, *Smithereens* capitalizes on Wren's and the city's momentum without wholly committing to a punk ethos, befuddling critics who wanted to make easy sense of her. Judged by the misogyny of a culture that would not meet Wren or *Smithereens* on her/its terms, the film nevertheless persists as a unique document of New York in the early 1980s, foreshadowing elements of Seidelman's career in both subject-matter and critical regard.

Smithereens tells the story of Wren (Susan Berman), an energetic, twenty-something woman eager to make a name for herself in New York. While pasting photocopies of herself over subway posters, Wren meets Paul (Brad Rijn), an earnest street portrait artist and recent transplant from Montana who lives in his van. Wren's style signifies her place among the artists and musicians central to the scene that she wants to embody, and Paul is immediately drawn in. Wren is more interested in rising star Eric, played by musician Richard Hell (Television, Richard Hell and the Voidoids). Eric has more cultural capital to offer Wren, and she is just strange enough and eager enough to hold Eric's attention. Something between a groupie, a Warhol Superstar and what we would now call an influencer, Wren is driven by a desire for fame; why, she is not sure.[3] Wren's flyers ask, "Who is this?" and "Wren would very much like others to ask . . . though no one much does."[4]

Yet, Wren is the driving force of *Smithereens*. She has enough determination, or possibly delusion, to believe that she should be famous for being herself. As such, when Eric announces his plans to leave New York for California, he does not protest when Wren invites herself along. He does, however, see an opportunity. Needing money, Eric convinces Wren to help him rob a man. Eric skips town with the money, abandoning Wren. She returns to Paul's van, only to find Paul also gone, his van now housing neighborhood sex workers. Out of money and friends, Wren walks, as she spends much of the movie doing, down a street at sunset, looking for her next move. A man pulls up, seemingly soliciting her for sex, and although she tells him to get lost, the film freezes on a moment of contemplation, suggesting that she could just as easily get into his car as she could keep walking.

Smithereens' appeal lives its naturalistic quality, a result of the film's low budget, inexpensive location shoots and the ambiance of New York. After raising about $20,000 through friends, family and an inheritance left to her by her grandmother, Seidelman approached another recent film student, screenwriter Ron Nyswaner, with a stack of notes and a story idea.[5] With the help of Peter Askin, the notes eventually became the *Smithereens* screenplay.[6] From there, a cast of mostly amateur or up-and-coming actors and filmmakers began production in late 1979. Production quickly came to a halt when Berman broke her ankle, and shooting resumed several months later.[7] Seidelman used that time to adjust both script and cast. Story tweaks foregrounded Berman's strengths as an actress, and the original actor cast as Eric was replaced by Richard Hell. In a director's commentary, Seidelman says that many filmmakers were casting musicians and that the "energy" of mixing film with music drew her to this combination.[8] Pierre Henri Deleau selected the film for the Directors'

Fortnight at the Cannes Film Festival "after seeing the first print out of the lab. However, when the Festival director Gilles Jacob came to New York to pick films for the main competition," Jacob moved *Smithereens* into that category.[9] When Seidelman learned she needed an additional $20,000 to $25,000 to blow up *Smithereens* to 35mm and hire a publicist for the festival, foreign sales agents sitting near enough to hear the conversation offered the money if they could represent *Smithereens* internationally, allowing *Smithereens* to become the first American independent film in competition at Cannes.[10] Once New Line picked it up for international distribution, they cut several minutes and added additional music to accelerate the pace for American audiences.[11]

With both a domestic and international theatrical run, *Smithereens* was a success. In announcing the film's return to New York, Annette Insdorf wrote:

> The surprise hit of international film festivals from Cannes to Telluride has come full circle to its home town: "Smithereens," an affectionate exploration of lower Manhattan's rock club aficionados, is currently at the Waverly Theater, basking in favorable critical and popular esteem.[12]

It held court at the Waverly for several months,[13] and Janet Maslin called it "resourcefully directed" and "ragged, funny and eccentric. It has as much life as the indefatigable Wren, and that's plenty."[14] Maslin noted that Seidelman presented Wren with "wit, style, and even more nerve than the heroine's own,"[15] suggesting a deepened relationship between character and director that extends beyond the screen.

As a film school graduate, Seidelman drew from film history and incorporated it, creating something of a neo-realist, new wave hybrid – a *Nights of Cabiria* by way of the now legendary New York scene. Over time, the "documentary," cinema verité or neo-realist elements of the film, whatever one prefers to call them, became increasingly prominent, resulting in a sort of verité fiction. Because the New York of *Smithereens* seems impossible, if not mythical,[16] compared to the city that now exists, the film's footage of cityscapes and venues gives the film an arresting quality. Much of the film is shot on the street, in parking lots or in available locations such as the Peppermint Lounge and the subway, giving it a verité quality that contributes to the sense that, while *Smithereens* initially told Wren's story, as time has passed, it now tells New York's. Johan Andersson suggests that numerous films coming out of New York during the 1980s, including Seidelman's follow-up *Desperately Seeking Susan*, could be described as picturesque, meaning that they aestheticized poverty, dispossession, eviction, unemployment and motifs of ruin in post-industrial settings.[17] *Smithereens*, however, might be seen as a bridge between the punk and the picturesque, as its do-it-yourself aesthetics, naturalistic performances, urban location shooting, hand-held cinematography, ambivalent character arcs and lack of narrative closure[18] connect *Smithereens* with the punk cinema circulating at the time of its release, which Jay McRoy argues invokes Italian Neo-Realism.[19] Although McRoy does not mention *Smithereens*, its style affords it the same street cred that Wren works to achieve in the film's story, contributing to its legacy as a document of punk.[20]

Chirine El Khadem's cinematography lingers to capture New York as it exists around Wren. When Wren leaves the Peppermint Lounge early in the film, for example, the camera stays, observing reactions to Wren's departure and capturing the band on stage as a marker of space, time and scene. Many films now labelled neo-realist incorporated loose or episodic plots reflecting contemporary urban struggles within "a radically changing social and political environment."[21] If *Desperately Seeking Susan* moves into New York as fairy-tale, one that *Sex and the City* secures as a playground for the rich, *Smithereens* presents a city on the cusp: an oasis of gravel and concrete, where one could park on the lower east side for free, create a one-man van island among bridges and dilapidated buildings, go unnoticed spray-painting a wall and wander until finding a soon-to-be-famous musician's mattress to share, knowing change is on the horizon. *Smithereens* captures New York observationally, cinematically and psychically through Wren's energy and commitment to her desires in these spaces.

The pacing of the camera and editing also mimics Wren's and through the cinematography reflect her embeddedness in the fabric of New York. Early on, the camera's pace picks up when she leaves work, the lighting separating her from dark city streets and unlit apartment hallways. Later in the film, the camera walks with Wren, pausing on random people on stairs and in bathrooms. While Wren stands out because of how present she is, both posting images of herself and making herself an annoyance to others, such as Eric and the patrons of the Peppermint Lounge, she also connects herself to their identity. Although *Smithereens* is not a musical proper, both Wren and the film reflect the idea that "American punk-musical films fed into and off of the emerging independent sensibility; not particularly genre-oriented, they are preoccupied with fan culture and with punk's social or ethnographic impact and influence."[22] Wren is part of that fandom, both contributing to and leeching off its vibe. By the end of the film, she rides the subway with nowhere to go as people sleep around her – the ultimate sign that one has adapted to New York life. Even though she again stands out at the end of the film as a pedestrian on a traffic-heavy bridge, the sun flare reads as potentially hopeful. She moves more slowly now, not as frantically, indicating that, although it is unclear whether she has grown as a person, she is changed.

Smithereens' aesthetics connect with Siegfried Kracauer's "realistic tendency" in film, which privileges physical reality, raw material and objective movement over the staged realities on which most cinema would eventually rely (what he calls the "formative tendency"). Kracauer says that films made in the realistic tendency capture "objective" movement shot by a static camera and "subjective" movement, which might involve a mobile camera and editing to emphasize or alter movement.[23] Furthermore, audiences "may have to identify himself with a tilting, panning, or traveling camera which insists on bringing motionless as well as moving objects to his attention."[24] Through this tendency, "films may seize upon physical reality," and Kracauer privileges the "raw material" rather than the "gist" of it.[25] Filming a scene on a mountain rather than on a studio set, he says, allows for "emanations" of the place itself to give a film its "soul."[26] *Smithereens*' cinematography and use of location shooting captures the cinematic "soul" of New York, rather than its "gist."

The film's opening focuses on watching and being watched within a city full of life. Centered in the opening shot are the plastic, black-and-white checkered sunglasses that immediately become part of Wren's signature style. While a woman waiting for the subway swings them slightly in her hands, creating movement in the frame to emphasize the glasses, Wren quickly grabs them and runs into the subway. Movement attracts movement. Then, as Wren posts photocopies of herself over subway advertisements, Paul watches her. She catches his eye and smiles, cultivating this audience of one. Here she reads as a potentially famous person, because of her confidence, style and bravado with which she defaces public property with images of her own face. Paul is drawn in, and he follows her off the subway to her job at the copy shop. However, he waits outside, watching her through the glass. A shot-reverse-shot pattern captures both of their faces, connecting them in space and time, before a shot brings them together in one frame: Wren inside making copies while Paul's reflection in the glass becomes observable to the audience. She is literally the insider and he the outsider. When he walks away, the camera stays on the street, documenting the energy of the city in which they both circulate. On the sidewalk, roller-skaters glide by after Paul walks away. The camera remains, capturing changes in light as the sun sets before streetlights and traffic lights illuminate the darkness. Paul returns, following Wren again and introducing himself: "Small world, isn't it?" As seen through the objective lens of this static camera, it is. Wren and Paul, then, walk quickly down the street toward the camera, Wren setting the pace for Paul and the camera, until Wren hands him another photocopy and continues alone. She places photocopies on car windshields before jumping the Peppermint Lounge line, waving her hand and yelling: "I'm on the guest list!" This introductory scene establishes Wren as the center of this world and the city as her heart. The camera captures the city outside her workplace while waiting for her to re-enter it, creating the sense that the city continues moving without her but moves more energetically with her present. She is part of its soul. The interior spaces throughout the film, including the bar she is just about to enter, the copy shop, the hallway of her apartment and domestic spaces, in general, restrict her energy and movement. Inside, she often is an outsider. Outside, she is a life force of and for the city, feeding it and feeding off it.

Wren's movement within the city, and the camera's attention to her pace, symbiotically connects both with the film's rhythm. Wren is constantly on the go, but the editing and handheld camera illustrate also when she is out of place; she walks fast and, at times, awkwardly and excessively. Yet, she simultaneously creates presence for herself with her red lipstick, blue shirt, green belt and checkered skirt and glasses, even if the way in which she fits in remains unnatural, creating tension between herself and her surroundings. Seidelman has discussed how important energy is to the film, so much so that she recut the opening sequence to match the "nervous energy" of The Feelies' music that sets its pace.[27] Further, the energy of low-budget filmmaking creates its own presence in the film, echoing the vitality of its main character, or vice versa. Seidelman says:

> By working independently, you generate a real energy. [. . .] For example, we had to sneak into the subway at 2 A.M. and hide the camera in a travel bag, hoping that the subway police wouldn't throw us off the trains. We were trying to sneak a shot here and there, but the thing that pleases me so much about working this way is the energy that is generated.[28]

Stacy Thompson argues that do-it-yourself resourcefulness and energy is key to the nature of "punk," and one articulation of punk cinema aesthetics includes "speed, frenetic energy, anger, antiauthoritarian stance, irony, style, anomie, or disillusionment."[29] Thompson ties punk aesthetics to the economics of creation to ensure it goes beyond just a film's formal elements:

> In order for the term *punk cinema* to carry some weight, to describe something more than a consumable aesthetic, it must bear, aesthetically and economically, a filmic version of the old punk democratizing dictum, "This is a chord. This is another. This is a third. Now form a band." Just as anyone can produce punk – and should – anyone can produce punk cinema – and should.[30]

In defining a punk approach, he says that films made by Hollywood studios or with "prohibitive financial investments" do not qualify; punk productions instead might be considered a "project" that aesthetically and/or economically resists capitalist assimilation.[31] Further, creators should not have "specialized training."[32] Seidelman notes that, when she was making *Smithereens*, the do-it-yourself energy around music, art and filmmaking was less focused on intentionally branding oneself; hence, while Wren engages in this activity, it was more about scene and art, and less about capitalism:

> I don't remember that kind of calculation. By the mid-to-late '80s, the culture changed. It was the beginning of the yuppie culture. I think that sense of branding and being aware of your commercial value [. . .] started to come into play more.[33]

Still, these definitions of punk cinema both include and exclude *Smithereens*. As a director, Seidelman had specialized training, reflected in her use of cinematic elements such as continuity and rhythmic editing. The filmmaking is mannered. She also drew from film history, so while *Smithereens* refuses closure for Wren, it does so in a way familiar to European cinema enthusiasts. Perhaps it is no surprise that the French first embraced the film. Yet, the film was independently created outside of Hollywood using certain guerrilla tactics and intended as a portfolio piece: "I didn't even think about what would happen to the film after it got made. I didn't think of film festivals or distributors."[34] Like punk music, energy drives the film, and Wren's amateur photography, with its ransom-note lettering, suggests both punk zines and the idea that anyone can participate.

Wren herself, however, is not necessarily "punk." Like Madonna/Susan who follow her in *Desperately Seeking Susan*, Wren is more of an influencer with a punk aesthetic than someone uninterested in capitalism and its trappings. She steals and squats because she goes after what she wants, not to make a statement. Wren dresses to self-actualize, to construct an exterior version of herself reflecting the woman in the Xeroxed images – the physical, fashionable embodiment of the woman destined for fame – not for rebellion. She can be read as a groupie but does not have the wherewithal to be a band manager; she wants to be famous, and other famous people might get her there. She is the star of her story, whether based in fantasy or delusion.

Ultimately it matters less if *Smithereens*, Wren or Seidelman herself fit neatly into definitions of "punk" than how each troubles easy categorization, even within the context of their emergence. Readings of the roguish Wren, for example, vary dramatically. Pamela Hutchinson is drawn to Wren's vivacity, calling the film a "punk picaresque" and noting that "Berman provides an engaging anti-heroine, just human enough to elicit our sympathy and monstrous enough not to care."[35] David Laderman says that Wren's "punk identity" is articulated through her "alienated sense of displacement" as she "somewhat desperately" searches for "a figurative place in the New York punk scene."[36] He also characterizes Wren as "a brazen self-promoter and cutthroat entrepreneur" who anticipates neo-conservative capitalism: "lacking talent and a product, she just wants to exploit the punk scene however she can."[37] Janet Maslin sees Wren's lack of character arc as derivative:

> PUNK screen heroines, of whom there are now a couple, are a little like the French movie waifs of yesteryear. They seem to wake, sleep, live and breathe with an utter spontaneity bordering on recklessness, and to enjoy their freedom inordinately while it lasts.[38]

Still, many critics admire Wren's steadfast forward momentum. Hutchinson says Wren "hustles through" the city "hot on the trail" and "hunting for a break."[39] Maslin describes Wren as "march[ing] fearlessly" as the camera "tracks" her "around a series of locations."[40] Eventually Maslin decides that "neither Wren nor the movie is going anywhere, since the character never becomes any more thoughtful or less selfish than she was to begin with."[41] Critics seemingly want Wren to "go" somewhere emotionally or politically, to add up to more; traversing the city finding herself is not enough.

Several critics use Wren's aimlessness against her, uncertain of her character type. Generous readings suggest that she reflects women's liberation; many call her a prostitute. This second label might merely reflect critics' knowledge of *Nights of Cabiria* – Federico Fellini's 1957 film in which Giulietta Masina plays Maria/Cabiria, a prostitute so eager to find love that men take advantage of her, eventually leaving her destitute – which Seidelman cites as an influence for *Smithereens*. Yet, the contempt with which (mostly male) critics wrote about Wren suggests unease with floundering female characters. Emanuel Levy calls Wren a "hustler" and "village groupie who wants fame but lacks discernible talent for anything."[42] He reiterates this, noting that she "lacks talent and personality" and is "energetic" and "desperate to score," yet ineffective because she is "too eager," "inept" and "shallow."[43] He calls Wren a "dislikable character, repeatedly humiliated"; "[b]rassy and indefatigable, cocky and calculating, Wren is essentially a loser."[44] All the while, she also is drifting "toward prostitution."[45] He then quotes Stanley Kauffmann, saying that Wren is the product of "everything hateful in pop culture."[46] (For contrast, Paul is described as "innocent" and Eric as "indifferent," although neither get much mention in the review.[47]) Ultimately, Levy calls *Smithereens* a "cautionary tale about ragamuffin punks";[48] the review's rhetoric suggests that he sees it as a cautionary tale about adventurous women.

Critic Mas'ud Zavarzadeh also sees Wren as a "talentless woman," yet he suggests that *Smithereens* reflects changing American cultural norms from the 1960s to the 1980s.[49] Zavarzadeh says that Paul, a painter from Montana passing through New York on his way to New Hampshire, is reminiscent of 1960s men through his quiet "contemplation and depth"; he can "see through" the "futility" of Wren's world.[50] Wren, on the other hand, is "characterized by re-production instead of production" via her copy-shop job and the photos of herself she reproduces and posts around the city; she is both driven and dehumanized by hype.[51] He writes:

> Her indifference to the actual human predicament and her inability to appreciate the subtle negotiation of the real in any complex human situation gives her thoughts and acts a raw quality and brutal tone that the film expands and associates with contemporary punk rock. The crude, narcissistic and relentless pursuit of power, which marks punk rock music, is seen in the film as the underlying order in the night clubs and bars that Wren and the others frequent and [. . .] shapes their relationships.[52]

Eric, then, embodies punk as "a form of fascism" for "feeble-minded" and powerless youth who submit themselves to it for visibility.[53] In contrast, he calls the landlady who kicks out Wren "decent," "hardworking" and a character with which the bourgeois audience can sympathize.[54] This reading suggests empathy for Paul as the moral center of the film, but Zavarzadeh notes that, by ignoring Paul's romantic intentions and lectures on being a better person, Wren "transgresses the laws of exchange, and it is for this that she is 'punished' in the film."[55] Zavarzadeh sees the laws of exchange following Wren in the closing scene, when she is propositioned by another man.[56] Ultimately, he says the film reassures middle-class values, because rather than engaging with social causes, it trades in moral issues; the film, he says, has an "underlying moral anger."[57] In other words, these characters, and Wren especially, are either bad people or making bad choices; society itself is not taken to task. Yet, Wren breaking the cycle of exchange seems important. One might imagine her relenting and moving to New Hampshire with Paul to start a safer but boring life. Audiences might even have rooted for it as a reflection of internalized 1960s norms. But Wren embodies both self-reproduction and resistance to becoming someone else's mode of exchange. As such, she remains a conundrum for audiences to decipher.[58] Who, indeed, is this girl?

This ambivalence toward Wren and the subcultures she roams speaks to her transition from suburban to urban, New Jersey to New York, and to the city itself at a time of cultural change. Movement is key, and *Smithereens* includes numerous images of Wren or her feet walking or running, a deliberate motif. Wren is "always on the go."[59] She may not stay long or find her stay satisfying, but her feet in motion suggest new possibilities continually on the horizon. Part of why Eric attracts her is because their energy matches, unlike Paul, who is more stationary. Despite Paul owning transportation, his van rarely starts. Put another way, Seidelman also calls Wren an "urban cockroach."[60] The film's verité quality strips it of nostalgia, making it a document of an imperfect city that once was, the film's characters reflecting the people who brought it to life – "cockroaches" maybe, or songbirds filling decrepit spaces with art, music and style. Unpredictability is part of the allure of both this film and moment in New York, where an artist or musician could be made via a single chance encounter (say, when a nearby café patron fronts the cost of a 35mm film print for Cannes). Additionally, the film reflects charming elements of this period in one's life, when breaking into a padlocked apartment seems less like breaking the law and more like problem-solving; marrying a charismatic musician after a week seems romantic and full of possibility; traveling to Los Angeles or New Hampshire in a van with someone you barely know sounds like an adventure, not a dead end. None of these people, except possibly for Paul at the beginning of the film, are wholly trustworthy or stable. They are flawed but interesting, driven by desire and boredom, and willing to use people along the way knowing others will scuttle by shortly.

Wren is, however, judged harshly as a character because she is out of step with her prescribed gender role in her unwillingness to settle down, stay inside/contained and be nice – but that does not mean that it was not by design. Seidelman explains:

> I wasn't trying to provoke the audience. I just knew people like her, men and women. There are people who are cutthroat and manipulative and cruel, but she's kind of bad at it in a way. To me that's what made her likeable to a certain extent. You can feel the vulnerability.[61]

Seidelman also notes creating women characters who are "too perfect or too virtuous [are] unreal" and can reinforce limiting images.[62] Seidelman aimed to overturn expectations that interesting women characters needed to be likable. Many women filmmakers of the 1970s working outside of the mainstream, like Seidelman, according to Christina Lane, came from a "tradition of counter cinema that challenges the supposed mastery and coherence of any spectatorial position."[63] As such, spectators are "geared toward destabilizing subjectivity" and discomfort via any number of cinematic elements, including flawed female characters or rejection of the "closure traditionally provided by classically structured narratives."[64] These films "complicate easy identifications" and appropriate "dominant codes in order to attend to female subjectivities and modes of seeing – female spectacle becomes female point of view."[65] Certainly Wren complicates "easy identifications," and *Smithereens*' focus on looking throughout foregrounds women's seeing and being seen. It is also a core issue with which Wren struggles: she controls the reproduction of her image but not how it circulates. Mostly, she just wants to be sure it does – that even her image has energy and movement and makes space for her in her absence. She spray-paints her name on a building with a line leading to her image, maintaining her space in an empty lot. She also removes the images of Eric's wife (Kitty Summerall) from his apartment – tears them up and burns them – before replacing them with her own, installing herself as art in his domicile. This destabilizes but instates her own subject position; she commands an audience regardless of her presence.

The theme of trading people for one another also runs throughout the film, most prominently in the triangle between Wren, Paul and Eric. In discussing *Desperately Seeking Susan*, Kristin Thompson identifies a "parallel-protagonist" story structure that incorporates a character "desperate for something that the other can supply or aid in gaining" and ending "either in intense friendship or love between the two characters," as one character is elevated to "equal or nearly equal status" as the other, "envied" character.[66] Although *Smithereens*' resolution leaves Wren alone, rather than on parallel status with Eric or Paul (who end as something of parallels to one another in their absence), Wren is 'desperate' for what she believes Eric can help her gain – public visibility and a secure place in the scene. The equally opportunistic Eric wonders what Wren might do for him. Wren intrigues him enough that he invites her to his apartment and even chases her a time or two. However, their relationship is not exactly friendship, and certainly not love. The final time Eric seeks her, it is to con her. He reads her desire to impress him and ups the ante, amassing enough money to travel to Los Angeles, abandoning Wren as she packs. No character in *Smithereens* is particularly "good" or "bad." No one is deceived more than anyone else, and all are deceitful. Wren exaggerates her connection to Eric throughout the film, so the audience is primed for her to believe what she wants to believe. And Eric is no stranger to using women. He does so in front of Wren, leaving his wife behind multiple times. During a slap-fight between Wren and a woman hoping to manage Eric's career, he grabs his lunch, leaves the restaurant and laughs from outside, amused and unconcerned. Between Wren, Paul and Eric, Eric is the best of the three at being a con artist. He has real talent, charisma and just enough notoriety that people let him use them, hoping some of his aura will rub off. Wren wants to be Eric's "parallel," but he is not interested. Similarly, Paul looks to Wren for a hook into the city. Of all characters in the film, he is the one asking: "Who is this?" He does not exactly believe that Wren is in the scene, but she is more part of New York than he is. Also, Paul is unsure if he wants in. He does, at least initially, want Wren, however. A more conventional film might use his love interest to tame or settle her, but Wren's yearning is not to be romantically coupled like her sister in Queens. On her first date with Paul, after all, Wren leaves the horror movie while a monster sucks the life out of a woman onscreen. *Smithereens* thwarts this parallel-protagonist structure, as the characters hook into one another for status or love, with the men ultimately unhooking and driving away, leaving Wren with her first love, New York.

Toward the end of the film, one scene, according to Lane, suggests the possibility of evolution through female community, even though Wren denies it.[67] Here, Wren discovers that Eric's girlfriend is really his wife and that she, too, was going to manage his band. Eric also has abandoned her. This moment

> offers up a rare glimpse of one direction of hope for Wren [. . .]. The recurring reference to Wren's troubled yet compelling relationship to her own image finds an answer in an alternative female-female representation, the feminist bond of friendship. The two women are linked by a sudden mutual understanding of Eric's misogyny.[68]

Through this interaction, Wren sees a different kind of copy of herself – another woman embodying the trajectory of life with Eric. Although Lane sees this moment as a "missed opportunity,"[69] it is consistent with Wren's tunnel vision. She inserts herself into community; she does not build it. The film suggests that Wren has roommates, because someone is sleeping in her apartment, but the audience never meets them. And Wren invites Cecile (Nada Despotovich) to Eric's place, but the invite is to prove that Wren knows Eric, not an act of friendship. Wren does interfere when Eric's predatory roommate Billy (Roger Jett) hits on a very drunk Cecile, suggesting that Wren follows some kind of girl code, but Wren's ambitions still keep her singularly focused. She embodies tensions between female community and urban individualism, in part because her desire to be anywhere but New Jersey keeps her in motion.

The observational camera, however, does not judge Wren. She is part of New York, and while not exactly a "good" person, she fits into the fabric of the moment. Wren, as her name implies, might even go unnoticed in the city – someone who flew in from elsewhere and is adapting – but she possesses a wren's complexity and trickery. Wrens are, after all, the "king of birds" for understanding when to hitch a ride via the strongest bird, emerging at that bird's height to sail above it and claim the king's title. The character Wren similarly strategizes how to embed herself, yet be noticeable, in the city where she belongs. She wants to perpetuate her self-made image in New York and be an urban king of birds. And in many ways, she is succeeding. Despite the bleak ending of *Smithereens* – the freeze frame of Wren on the bridge, broke with no place to go and contemplating hitching a ride with a new creep – the film suggests that Wren's image saturation campaign is working. She has left several pieces, smithereens if you will, of herself behind. Her image remains on Eric's apartment walls, and her spray-painted name marks the building by the van's parking lot. A new image of her, a portrait created by Paul, now hangs in the van, replacing his former girlfriend. This indicates that others are carrying out Wren's legacy, taking on the task of replicating and elevating her image. Although the van is now populated by prostitutes, Wren's portrait hangs prominently on its carpeted walls, a marker of her time or influence

Figure 4.1 Susan Berman (standing) and Susan Seidelman (squatting) on the set of *Smithereens*, 1982. (Photograph by Owen Franken. Courtesy of Owen Franken and Susan Seidelman.)

there. Paul even learns survival from her as he cons the pimp into buying his non-functional van at a functional van's price, an indication of how Wren and New York have changed him. He leaves New York touched, perhaps stronger, by Wren's survival instincts.

Despite its punk legacy, *Smithereens* has been called a "crossover" film, part of a batch of movies "bridging the gap between Downtown subculture and popular appeal."[70] This bridge was extended by Seidelman's follow-up, *Desperately Seeking Susan*, which also sees Roberta (Rosanna Arquette) leaving New Jersey for adventure in the city. One might even say that the eponymous Cookie (Emily Lloyd) echoes elements of Wren as she navigates her way into the New York mob, as does *Sex and the City*'s lead flaneuse Carrie Bradshaw (Sarah Jessica Parker). While Wren plasters images of herself around lower Manhattan, Carrie's column of dating adventures is disseminated around New York. Lane even suggests that Carrie pausing in the show's opening credits to notice her own image on a city bus forces Carrie to confront "her identity as commodified femininity," and she wonders "how different is this encounter" from Wren encountering her fliers as moments, perhaps fantasy, of subject/object inquiry?[71] Paul's painting of Wren – a reinterpreted, possibly idealised, version of her – might foretell the bus image of Carrie, publicity for a person as brand. But Paul, who sells images, has not sold Wren's. The portrait hangs among sex workers, perhaps equating selling images of bodies with selling access to bodies, but the unseen act of painting seems important as one of desiring something one cannot control. In contrast to Eric, who abandons, Paul bequeaths, advancing Wren's legacy while allowing her to remain outside of commodification in a city full of it – at least until the final shot when her commodification is up for grabs.

As a debut feature, *Smithereens* broke ground and continues defying categorization as a document of New York and a story about an unconventional woman, portending numerous other Seidelman productions interested in women aspiring to more. And just as many critics were unready to meet *Smithereens* or Seidelman on their terms, they nevertheless remain intrigued by this film that set in motion a lengthy career. Like Wren, Seidelman continued energetically moving with shifting cultural landscapes, differentiating herself as a creator. "Who is this?" remains an apt question for both filmmaker and film, and one perhaps even they did not yet know.

NOTES

1. Susan Seidelman, moderated by David Gregory, "DVD Audio commentary," Blue Underground, 2004.
2. For discussions of these cinematic categories, approaches and filmmakers, see, among others, Vera Dika, *The (Moving) Pictures Generation: The Cinematic Impulse in Downtown New York Art and Film* (New York: Palgrave MacMillan, 2012); Maura Edmond, "Deracination, Disembowelling and Scorched Earth Aesthetics: Feminist Cinemas, No Wave and the Punk Avant Garde," *Senses of Cinema*, 80 (September 2016); Rachel Garfield, *Experimental Filmmaking and Punk: Feminist Audio Visual Culture in the 1970s and 1980s* (London: Bloomsbury, 2005); Joan Hawkins (ed.), *Downtown Film & TV Culture 1975–2001* (Chicago: Intellect, 2015); Emanuel Levy, *Cinema of Outsiders: The Rise of American Independent Film* (New York; London: New York University Press, 2001); Nicholas Rombes (ed.), *New Punk Cinema* (Edinburgh: Edinburgh University Press, 2005); Roger Sabin, *Punk Rock: So What? The Cultural Legacy of Punk* (London: Routledge, 1999); or Stacy Thompson, *Punk Productions* (Albany: SUNY Press, 2004).
3. One poster tagline for the film read: "She was a legend in her own mind."
4. Rebecca Bengal, "Smithereens: Breakfast at the Peppermint Lounge," *Criterion Collection*, 20 August 2018.
5. Judith M. Redding and Victoria A. Browning, *Film Fatales: Independent Women Directors* (Seattle: Seal Press, 1997), 148.
6. Seidelman, "DVD Audio commentary."
7. Ibid.
8. Ibid.
9. Annette Insdorf, "'Smithereens' – The Story of a Cinderella Movie," *New York Times*, 26 December 1982.
10. Seidelman, "DVD Audio commentary."
11. Ibid.

12. Insdorf, "Smithereens."
13. Seidelman, "DVD Audio commentary."
14. Janet Maslin, "Smithereens," *New York Times*, 19 November 1982.
15. Maslin, "Smithereens."
16. In *New Punk Cinema*, Nicholas Rombes argues that punk's US identity "was solidified" in New York (9).
17. Johan Andersson, "Landscape and Gentrification: The Picturesque and Pastoral in 1980s New York Cinema," *Antipode* 49, no. 3 (2017), 539–56.
18. These components of punk cinema are compiled from Maura Edmond's "Deracination, Disembowelling and Scorched Earth Aesthetics," Jay McRoy's chapter "Italian Neo-Realist Influences" in and Nicholas Rombes' "Introduction" to *New Punk Cinema*, as well as Stacy Thompson's book *Punk Productions* and chapter "Punk Cinema."
19. Jay McRoy, "Italian Neo-Realist Influences," in *New Punk Cinema*, edited by Nicholas Rombes (Edinburgh: Edinburgh University Press, 2005), 39–55.
20. For another take on *Smithereens*' relationship to punk cinema, see Maya Montañez Smukler's chapter in this volume.
21. Jay McRoy, "Italian Neo-Realist Influences," 42–43.
22. David Laderman, *Punk Slash! Musicals: Tracking Slip-Sync on Film* (Austin: University of Texas Press, 2010), 103.
23. Siegfried Kracauer, *Theory of Film: The Redemption of Physical Reality* (Princeton: Princeton University Press, 1997), 33–34.
24. Ibid. p. 33–34.
25. Ibid. p. 34–35.
26. Ibid. p. 35.
27. Seidelman, "DVD Audio commentary."
28. Insdorf, "Smithereens."
29. Stacy Thompson, "Punk Cinema," in *New Punk Cinema*, edited by Nicholas Rombes (Edinburgh: Edinburgh University Press, 2005), 24.
30. Thompson, *Punk Productions*, 159–60.
31. Ibid. p. 159–60.
32. Ibid. p. 160.
33. Rich Juzwiak, "Susan Seidelman on How the 'Woman Director' Label Went from Pejorative to Political," *Jezebel.com*, 24 August 2018.
34. Ibid.
35. Pamela Hutchinson, "Smithereens," *Sight & Sound*, 28, no. 10 (October 2018), 87.
36. Laderman, *Punk Slash! Musicals*, 100.
37. Ibid. p. 102.
38. Maslin, "Smithereens."
39. Hutchinson, "Smithereens."
40. Maslin, "Smithereens."
41. Ibid.
42. Emanuel Levy, "Smithereens," *EmanuelLevy.com*, 1 May 2006.
43. Ibid.
44. Ibid.
45. Ibid.
46. Ibid.
47. Ibid.
48. Ibid.
49. Mas'ud Zavarzadeh, "Review: *Smithereens* by Susan Seidelman," *Film Quarterly*, 37, no. 2 (1983), 55.

50. Ibid. p. 57.
51. Ibid. p. 55.
52. Ibid. p. 56.
53. Ibid. p. 56.
54. Ibid. p. 56.
55. Ibid. p. 59.
56. Ibid. p. 59–60.
57. Ibid. p. 57.
58. See Maya Montañez Smukler's chapter in this volume for a further examination of Wren as an "unruly" woman.
59. Seidelman, "DVD Audio commentary."
60. Ibid.
61. Juzwiak, "Susan Seidelman on How the 'Woman Director' Label Went from Pejorative to Political."
62. Linda Seger, *When Women Call the Shots: The Developing Power and Influence of Women in Television and Film* (New York: Henry Holt and Co., 1996), 162.
63. Christina Lane, *Feminist Hollywood: From Born in Flames to Point Break* (Detroit: Wayne State University Press, 2000), 18.
64. Ibid. p. 18–20.
65. Ibid. p. 18 and 24.
66. Kristin Thompson, *Storytelling in the New Hollywood* (Cambridge: Harvard University Press, 1999), 155.
67. Lane notes that this theme is picked up in many of Seidelman's later films.
68. Lane, *Feminist Hollywood*, 56–57.
69. Ibid. p. 57.
70. Kase, Juan Carlos, "The Centre Cannot Hold: *Blank City* (2010) and the Problems of Historicizing New York's Independent Cinema of the Late 1970s and Early 1980s," in *Downtown Film & TV Culture*, edited by Joan Hawkins (Chicago: Intellect, 2015), 323.
71. Lane, *Feminist Hollywood*, 64.

CHAPTER 5

Swapping the Suburban Housewife for the NYC Feminist: Susan Seidelman and her Personas

Ruth Wollersheim

In director Susan Seidelman's 1992 documentary *Confessions of a Suburban Girl*, Seidelman begins by narrating a story about the start of her rebellious phase in high school, which all began with an eye problem that "resulted in a kind of blurry vision." Seidelman narrates while driving by identical suburban houses located in her childhood neighborhood, an "instant neighborhood, built on what was once farmland" called Huntingdon Valley, twenty minutes outside of Philadelphia. Although she does not exactly say that the blurriness resulted in double vision, Seidelman does suggest that her vision problem caused her to start seeing her suburban neighborhood in a strange, new light. And while she said that she felt loved and protected, she also confesses that she felt as if she were growing up in a glass bubble and that being too protected was "the problem."

Reminiscent of Betty Friedan's investigative-like inquiries into the lives of desperate suburban housewives experiencing "the problem that has no name" in *The Feminine Mystique* (1963), Seidelman seeks to uncover the secrets and untold stories behind the hundreds of new, identical model houses: split-level, colonial and ranch-style, all on identical plots of land in which her parents and her friends' parents invested in the 1960s. Seidelman, dressed in a black leather jacket, takes viewers through her old neighborhood, explaining that she has not been back in twenty years since she left to live in New York City. She wants to show us her childhood house, a "colonial model" that her parents called their dream house, but she cannot because the present owners are "being difficult." Like a good detective, however, she drives by slowly so that we can "get a peek," and promises to come back a little later with a long lens and to sneak some shots. The idea that there is something that a suburban girl has to confess, or that there is something to uncover inside these suburban homes is a theme that Seidelman explores throughout her work as a filmmaker. Like

Friedan, Seidelman wants to set free and liberate the suburban girl from these suffocatingly identical homes and lives without drama or adventure.

In order to see how suburbia shaped those who lived there, Seidelman interviews several of her old neighborhood friends, now at age forty. Despite fond memories of their childhood, most of her old friends confess that their lives did not quite turn out like the suburban fantasy promised. After they describe their high school obsessions with boys, beauty and the local bowling alley, in the end, they disclose that adult life ended up being much more difficult than they had projected. Some of them divorced, waited tables to support their children, or never had children at all. Likewise, Seidelman shows us how their childhood shopping centers and hangouts are now crumbling, deserted, or sparsely populated by grey-haired older women, implying that suburban life and the housewives who inhabited it did not quite live out the American dream.

Many of their confessions are filmed while the women stand in front of their childhood houses. The houses act as looming, even monstrous figures behind their former inhabitants. They also tell their stories in front of brightly colored screens, sitting together in pairs confessing their discontent to Seidelman, who presumably sits behind the camera. The paired women look like doubles, with the same dark, chin-length wavy hair and both dressed in black, long-sleeved shirts. Seidelman juxtaposes these confessionals with footage from *Desperately Seeking Susan* (1985), *She-Devil* (1989), *Cookie* (1989) and *Smithereens* (1982), suggesting that the stories of suburban life gone wrong are echoed in her fictional films as well. What ultimately saves Susan Seidelman as a young suburban teenager (as well as her fictional film housewives) from a life of quiet desperation is to take on a rebellious persona, what she calls a "mild form of badness," for which she gathered inspiration from the tough Italian girls who lived on the other side of the shopping center. In a black-and-white segment meant to signal a recreation of her past, two cool Italian girls get into a fistfight with two Jewish suburban girls, one of them playing young Susan Seidelman. Even though Seidelman comes away with a few bruises, she is proud that she could somewhat hold her own, and those tough girls "became her heroes." After the segment, Seidelman cuts to a scene from *Desperately Seeking Susan* where her later character Susan (Madonna) sticks her face through the prison bars so that the prison guards can light her cigarette. Ultimately, inspiration from these "coolest girls in the world" pushes her and her subsequent film characters out of the suburbs and onto the streets of New York City to live out lives of drama and adventure.

DIRECTING PERSONAS

In 2012, film critic and festival director Miriam Bale coined the term "persona swap," taken from Ingmar Bergman's 1966 film title *Persona*, to describe a subgenre of films that feature a "distinctly feminine experience" where two women

Figures 5.1 and 5.2 Juxtaposed stills from *Confessions of a Suburban Girl*, 1992.

swap, steal or merge personas, ultimately to "solve the mystery of who she is" and also perhaps of "what it means to be a woman."[1] The difference between other "chick flicks" or films that feature "mini-sisterhoods" and the subgenre of persona swap films is that women talk about other things besides men and that they are not necessarily positioned against men.[2] Instead, the persona swap film is about the identities, desires and dreams of (usually) two women, who by their friendship or their influence on one another, become more like each other. As Seidelman later describes to Bale in a 2020 interview for the Indie Memphis Film Festival, the romance is between women, where one woman pursues another "like a girl crush," where guys are merely sidekicks and "romances are secondary."[3] However, Seidelman also says that male directors tend to make this girl crush sexual.[4]

Ingmar Bergman's *Persona* is a strange, unsettling and haunting touchstone to this subgenre where the undercurrent of sexual desire is palpable. In *Persona* the swap happens between the actress Elisabet (Liv Ullmann), who has stopped speaking after some kind of mental trauma, and Alma (Bibi Andersson), her younger, talkative nurse. Bergman explains that he was inspired to write the film after observing what he subjectively describes as an "uncanny resemblance" between the two actresses after seeing them on the street together.[5] However, at the time of shooting the film, Bergman was also in a romantic relationship with Bibi Andersson and during the process seemed to "turn his attention" to Liv Ullmann.[6] In a much later interview with Bibi Andersson in 2007, Andersson remembers how Bergman seemed interested in her female friendship with Ullman: "He almost made it into something between a man and a woman! He saw our friendship, and he wanted to get. . . inside it. Involved."[7] Eventually, the scenario takes Alma and Elisabet to a seaside cottage loaned to them by Elisabet's psychiatrist, where they spend the days together eating, drinking, sunbathing and wearing similar black turtlenecks and other accessories. Alma fills the silence with chatter and then one night confesses a secret about a sexual experience she had on the beach with another woman and two younger boys, resulting in pregnancy and abortion. After her disclosure, Alma asks Elisabet: "Is it possible to be one and the same person at the very same time?" And then, describing herself looking in the mirror after seeing one of Elisabet's films one night: "I thought 'We look alike.' Don't get me wrong. You're much more beautiful. But we're alike somehow. I think I could turn into you if I really tried." The most iconic and memorable shot in the film is a composite face, half Alma's and half Elisabet's, suggesting that they have merged identities. Despite these psychological and sexual fantasies of a male director, however, the film does offer some more complexities in female friendships and identities than merely a simple persona merger or exchange. In 1967, writer Susan Sontag wrote a complimentary review of *Persona* in *Sight and Sound*, where she disputes other critics who suggest that the two women in *Persona* merely become one another or exchange identities. Rather, the theme is about doubling itself and representation – "duplication, inversion, reciprocal exchange, repetition," and in doing so, the doubling reveals the cracks in the masks of our perfect façade.[8] More specifically, both women wear masks, and "in the course of the film, both masks crack."⁹ Yet, in *Persona* much violation, tension and violence occur in the process.

In the ten persona swap films that Bale details (described as "on the list of the favorite films of virtually every woman director or film critic I know"), only two are films directed by women: the Czechoslovak surrealist film *Daisies* directed by Vera Chytilova in 1966 and Seidelman's *Desperately Seeking Susan*.¹⁰ Seidelman's gender as a filmmaker may separate her film slightly from Bale's descriptive definitions of this subgenre, since some reviewers have critiqued the persona swap film as being more about men's insecurities about women than about female relationships. In an article for *Vulture* in 2017, titled "What *Persona* is Still Teaching Us About Women Onscreen, 50 Years Later," writer and filmmaker Emily Yoshida criticizes past male-directed persona-swap films as being about "men's anxieties about women left alone, because it was men who were writing and making the movies [. . .] hence the unreality of that so many of these films exist in."¹¹ Essentially, to correct this trend, Yoshida "proposes that the persona-swap film be the domain of female filmmakers for the next two decades."¹² Differently structured than these male anxieties, Seidelman's persona-swap films use plot devices to transform one woman who lives in a kind of unreality, what Betty Friedan calls the "comfortable concentration camp" of the suburban home, into the life of another more free and independent woman, living autonomously out in the world.¹³ And while Chytilova's film may not have much of a plot, Seidelman categorizes *Daisies* as a feminist film because the female characters and friendship resemble the punk riot grrl personas that she admires, which is different from the "genuine phonies" she sees in some male-directed persona swap films.¹⁴

While Bale's 2012 persona swap article initially critiques Seidelman's lack of emotional thread or friendship between the two protagonists, Susan and Roberta (Rosanna Arquette), this initial contrast or lack of connection between the two characters is actually Seidelman's narrative strategy, which advances (rather than merges) the personas of the main characters. In film scholar Kristin Thompson's chapter on *Desperately Seeking Susan* in her book *Storytelling in the New Hollywood*, Thompson describes the characters Susan and Roberta as "parallel protagonists" whose lives have little connection until one "develops a fascination with the other."¹⁵ In this way, the personal ad – desperately seeking Susan – "becomes a dangling clause" that enacts a classic goal-oriented Hollywood plot structure where, in searching for each other, "hidden similarities between the two are gradually revealed" and one character eventually becomes more like the other.¹⁶ Although Thompson critiques the exaggeration in the movie poster's parallelism between the look of the two characters in matching jackets and the tagline – "It's a life so outrageous, it takes two women to live it" – Thompson does suggest that the film "seeks a happy medium" in the protagonists' personas, where each of them redefines themselves not as "either Susan or the old Roberta."[17] More specifically, in Seidelman's persona swap film, the desperate, passive housewife Roberta becomes activated into a more independent and even feminist persona, more like the Susan character, but still able to maintain her independence.

In a 2020 interview with Miriam Bale, Seidelman describes herself as a "narrative filmmaker," positioning herself away from Jaques Rivette's 1974 *Celine and Julie Go Boating*, which was an inspiration for *Desperately Seeking Susan*.[18] It is not that Seidelman is uninterested in these female friendships. Rather, Seidelman uses narrative devices (such as Roberta's amnesia) as an active strategy to unmask and uproot the unhappy suburban housewife character from her terribly unfulfilled life by following and eventually adopting a persona more like an urban and/or working woman that she admires. In other words, Seidelman's take on the persona swap throughout her work is a distinctly feminist strategy, a way to break the housewife out from her suburban façade, where she can become a more independent, free person inhabiting the gritty streets of New York City. This autonomous persona is one that seems more real than the characters in the dream-like Ingmar Bergman, Robert Altman and David Lynch films that both Bale and Yoshida describe.

In Bale's original description, persona swap films are "buddy action" films, starring two women who "speak of [. . .] identities."[19] The films recognize that "any distinctive personality is a performative act" and that the films are "primarily about women in a world removed from men."[20] In the case of Seidelman's *Desperately Seeking Susan* and *She-Devil* (1989), her two most notable persona swap-like films, the protagonists are not initially so-called buddies at all. The distinctive housewife personas/performances (Roberta in *Desperately Seeking Susan* and Ruth in *She-Devil*) are so trapped in their suburban identities that, in order to break free of these traps of femininity, they must find a more radical, interesting performance of female identity, which they seek to find either on the streets of New York City, or in working women who are not tied down by children and husbands. Miriam Bale calls "a swap of position, not persona," part of a "proto-genre" and not a true example of the subgenre.[21] Yet, "proto" does not seem like the appropriate description for the way in which Seidelman is directing her persona swap films. While the desperate housewife does swap out her position for a more independent one in Seidelman's films, the housewife develops a "girl crush"[22] on the more independent woman showcasing how "women can make an impact on each other" in a sort of consciousness-raising way, "liberated by the elasticity of [. . .] superficial identities."[23] In other words, Seidelman's housewives are activated by her counterpart and ultimately become a new version of herself, rather than passively symbiotic with the other woman.

In *The Feminine Mystique*, Betty Friedan also describes the problem that has no name plaguing suburban American housewives of the 1950s as a problem of passivity. The American woman lacks a private image apart from the public image of the mediated happy housewife, smiling on the faces of women's magazines.[24] American housewives had unhappily adjusted to an unreal image, a mask or phony ideal. The problem continued generationally when the children of suburban housewives developed an unhealthy symbiosis with their mothers.[25] Suburban mothers could not give their children the image of a successful career woman; thus, many in Friedan's generation "knew that [they] did not want to be like [their] mothers," even though they were not entirely sure who they wanted to be.[26] Friedan, too, suggests rebellion to battle against this image in order to reach full "self-actualization," which Friedan spends much of "Chapter 13: The Fortified Self" unpacking.[27] Under the suburban façade, self-actualization was "hardly possible at all for women in our society."[28] The mediated persona of a housewife pushes her toward "a complete merging of egos and a loss of separateness" from her husband.[29] Friedan's solution to the problem was not prescription pills, as many doctors were prescribing at the time. Instead, the housewife was to push for growth and realization of one's own identity though "self-fulfillment – autonomy, self-realization, independence, individuality."[30] Likewise, for Susan Seidelman's unhappy housewife characters (and for herself), in order to grow, they cannot keep themselves merged with their husband's ego. Instead, their growth is activated by separating from their housewife identities and initially merging with rebellious female personas who do not fit public images of housewives at all, as well as by seeking urban environments outside the suburban trappings of the middle class. Whereas Betty Friedan ultimately offers education and fulfilling work as a housewife's self-actualization strategy to break free of the feminine mystique, in Seidelman's narratives, the housewife must physically leave her suburban prison (or literally burn it down, as does Ruth in *She-Devil*) and find a kind of so-called private image or autonomous rebelliousness in order to grow and seek out independence. In order for this cause-and-effect persona transformation to happen, Seidelman uses some basic elements of screwball comedy plot design and twists them to explore the characters in whose transformation she is most interested.

SUSANS SEEKING SUSANS

In the *Criterion* interview "Susan Seidelman and Susan Berman on *Smithereens*," Seidelman explains how her success at the Cannes Film Festival with her first feature-length, independent film *Smithereens* put her in touch with agent Brenda Beckett who began to send her scripts. Seidelman felt nervous about picking her first studio project as a female director, especially afraid of "a heavy-handed producer looking over [her] back."[31] She describes two obstacles: first, "I was a female director"; and, second, "I was a female director who wanted to make

Figure 5.3 Susan Seidelman and Susan Berman on the set of *Smithereens*, 1982. (Photograph by Owen Franken. Courtesy of Owen Franken and Susan Seidelman.)

movies about female characters."[32] However, instead of rejecting the challenge of trying to make something more popular, she tried to carefully discern and search for scripts that would examine feminism in popular culture. It took her about a year and a half before she was sent the script for the aptly named *Desperately Seeking Susan*, which "felt like a sign."[33] The theme resonated with her as well:

> I've always been interested in [. . .] a suburban housewife who feels this vague dissatisfaction about the [. . .] life she's living and kind of wants to cross over to another world, wants to have an adventure. The theme [. . .] was personal too because that could have been me.[34]

Susan Seidelman had already escaped the suburbs of Huntingdon Valley, graduated from film school in New York City and made the successful independent, low-budget film *Smithereens*, thus first establishing herself as a more Susan-like persona before taking her second big film-directing project. Seidelman connects the narratives of her first two feature films, swapping Susan Berman's character with Susan/Madonna and giving Roberta the chance to try on these personas, in a way in which one may try on accessories such as jackets, earrings and shoes.

Rather than a story about transformation, *Smithereens* already begins with a main character who has crossed over to another world, the punk scene in New York in the early 1980s. The feisty main character Wren, played by Susan

Berman, had already escaped New Jersey for New York City, where her independent identity is not only established at the start of the film, but she is promoting her punk persona on self-made flyers which she pastes wherever she feels like. In the first few scenes in the movie, Wren steals a pair of sunglasses from an anonymous woman's hand, runs down the stairs to the subway, hops on and starts gluing photocopies of her face to windows and a map, and even handing one to her future love interest Paul (Brad Rijn). The actress Susan Berman describes her own difficulties in becoming a bolder persona like Wren for the role. After breaking her ankle falling on a fire escape early in the filming process and having to take a three-month break from filming, Susan Berman came back from her recovery to learn that Susan Seidelman had changed the actor and role for the part of the other male lead named Eric, to legendary punk singer Richard Hell. Not only was Berman initially scared to work with the famed Richard Hell, but she was also anxious to adopt a more spirited version of Wren's role than she had initially thought. Susan Seidelman asked her to play a version of Giulietta Masina's scrappy prostitute character in Federico Fellini's 1957 film *Nights of Cabiria*, perhaps also reminiscent of the rebellious Italian girls from the other side of the shopping mall that she describes in *Confessions of a Suburban Girl*. Susan Berman felt "completely intimidated" because she could not "imagine [herself] doing that."[35] Nonetheless, Seidelman's direction, as well as costuming, helped Berman transform into the more fame-seeking, confident and idiosyncratic Wren. Later in the interview, Seidelman describes Wren's persona as having a connection to Madonna and how she imagined the character of Susan in *Desperately Seeking Susan*; she even gives Richard Hell a cameo as Susan's murdered lover in the first part of the movie.

Rather than the streets of New York City, *Desperately Seeking Susan* begins in a beauty salon in New Jersey where the camera juxtaposes shots of women attempting to achieve the feminine mystique by getting their legs waxed, nails painted, make-up applied and hair done. The housewife Roberta sits on a salon chair, reading the personal ads in the newspaper, while her sister-in law Leslie (Laurie Metcalf) pages through a beauty magazine with foil in her hair. It is Roberta's birthday, and Leslie insists on Roberta getting something special done. The hairstylist announces: "Don't worry, her husband will love it." The desperateness of the suburban housewife is immediately apparent when, sitting under the hair dryers, Roberta reads a personal ad sent by Jim (Robert Joy) who is "Desperately Seeking Susan." Roberta declares breathlessly: "Desperate. I love that word. So romantic." Leslie replies: "Everybody I know is desperate except you." And Roberta counters: "I'm desperate. . . sort of." In fact, Leslie's character seems to function as a gauge of Friedan-like descriptions of suburban desperation throughout the film. For example, after Roberta disappears from home, she asks Roberta's husband Gary (Mark Blum), the "spa king of New Jersey," questions about Roberta's happiness, similarly explored in *The Feminine Mystique*. Leslie asks, "Does Roberta have orgasms?" and wonders if she is a lesbian, citing "one-fifth of prostitutes are lesbians," after Roberta gets thrown in jail, suspected of prostitution. Leslie describes a "not uncommon" magazine story that she just read of one housewife who turned tricks from nine to noon and then shopped all afternoon before coming home. Similarly, after Gary worriedly overeats, Leslie implores him to do what nervous housewives have been over-prescribed since the 1950s: "Take a Valium like a normal person." The film again reminds us of Roberta's desperation later when Susan finds her diary and her reading material tucked away in her panty drawer next to her side of the bed, including *How to Be Your Own Best Friend*, *I'm OK – You're Ok* and *Dr Ruth's Guide to Good Sex*. By using these props and dialogue cues, Seidelman attempts to process the meaning of feminism in a more popular movie script.

However, it is a commercial for her husband's spa company, Gary's Oasis, that seems to be a tipping point of desperation for Roberta. In the midst of a party, Gary turns on the television for all the guests to watch his "10:58 spot" during the nightly news. At the end of the commercial where four blonde women in swimsuits pull Gary into a showroom hot tub and the voiceover narration describes "Gary's Oasis where all your fantasies can come true," Roberta instead stares at her fuzzy reflection on the screen door. Her hair is perfectly pinned on her head, and her pale pink dress collar primly covers her neck. She opens the door and looks out longingly. In a shot-reverse-shot, the camera cuts to an image of the George Washington Bridge connecting New Jersey to New York City, back to Roberta, and then back to the bridge and a bus with a New York City marquee, out of which Susan eventually steps. Although the romantic desperation of the earlier personal ad acts as the initial pull, the glittering lights of the city across the bridge also seems like a path away from her desperation, suggesting that Roberta's fantasy is clearly different from her husband's.

While it is true that Roberta and Susan do not establish a friendship throughout the narrative (with the exception of the implication that they become real friends at the end), they do swap roles and try on each other's clothes, spaces and lives in intimate ways, or ways which intimately signal their identities and desires. Roberta carries around Susan's skull-bone circular suitcase, wears her bedazzled pyramid coat, applies her colorful make-up and puts on her (stolen) jewelry and sparkly clothes. She almost enacts a role that a close friend of Susan would likely have when Roberta becomes romantically involved with Jim's best friend, Dez (Aidan Quinn), and finds a job as an illusionist's assistant at the Magic Club to replace Susan's curly-haired, bespectacled friend Crystal (Anna Thompson). Both Crystal and Roberta transform into a sexy and glamorous sidekick with the help of a blonde wig and gaudy make-up. Likewise, Susan spends some time at Roberta's suburban house, exclaiming, "Nice place you got here, Gare," while walking into Gary's and Roberta's pink wall-papered bedroom and spraying Roberta's perfume on her neck. She pulls out Roberta's white panties from her drawer, walks into Roberta's closet and puts on a sparkly black jacket. Susan steps on Roberta's scale, trying to determine if they are approximately the same size. They are. She steps into their big spa-like brown tub, in which Susan declares: "You know, I could get used to a place like this." However, when Gary describes how installing these popular tubs can increase the resale value of the home, Susan stops him: "I didn't say I wanted to buy one." In other words, while it is nice to fantasize about living luxuriously, Susan is not going to entirely give up her punk persona and city-dweller life for suburban comforts. Even as Susan lounges by Roberta's pool with a bowl of cheese doodles and half-finished bottles of wine, when she gets out of the pool, she is costumed with a black, lacy bra and men's boxer shorts, rather than a feminine or frilly swimsuit, setting her apart from the spa girls in the commercial for Gary's Oasis or the housewife persona that Roberta left behind. When Susan's boyfriend Jim exclaims, "I think she's ready to settle down," Dez corrects him: "She'd never do that. She's really not the type. . . She's too wild. That's what's so great about her." In Seidelman's take on the persona swap, the characters get to keep attributes about themselves that make them "great," rather than completely transforming their personas into someone they are not. This is a theme that Seidelman carries over into her other big persona swap film *She-Devil*, dramatically shifting the outcome of the original source novel.

CAREER DEVILS

While Susan Seidelman's film *She-Devil* does not immediately appear to be a persona swap film in the same way as *Desperately Seeking Susan*, Fay Weldon's 1983 source novel *The Life and Loves of a She-Devil* is clearly a story about a desperate housewife, Ruth, who, through lots of expensive plastic surgery, literally swaps out her body and life to become Mary Fisher, the romance writer who was having an affair with Ruth's husband, named Bobo in the novel. Ruth, the housewife scorned, goes through several years of painful, cutting-edge surgeries (taking out all her teeth to trim three inches off her jaw and transform her face, sawing her femur bones to shorten her 6'2' frame down to 5'6' and so on) done by world-renowned Frankenstein-like plastic surgeons so that Ruth can fully become the body and persona of Mary Fisher, the feminine ideal. Weldon describes Mary as "small and pretty and delicately formed, prone to fainting and weeping and sleeping with men while pretending that she doesn't."[36] She also has size-four feet, no children and lots of orgasms with Bobo. This complete persona swap or identity shift, however, is not how

Seidelman chooses to adapt the novel. Instead of subsuming Ruth's total look and identity into Mary's, Seidelman changes the script and at the end of the film gives Ruth (Rosanne Barr) her own successful business and life as herself. Additionally, Seidelman allows Mary Fisher (Meryl Streep) her own transformation from trashy romance novelist to a more serious writer, shown in an interview wearing baggy, black clothes and oversized glasses on the Sally Jessy Raphael Show, where she is introduced as a "former romance novelist." Ruth's voiceover states: "People can change. Even Mary Fisher." This is in contrast to the source novel where the distraught Mary Fisher develops cancer, loses her hair and dies alone. In other words, Seidelman renegotiates the meaning of the she-devil, redefining tropes of popular feminism in popular texts.

Using the characterization of a she-devil to describe an angry or independent woman who does not possess the feminine mystique or conform to postwar suburban mandates is a familiar trope. In Chapter Two of *The Feminine Mystique*, titled "The Happy Housewife Heroine," Betty Friedan spends a good deal of the chapter analyzing the striking way in which advertisements, articles and short stories in women's magazines dramatically shift from the 1930s and 1940s to the post-war 1950s in retrograde and harmful ways. Earlier magazine heroines, largely written by women, passionately pursued both careers and men and did not have to give up one for the other.[37] In contrast, the 1950s housewife-mother heroines, considered "the model for all women," gave up their careers for marriage, and their stories were written largely by male writers.[38] Friedan describes a schizophrenic split in the image of women in magazines beginning in 1949, as between either a feminine woman or a career woman. The career woman or the temptations of a career are frequently described as the devil. Friedan elaborates:

> The new morality story is the exorcising of the forbidden career dream, the heroine's victory over Mephistopheles: the devil, first in the form of a career woman, who threatens to take away the heroine's husband or child, and finally, the devil inside the heroine herself, the dream of independence, the discontent of spirit, and even the feeling of a separate identity that must be exorcised to win or keep the love of husband and child.[39]

Often, at the end of these short stories, the heroines disappear altogether as separate self and "the subject of her own story. The end of the road is togetherness, where the woman has no independent self [. . .] she exists only for and through her husband and child."[40] In other words, as a narrative device in popular stories, the devil provokes the housewife out of her suburban façade and away from her husband and children. If she stays, she remains someone's wife and mother. If she leaves, she becomes her own independent, liberated self – a she-devil.

As a narrative device, the devil in Weldon's text functions slightly differently from the one in Seidelman's adaptation. Through Ruth's narration, Weldon's novel spends a good amount of time describing Ruth's neighborhood – "green, leafy, prosperous [. . .] a thousand or more similar houses [. . .]. A suburb" – in contrast to her unfeminine body, her tall frame, broad shoulders, hooked nose, fleshy hips and hairy face moles – "I was unlucky, you might think, in the great lottery that is a woman's life."[41] As a figure opposite to Mary, Ruth wonders: "And how, especially, do ugly women survive?"[42] Even though Ruth is called "such a good wife" by her mother-in-law and desperately tries to fulfil her "matrimonial duties" by reciting to herself the "Litany of the Good Wife" in her bedroom after ruining dinner with her in-laws, the answer to Ruth's survival and drive lies in the devil: "Hate obsesses and transforms me."[43] When, out of anger, Bobo calls her a "she-devil," Ruth finally finds liberation, declaring: "This is exhilarating! If you are a she-devil, your mind clears at once [. . .]. There is only, in the end, what you want [. . .]. Nothing is impossible for she-devils."[44] And when Ruth later stands naked in front of the mirror, wanting change, she says: "Peel away the wife, the mother, find the woman and there the she-devil is."[45] When the mask of wife and mother cracks, the face underneath is a she-devil, and the eyes glitter "so bright, they light up the room."[46] Within the novel, Ruth's new persona and transformation is clearly against God's wishes. At one point during a lightning storm, her plastic surgeon Mr. Ghengis remarks: "God's angry. You're defying him." To which Ruth replies: "Of course He's angry. I'm remaking myself."[47] While Ruth's she-devil persona drives her to burn down her suburban house, leave her kids with Bobo and Mary Fisher, start her own business, endure insane surgeries and basically steal enough money to buy Mary Fisher's crumbling high tower by the sea, it does not ultimately bring her self-actualization. Instead, she does not rest until she becomes so very much like the image on Mary Fisher's book cover that she is willing to insist on surgeries that will cause her life-long pain, screaming at night. In the last few pages of the book, she writes a novel like Mary Fisher, just to see if she could. But even though Ruth has completely swapped personas in the novel, she still seems sad and stuck in a different kind of feminine mystique. The last two lines of the book are: "I am a lady of six foot two, who had tucks taken in her legs. A comic turn, turned serious."[48] Aside from the suggestion that neither housewife nor childless career woman personas are truly fulfilling, the reader is also left unsatisfied, wishing both Ruth and Mary would have found their own path, not contingent on sleeping with a man or achieving an ideal beauty mystique.

Seidelman describes her position on trying to deliver a feminist message in a mainstream movie. In an interview with *Premiere Presents*, Seidelman talks about the opportunity to make a film "about the politics of beauty and the politics of femininity [and] how often a woman's power is based on how she looks."⁴⁹ She does not want her character of Ruth to swap roles with Mary Fisher, transforming her into some sort of phony feminine ideal. In the film, Ruth keeps her name and her body. Aside from removing the hairy mole on her face, there are no plastic surgeries, no dramatic weight losses, no pseudonyms and no sleeping with priests or judges to achieve her goals. In fact, Seidelman's notes on the shooting script show that she eliminates parts of the script at the end of the film where Ruth is supposed to be working toward a more ideal body. In a line about Ruth stepping on a scale with "encouraging" results, Seidelman crosses out "encouraging" to "– well, who cares." Instead, Seidelman transforms the script to give Ruth her own identity, some meaningful female friendships and a successful business. While the Vesta Rose Employment Agency also appears in the novel, in the film it takes on a much bigger role in transforming Ruth and the lives of other female characters "who just needed a little support and encouragement" to develop into successful career women, becoming part of Ruth's "own personal army" or sisterhood. Seidelman gives nods to strong female role models and popular feminism. For example, hanging on the walls of the Vesta Rose Employment Agency are framed black-and-white photos of other successful, independent women: Mother Theresa, Oprah, Gloria Steinem, Eleanor Roosevelt and Jane Fonda. At one point in a clear demonstration of defiance against the romance novels that her daughter writes, Mary's mother, Mrs. Fisher (Sylvia Miles), is sitting on the lawn of Mary Fisher's expansive sea-side home, drinking a pina colada with an umbrella and reading a copy of *The New Our Bodies Ourselves*. Finally, Seidelman ends *She-Devil* with an homage to the film *Tootsie* (Sydney Pollack,

Figure 5.4 Roseanne Barr in the ending shot of *She-Devil*, 1989.

1982) where Dustin Hoffman transforms himself into a woman to become a successful New York working actress. The last shot uses a telephoto lens and watches Ruth, clutching Mary Fisher's latest and more serious novel, walking confidently toward the camera with her army of career women on the streets of New York City. This is a contrast to the novel's ending where Ruth-as-Mary sits up alone with her deranged husband in the high tower by the sea. In an interview about her role in the film, Rosanne Barr sums up what seems to be Seidelman's directorial take on the she-devil: "I think she-devil is a pretty empowering word. It just means you take control."[50]

HOUSEWIFE LIBERATION

Although the feminist persona swap strategy does not continue with the same fervor in Seidelman's films after *She-Devil*, there are many thematic overlaps in her subsequent work. The narrative arc of the unhappy suburban housewife who goes through a feminist transformation is still prominent in many of Seidelman's later films, showing the importance of this storyline to her work as a director.

In the 1990s, she directed a short called *The Dutch Master* (1993) where a young dental hygienist (Mira Sorvino) engaged to a New York police officer fantasizes about swapping places with a seventeenth-century Dutch maid in a museum painting to fulfil a desperate sexual desire. As the wedding date becomes close to a week away, her friends and family start to get worried. In a technique she would later use again in episodes of *Sex and the City*, characters turn toward the camera, breaking the fourth wall to explain their concern. Theresa's mother fries sausages in hair rollers and explains the changes in her daughter: "She says she's afraid that once she gets married, her life will be boring." Later, when Theresa shows up to clean teeth in a Dutch bonnet, her hygienist friend exclaims: "It was so weird. I mean it was like she'd become one of those Stepford wives or something." On the night before she is going to get married, Theresa hides in the museum bathroom with her bonnet and lacy bustier until after closing. With her flashlight, she seemingly walks into the painting and closely kneels by the bed to watch the two lovers. When the woman in the painting clutches her arm in a moment of ecstasy, Theresa faints, and the museum guard finds her passed out on the museum floor in front of the painting. The next day, Theresa does not show up for her wedding. And while her family members shake their heads and her scorned fiancé swears that she will be found, Seidelman seems to suggest to us that Theresa has vanished forever into the painting. In the last shot, Theresa is laying on the same bed where she watched the painted lovers the night before, clutching her heaving chest in a see-through negligee. While the seventeenth-century painting and the Stepford-like bonnet might seem retrograde to her friends, Theresa escapes her fate as a contemporary housewife and achieves sexual fulfillment, in a plot similar to a romance novel. Instead of ending in marriage, this narrative continuously repeats the excitement of an affair.

Of the three episodes of *Sex and the City* that Seidelman directed in 1998, episode 10, called "The Baby Shower," serves as a cautionary tale of what can happen when city girls get married and move to the suburbs to become Stepford wives. The four New York friends receive an invitation to a baby shower from once-wild city girl Laney Berlin (Dana Wheeler-Nicholson). Flashbacks from eight years ago show Laney at a bar, stripping off her shirt and bra, both a sign of sexual freedom and reminiscent of the pop culture trope of feminist bra-burning. Miranda (Cynthia Nixon) declares: "Those things make so many public appearances, they need a booking agent." However, Carrie (Sarah Jessica Parker) describes in her narration that Laney did "the most shocking thing of all. She met a Wall Street Investment Banker, married him and moved to Connecticut." This move was not supposed to happen; "She was supposed to have sex with Sid Vicious and move to heroin." The friends lament having to leave New York and drive to the suburbs, "a place so filled with nature [yet] so unnatural," and describe baby showers as "cults" where all the women "think the same, dress the same and sacrifice themselves to the same cause. Babies." As Carrie, whose period is seven days late, walks to Laney's bathroom to pee, she anxiously wonders whether she is next. Seidelman directs cinematographer Michael Barrow to film Carrie's walk as frenetic and shaky in slow motion and Dutch angles, giving it a horrific feel, more like *Rosemary's Baby*. As Carrie gazes at a photograph on the bathroom wall of a nude, pregnant Laney (replicating Demi Moore's 1991 *Vanity Fair* photo), she wonders what was "still buried deep inside the mommies downstairs?" In the next few sequences, Seidelman films baby shower guests confessing directly to the camera what they used be like or do as a career before having kids. They slept around. They were senior vice presidents. They fantasized about dating women. They smoked pot. These desperate confessions are reminiscent of the confessional tone in Seidelman's *Confessions of a Suburban Girl* documentary. Toward the end of the episode, Laney, eating a pickle in her kitchen, calls Carrie who is getting ready for Samantha's "I don't have a baby" shower party. Seidelman shows the two talking in split screen, juxtaposing two very different outcomes between friends who once shared similar, fun, single lifestyles. When Laney shows up unexpectedly to Samantha's party, wanting to join in their fun, she ends up looking ridiculous, trying to drink alcohol and exclaiming: "Hey you fuckers, who wants to see my tits?" While one lone dude raises his hand, the others look at her in horror while she struggles with her maternity top. Whereas Samantha (Kim Cattrall) declares it "the most fabulous validation I've ever gotten in my life," Laney laments to Carrie: "One day

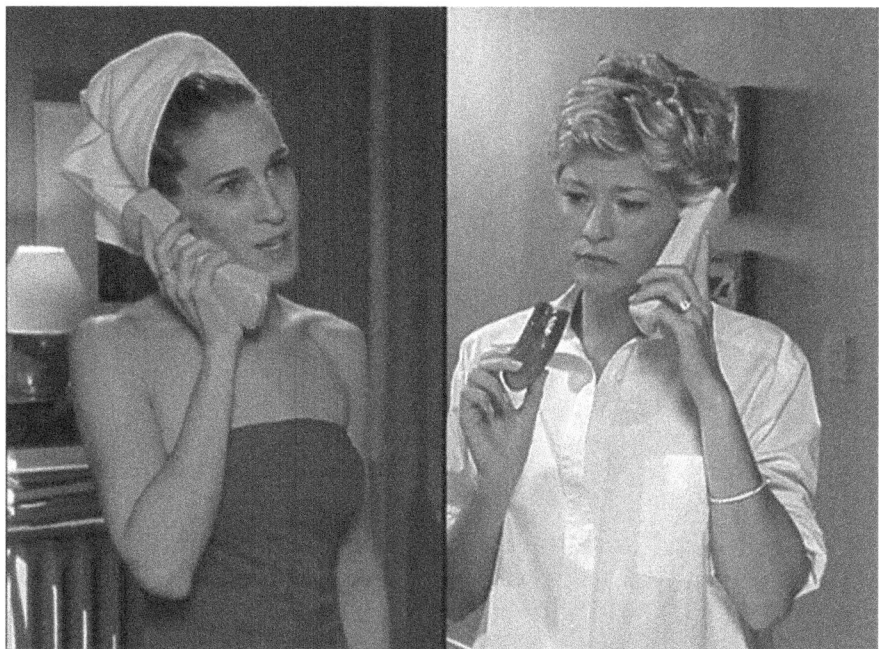

Figure 5.5 Carrie Bradshaw (Sarah Jessica Parker) and Laney (Dana Wheeler-Nicholson) talk on the phone during "The Baby Shower" episode of *Sex and the City*, 1998.

you're going to wake up and you're not going to recognize yourself." When Carrie sits in the park the next day watching children play, wondering "would I somehow manage to stay me?" she seems relieved when she gets her period on the way home and is liberated from having to answer that question.

In the twenty-first century, Seidelman takes scripts that speak to later generations of housewives who are no longer young or have already raised their kids. In *Boynton Beach Club* (2005), which was actually co-written by Florence Seidelman, Susan Seidelman's mother, widowed character Jack (Len Cariou) is surprised to learn that his late wife, Phyllis, wanted more than to "get married and have kids" when his punk-rock granddaughter, who has been reading her old diaries tucked into her closet, announces: "Did you know Nana wanted to be a psychiatrist? I read it in her diary." She continues: "Actually, she always regretted marrying so young and not going to college." He replies: "Really. All those years together I thought I knew everything about her." This conversation is interrupted when the phone rings from another member of the Bereavement Club, Sandy (Sally Kellerman), who is currently dating Jack and is more open about her sexual desires and needs, a persona seemingly opposite to Phyllis. Seidelman even includes a shot of her baring her breasts to Jack, again signaling a more rebellious or feminist persona. But that night

Jack is not ready to embrace the different kind of woman yet, when he asks Sandy to "just cuddle."

Likewise, in *The Hot Flashes* (2013), Beth's (Brooke Shields) unhappy marriage is crumbling. Seidelman includes many shots of Beth's husband Laurence (Eric Roberts) sitting on the couch drinking beer and making snide remarks about Beth's lack of accomplishments. Later, we learn that he is having an affair. Although Beth does not swap personas, she does transform from a menopausal married woman experiencing early hot flashes to a confident single woman athlete and profitable blogger at BethWon'tShutUp.com. This transformation happens with the help of a sisterhood of friends whom she organized to play basketball as a fundraiser for Tess Mulldoon's Mobile Mammography truck, after it lost its state funding. Beth's basketball team "The Hot Flashes" plays against the competitive high school girls' team "The Armadillos" and beats them. As Beth walks down the halls after the game, she confronts her husband and tells him that it is over. Laurence says: "Beth, face it. You can't make it all alone. At your age?" Beth replies: "You're right. I can't. But I'm not alone." After the "6 months later" intertitle, we see Beth meeting her girlfriends for coffee, laughing and talking about all their current accomplishments. Particularly, Beth's next blogpost is called "Tools for Goin' it Alone," which they jokingly comment might be misunderstood as an article about vibrators. The blogpost title is also a response to her former husband's snide remarks, since with her girlfriends Beth is never really alone.

RUTH'S CONFESSIONS

Although the editor of this collection, Susan Kerns, may not want me to discuss the striking coincidences in our names, I cannot help but conclude with a bit of my own confession of gratitude for all the Susans that pull us Ruths (or Robertas) out of our desperation and give us inspiration for drama, adventure and "a mild form of badness." As Susan Seidelman felt when receiving the script for *Desperately Seeking Susan*, it "felt like a sign" that my unmarried, childless and brilliant friend, Columbia College Chicago Film Professor Susan Kerns, wanted to edit a collection on film director Susan Seidelman, and one of the bullet points on the call for papers was "activist housewives in Seidelman's films." Like the characters in Seidelman's films, I have lived life as a former suburban girl and have often currently felt a like a desperate housewife, trying to be both a married mother of two young children and a teaching academic. But it is those Susan personas (Susan Sontag, Susan Seidelman, Susan Berman, Susan-Desperately Seeking and Susan Kerns) that help remind us of our worth and that we are not alone. The bullet point in the call for papers was my own sign, activating me to write this paper and pushing me to reclaim a sense of self outside my family. With a little bit of rebelliousness, a black leather jacket and maybe some amnesia or blurry vision, we can all become more like the liberated Susans we admire. Thank you to all the Susans. With love, all the Ruths.

NOTES

1. Bale, Miriam, "Persona Swap PT. 1: Past," *Joan's Digest: A Film Quarterly*, Spring 2012.
2. Ibid.
3. Indie Memphis Film Festival, "Virtual Discussion with Susan Seidelman (Desperately Seeking Susan)," *YouTube.com*, 2 June 2020.
4. Ibid.
5. Dan Callahan, "A Woman's Face: Bibi Andersson & Persona at BAM," *Slant Magazine*, 21 November 2007.
6. Ibid.
7. Ibid.
8. Susan Sontag, "Persona Review," *Sight and Sound: Scraps from the Loft*, 16 October 2016.
9. Ibid.
10. Bale, "Persona Swap PT. 1: Past." Besides *Persona*, the others are *Gentlemen Prefer Blondes* (1953), *Performance* (1970), *Céline and Julie Go Boating* (1974), *Freaky Friday* (1976), *3 Women* (1977), *Single White Female* (1992) and *Mulholland Drive* (2001).
11. Emily Yoshida, "What *Persona* is Still Teaching Us About Women Onscreen, 50 Years Later," *Vulture*, 12 May 2017.
12. Ibid.
13. Betty Friedan, *The Feminine Mystique* (New York: Dell Publishing Company, 1963), 306.
14. Indie Memphis Film Festival, "Virtual Discussion."
15. Kristin Thompson, *Storytelling in the New Hollywood: Understanding Classical Narrative Technique* (Cambridge: Harvard University Press, 1999), 46.
16. Ibid. p. 159, 46.
17. Ibid. p. 157, 171.
18. Indie Memphis Film Festival, "Virtual Discussion."
19. Bale, "Persona Swap PT. 1: Past."
20. Ibid.
21. Ibid.
22. Indie Memphis Film Festival, "Virtual Discussion."
23. Bale, "Persona Swap PT. 1: Past."
24. Friedan, *The Feminine Mystique*, 273, 68.
25. Ibid. p. 277–78.
26. Ibid. p. 65.
27. Ibid. p. 280.
28. Ibid. p. 310.
29. Ibid. p. 312.
30. Ibid. p. 314.
31. "Susan Seidelman and Susan Berman on *Smithereens*," *The Criterion Channel*, 2018.
32. Ibid.
33. Ibid.
34. Ibid.
35. Ibid.

36. Fay Weldon, *The Life and Loves of a She-Devil* (New York: Ballantine Books, 1983), 2.
37. Friedan, *The Feminine Mystique*, 37.
38. Ibid. p. 47.
39. Ibid. p. 40.
40. Ibid. p. 41.
41. Weldon, *The Life and Loves of a She-Devil*, 4–5.
42. Ibid. p. 7.
43. Ibid. p. 26, 3.
44. Ibid. p. 48.
45. Ibid. p. 49.
46. Ibid. p. 49.
47. Ibid. p. 269.
48. Ibid. p. 278.
49. Premiere Presents, "She-Devil Behind the Scenes 1989," *YouTube.com*, 3 December 2017.
50. Ibid.

CHAPTER 6

Original *She-Devil* Ending Screenplay Pages

Written by Barry Strugatz and Mark R. Burns and based on the novel *The Life and Loves of a She-Devil* by Fay Weldon, the screenplay pages reproduced here were filmed before another ending was written, shot and included in the film as it exists today. Markings on these pages are Susan Seidelman's notes.

106 ORIGINAL *SHE-DEVIL* ENDING SCREENPLAY PAGES

223A.
She's dressed in a sweat-suit, and working out on a hi-tech exercise bicycle.

ON THE TV:

          SALLY
Yes...

          MARY
We may as well be blunt.

          SALLY
Okay. But your new book has gotten fantastic reviews--

          MARY
Yes, and from the serious critics.

          SALLY
It's a real departure from anything you've ever done before. Your heroines are more complex -- you could say less romantic. Why is that?

          MARY
You know, Sally, to write about something, you must have a personal belief system. One day I looked in the mirror and realized that there were a lot of things I no longer believed in.

          SALLY
Like what?

          MARY
Like Romantic Love. I wonder if it can exist in a world trashed by greed and infidelity.

          SALLY
You sound cynical.

          MARY
Cynical, no. Bruised and skeptical, yes -- although ten months of therapy have helped me recover from a dysfunctional relationship...And I no longer subscribe to certain patterns of emotional dependency.
          (thoughtful)
I guess I've learned the hard way that love is a very complicated...thing...

          RUTH (VO)
...Yes, people can change...

Figure 6.1 Final pages of original *She-Devil* screenplay. (Courtesy of Susan Seidelman.)

ORIGINAL *SHE-DEVIL* ENDING SCREENPLAY PAGES 107

continued   (6/4/89)   1

> MARY
> ...And right now I'm very close to reaching a plateau of self-acceptance. I'm no longer the same innocent, vulnerable woman I once was. I've come to the conclusion that there's such a thing as being too nice...
>
> RUTH (VO)
> ...Of course, you can't expect miracles.

INT. RUTH'S OFFICE - AT THAT MOMENT

Ruth stops bicycling. She smiles to herself and climbs off the bike.

> RUTH (VO)
> ...But if you work hard enough at something...

Ruth steps onto a scale. It reads: 181.

> RUTH (VO)
> ...the results can be ~~encouraging~~ well, who cares.

CUT TO:

EXT. RIZZOLI BOOKSTORE - MANHATTAN - DAY

The window display on Fifth Avenue features copies of "Trust and Betrayal." A sign reads:

> MEET MARY FISHER
> AUTHOR OF
> "TRUST AND BETRAYAL"
> NOON TODAY!!!

Figure 6.2 Final pages of original *She-Devil* screenplay. (Courtesy of Susan Seidelman.)

ORIGINAL *SHE-DEVIL* ENDING SCREENPLAY PAGES

225. INT. RIZZOLI'S   225.

The store is packed. There is a long line of ACADEMIC-
TYPES waiting for Mary to autograph her book.

Mary is seated behind a table, signing copies.

AT THE HEAD OF THE LINE

DOUGLAS, an elderly man, hands Mary a copy of the book.
          DOUGLAS
   Could you make it out to "Douglas?"

          MARY
     (signing the book)
   "To Douglas..." Thank you

Mary hands the book back to Douglas and he walks off.
Mary automatically puts her hand out to take a copy of the
book from the next person -- <u>it's Ruth</u>.

Mary doesn't look up. She's been doing this all day.

          MARY
   How would you like me to inscribe it?

          RUTH
   Would you sign it: "To Ruth."

          MARY
     (writing)
   "To Ruth -- with thanks, Mary Fisher."

Glancing up, Mary hands the book back to Ruth.

          RUTH
   Thank you.

Ruth takes the book and walks away, by which time the next
fan has thrust a copy of the book into Mary's hand.

Mary is about to inscribe it, but something makes her look
up, just in time to catch Ruth exiting the book store.
For a moment we think she might even recognize
Ruth...Maybe?...Maybe not?...

     SEXY MALE VOICE (VO)
     (French accent)
   Would you please inscribe it to
   "Alain?"

Mary turns and sees ALAIN, a gorgeous thirty-ish professor
casual but stylish sweater and slacks. His beautiful
eyes meet hers -- Mary's enthralled.

          MARY
   Of course...

Mary starts to sign the book.

Figure 6.3 Final pages of original *She-Devil* screenplay. (Courtesy of Susan Seidelman.)

ORIGINAL *SHE-DEVIL* ENDING SCREENPLAY PAGES

225. continued (6/26/89)

>   ALAIN
> I saw you give a reading at the
> Institut Francais -- you were
> magnificent! Miss Fisher
>
>   MARY
> Thank you so much.
>
>   ALAIN
> (Your grasp of the post-modern
> metaphor is unparalleled, Ms. Fisher.
>
>   MARY
>   (aroused)
> Oh, please...call me Mary.

WE HOLD momentarily on Mary's aroused face.

226.   EXT. MIDTOWN STREET - MOMENTS LATER

Ruth walks down the avenue, Mary's book under her arm.
She has a spring in her step, a triumphant air about her.

CLOSE ON Ruth's face.

Ruth smiles confidentially as the CAMERA CRANES BACK AND
UP to reveal Ruth walking in a LARGE CROWD OF PEDESTRIANS
-- almost all of them are WOMEN -- short, tall, fat, thin,
attractive, ordinary, unremarkable, but all VERY REAL
WOMEN.

The CAMERA CONTINUES BACK until Ruth's face becomes just
one in the crowd.

227.*   EXT. MANSION - DAY

A limousine comes down the road and pulls into the drive-
way.

>   RUTH (VO)
> I can't hate Mary Fisher anymore...

The front gate opens and the limousine heads up the drive.

IN FRONT OF THE MANSION

the limousine pulls around the circular drive and stops
by the front steps.

>   RUTH (VO)
> ...She still writes her books about
> love...

The CHAUFFEUR hops out and opens the back door.

>   RUTH (VO)
> ...but now she knows that love is
> complicated...

Figure 6.4 Final pages of original *She-Devil* screenplay. (Courtesy of Susan Seidelman.)

ORIGINAL *SHE-DEVIL* ENDING SCREENPLAY PAGES

27. continued (6/26/89)

    WE SEE a woman's high-heeled foot step out onto the driveway.

                  RUTH (VO)
        She learned that from me...

    As the woman walks up the front steps the CAMERA reveals that she is Ruth.

                  RUTH (VO)
        ...the She-Devil.

    As Ruth reaches the front door, it opens and Nicolette, Andy and Fuzzy run past her and onto the front lawn to play.

    Standing there, WE NOW SEE a very handsome BUTLER. He smiles at Ruth as she steps inside the house.

    Ruth looks at him, then turns to the CAMERA and smiles knowingly. The butler closes the door behind her.

    SUPER TITLE in fancy script: <u>THE END</u>

Figure 6.5 Final pages of original *She-Devil* screenplay. (Courtesy of Susan Seidelman.)

CHAPTER 7

Unsettling Domesticity: *Desperately Seeking Susan*, Madonna and the Voyeuristic Politics of MTV Stardom

Michael Reinhard

When desperate housewife Roberta (Rosanna Arquette) looks through the coin-operated binoculars in *Desperately Seeking Susan* (1985), she finds the woman she was longing to be. The effortlessly cool Susan (superstar Madonna Louise Ciccone) smoking a cigarette in lace gloves and kissing her paramour greets the housewife's gaze. Susan Seidelman's direction underscores Roberta's voyeurism through repeated cuts to a medium shot of the housewife's act of looking. The binocular peephole-effect echoes this emphasis, recalling genre motifs that frequently mark romantic climaxes in women's literary and filmic genres. Roberta's voyeuristic desires, quasi-sexual and quasi-political, places Susan at the heart of the housewife's longing for her own independence from domestic life. This structure of looking relations, as I argue in this chapter, draws on the intertextual range of associations around Madonna's star image as an archetype of female celebrity in 1980s music television. Positioned in this way, Susan embodies the sexual and racial hierarchies of post-war urban and suburban space unsettled by the introduction of cable networks such as MTV.

Desperately Seeking Susan follows New Jersey housewife Roberta who forgets her identity after hitting her head while following downtown bohemian Susan, whose romantic exploits are chronicled in the personal ads that the housewife reads. A significant piece of direction and historical artefact, *Desperately Seeking Susan* captures 1980s anxieties around independent and sexually liberated women, domesticity and the recentering of the American city within national popular culture. Seidelman gathers the period's images of lifestyle advertising made dominant by television and explores the significance of this new female iconography as a rejection of domesticity and an embrace of the cross-racial and interclass mixing of the city. Recalling second-wave feminism's consideration of the housewife, Leora Barish's script owes debts to what Lisa Marie Hogeland has identified as the 1970s "consciousness-raising (CR) novel" that introduced "feminist ideas to a broader reading public [. . .] beyond the small-group networks that made up radical feminism."¹ These novels, so Hogeland observes, employed "feminist-inflected devices as the housewife's coming to consciousness and sexual awakening as political awakening," all elements that describe Roberta's exit from the home, even as *Desperately Seeking Susan* avoids political conclusions to this journey.² Compellingly, the ending, contrasting most Hollywood fare, refuses to reunite the film's central marriage. With this in mind, *Desperately Seeking Susan* features cultural commitments made popular by feminism's literary influences in that it explores female independence narratively, as Bonnie J. Dow also observes of prime-time television depictions of divorce, spousal death, changes to a living location, or job acquisition.³

To examine interconnections between feminism, anti-domesticity and female music celebrity, this chapter discusses Susan Seidelman's work in relation to MTV's depiction of female youth culture in the 1980s by interrogating *Desperately Seeking Susan* as representative of this cultural shift. "Unsettling Domesticity" analyses this history by looking at the development of music videos with a female address in the context of MTV's appeal to the coveted rock'n'roll audience. Against the masculine and white bent of rock musicianship, I study how MTV's music videos by female musicians such as Tina Turner, Pat Benatar, Cyndi Lauper and Madonna challenged gendered hierarchies in music by positioning female sexual agency against traditional attitudes about women's sexuality. Seidelman's work highlights this dimension of female stardom through the studio's decision to cast Madonna as Susan. This chapter, moreover, underscores how *Desperately Seeking Susan* dramatizes this new archetype of female stardom and its voyeuristic politics. Echoing 1980s commentary on how fans would dress up and impersonate the performer, Roberta's grappling with suburban domesticity (and her privileged experience of whiteness) embodies this impersonation as she loses herself in the persona of Madonna's Susan.⁴ While narratives of mistaken identity have often explored female identity as in Ingmar Bergman's *Persona* (1966) and Robert Altman's *Three Women* (1977), *Desperately Seeking Susan*'s makes legible how MTV's female stardom premised itself on a reclamation of female autonomy and sexual agency through a voyeuristic engagement with a sexually liberated form of female celebrity. Recalling "the new woman" archetype of early Hollywood film culture, *Desperately Seeking Susan* mythologizes MTV's female music celebrity for how it gathered critiques of domesticity, the restriction of women's bodily autonomy, and the need for sexual fulfillment, all observable themes in Seidelman's other projects such as *Smithereens* (1982) and *Sex and the City* (1998–2004).

The unsettling of suburban domesticity comes to the fore in *Desperately Seeking Susan* through Roberta's voyeuristic and vicarious experience of Susan's life. For the housewife, this voyeurism promises the possibility of self-expression, as her stalking gaze transgresses boundaries of urban and suburban space and its mapping of racial and sexual geographies. When Susan travels to the domestic enclaves of the suburbs, she brings not only the sexual heat of the city but also drugs like marijuana, culturally racialized due to the expansion of the War on Drugs by the Nixon, Reagan and Clinton administrations, presidencies that were defined, in part, by their framing of urban crises through a white political imaginary. To this point, the value of respectability, historically racialized and classed through the ennoblement of "true womanhood," has played a pivotal role in demarcating the social geographies of the suburbs in its racial identity and set of class expectations for women. *Desperately Seeking Susan* features Roberta sacrificing her respectability for the anonymity of the city, providing new autonomy over her body while bringing connotations of sexual and racial deviancy for her husband Gary (Mark Blum) and sister-in-law Leslie (Laurie Metcalf). Roberta's violation of this geography recalls the unsettling of key binaries in American public life of the twentieth century between urban/suburban space, Black/white racial identity and heterosexuality/homosexuality, which were amplified by MTV's influence of US popular culture.

Crucially, *Desperately Seeking Susan* represents New York as Other to the assumed social groups of the suburbs. The film, thus, casts urban space as the site of personal and sexual autonomy for women experiencing domestic malaise. For this reason, *Desperately Seeking Susan* is significant within longer histories of feminism on film and the resetting of cultural geographies in white, middle-class imaginings of the city. In "Desperately Seeking Difference," Jackie Stacey interrogates how the film recodes the traditional looking relations of classical Hollywood narratives. Importantly, Stacey attends to the "homosexual pleasures of female spectatorship," recognizing how traditional accounts of pleasure in dominant cinema are rooted in theories of sexual difference and the presumed absence of the female gaze.[5] While the object of the film's gaze remains a woman, the gaze's subject is Roberta whose desire propels the narrative forward. That said, Stacey's critical reading leaves unexplored urban iconography and the racial tensions that mark Susan's assertion of self-fulfillment. Contending with sexual respectability and marital dissatisfaction, *Desperately Seeking Susan* contributed to the iconography of modern-day liberal feminism by reclaiming urban space as a rejection of suburban domesticity. Importantly, the film also illustrates media synergy and cross-promotion that would become a mainstay of youth culture by the 1990s. When Susan is seen in white lace gloves, eating cheese puffs, her look of attitude gestures to the visual advertising pioneered by cable networks such as MTV, particularly through the splashy use of color and promise of urban coolness. These motifs crystallize in female-driven music videos that functioned as the promotional address to young female viewers on the network. This reclamation of urban space on MTV resettled urban geographies marked by racial and sexual paranoia by the late-nineteenth-century's ideology of domesticity. As Catherine Jurca observes, this suburban ideal functioned as a "a model of white middle-class community as well as of private domestic life" – a model of community that *Desperately Seeking Susan* explicitly rejects.[6]

An unexpected hit, *Desperately Seeking Susan* promised a new wave of female talent, yet its success was not assured. As Michael London observes in the *Los Angeles Times*, "sexual politics being what they are in Hollywood, a film with two women producers, a woman director, a woman writer, and two female lead characters wasn't destined to be an easy sale."[7] The project suffered various challenges from working with Warner Bros., moving to a new studio at Orion Pictures thanks to Senior Vice President Barbara Boyle and revising the script to add romance, danger and spectacle for various audiences.[8] This press coverage also illustrates how women in Hollywood are both celebrated and othered due to their gender identity. Female creatives are forced to work through and against this ambivalence as a particular experience of laboring in the film industry. To this point, Seidelman has stated: "I bristle a little bit when they say 'female director' or 'woman director' as though that's a way of saying, 'Well, she makes soft little sensitive movies that don't look very good and are technically sophisticated but they're gentle'."[9] Following its release, *Desperately Seeking Susan* announced the distinction of Madonna as not only a music and television talent but also a film one. During the release, producers Midge Sanford and Sarah Pillsbury took pains to qualify the superstar's casting:

> We feel it's important to tell people that this is about two women and not a Madonna film [. . .] forgetting who Madonna is, the Susan character represents freedom and living one's life in a liberated fashion, in contrast to the repressed Roberta.[10]

At the same time, the singer's inclusion reflected new archetypes of music stardom that drew influence from the bohemian downtown scene in New York. *Desperately Seeking Susan*, significantly, can be studied for how it mythologizes female stardom within the larger field of 1980s post-feminist culture.

With debts to the French New Wave and its generational questioning of "quality film," Seidelman's work interrogates new models of female celebrity popularized by MTV's arrival. This new archetype, rooted in a celebration of girl culture and a reclamation of female pleasure, can be studied through cultural texts such as *Desperately Seeking Susan*. Reflective of the cultural impact of cable networks, the MTV female star promised new forms of social representation for women through its youth culture address. As Lisa Lewis has observed, these videos appealed to female audiences by strategically appropriating street culture, dance as a symbolic mode of protest and female camaraderie as an ideal.[11] At a time when cable channels were rewiring the American consciousness, the film's interest in the relationship between Roberta and Susan was reflective of a new visual culture where the rules of female celebrity were being rewritten, in part, by a rejection of domesticity and an embrace of the forms of boundary-crossings, both sexual and racial, that drew on past histories of urban voyeurism. Echoing this reading, conservative cultural critics critiqued *Desperately Seeking Susan* as symbolic of an excessive sex culture for its casting of Madonna, thus encouraging audiences to read the film as part of a broader disruption of patriarchal control over women's sexuality arising from the sexual revolution.[12]

From its very beginning, *Desperately Seeking Susan* raises visions of suburban domesticity through its choice of locales and pastel color-schemes that mirror 1950s advertisements. At *Desperately Seeking Susan*'s beginning, beauticians are hard at work attending to their clients' grooming demands. Roberta sits reading the personal ads to her sister-in-law Leslie. The salon represents the racial and class insularity of Roberta's world, a space wrought with associations of middle-class white women seeking refuge from domestic responsibilities through their capacity as consumers. Roberta is taken by the erotic promises of romance that she reads in the personal ads: "beautiful stranger, red hair, green jump suit, walking dogs in Washington Square Park. Can't forget you. Give love a chance. Blackie."[13] Leslie, cynical and dismissive, chastises her: "Oh, Roberta, please. He must be some kind of a pervert. [. . .] Nobody named Blackie is sincere." This moment communicates the film's awareness of sexual fears about women and public space and the racialized assumptions that underwrite those concerns. From there, Leslie forces Roberta to style her hair differently for her birthday, telling the hairdresser to give her sister-in-law "nothing weird." Leslie's comment highlights concern over Roberta's cut being unflattering or expressing too much individuality. The salon worker understands Leslie's meaning and responds that "her husband will love it," thus depicting Roberta's lack of agency as rooted in the wifely demands of middle-class respectability on her body and self-image.[14]

Against these demands of respectability and visual conformity, Susan is distinguished from Roberta as the image of what Kathleen Rowe Karlyn has termed the "unruly girl," whose unruliness is "implicitly feminist because it destabilizes patriarchal norms."[15] As others discuss in this volume, *Desperately Seeking Susan* privileges this sense of unruliness through its critical depiction of suburban domesticity by emphasizing what Betty Friedan diagnosed in *The Feminine Mystique* (1963) as the lack of personal fulfillment experienced by housewives.[16] Through ideas about sexual unruliness, Roberta's relationship to Susan is privileged as a figure of personal freedom within a network of looking relations that pose her as a mirror to the housewife's discontents. Seidelman's first shot of Susan stresses her material excess with room service and playing cards scattered all around her as Foreigner's *Urgent* (1981) plays. Susan, unlike Roberta, is narratively marked by her ease of self-expression as a sexual subject, as she takes a polaroid of herself wearing an array of beaded necklaces that flow down into her cleavage. This moment of self-display, in particular, dramatizes the sartorial vogue of 1980s MTV entertainers such as Madonna for how they embodied promises of female empowerment through sexual self-expression. In contrast, Roberta is saddled with visits to house parties where she aids her sister-in-law's desire to find a good economic and romantic match in nothing less than a doctor. Underscoring this attention to masculine hierarchies, the party's guests watch the debut of Roberta's husband Gary's ad campaign for his hot-tub empire. The commercial insinuates his philandering behavior, as a group of buxom blondes flirtatiously pulls him into the hot tub. Stepping outside, Roberta looks at the New York skyline in the distance. In a cinematic cut that returns Roberta's longing gaze, Susan's life in the city enters the frame, reflecting a certain desire for Roberta to leave her suburban landscape. Through these juxtapositions, the film's titular, unruly subject is positioned as an embodiment of Roberta's desire for personal freedom by underscoring the feminist significance of the city within this network of meanings.

While Madonna's celebrity certainly communicated such unruliness by the mid-1980s, this circumstance was not immediately clear at the production's start. The performer's casting is only retrospectively an obvious recipe for success. *Desperately Seeking Susan* started as a risky project, marking the thirty-two-year-old Seidelman's move from the independent *Smithereens* (1982) with an $80,000 budget to one of about $5 million. In the production's beginning, film executives gravitated to more established film talent, not originally recognizing the potential of MTV and its youth audience, as Cher, Goldie Hawn and Diane Keaton were considered for the role of Roberta Glass. When casting had finished, Rosanna Arquette was considered the film's star for her work in John Sayles' *Baby It's You* (1983). Seidelman has admitted that Arquette's rising celebrity is a significant reason why Orion greenlit the project.[17] Regarding the titular Susan, Seidelman recounted that Orion initially recommended what she termed "a studio head's idea of a perfect blonde," which contrasted her vision of Susan as a "spicy blonde" who "floats through the funkiness in which she lives as if she were a princess."[18] Although the biggest star of the MTV era, Madonna's fame had been largely confined to a limited subset of America's youth, from music videos such as *Holiday* (1983) and *Borderline* (1984). As lore goes, it was the children of Orion executives petitioning for Madonna who helped her earn the role. Thus, her casting illustrates critical shifts in generational frameworks of celebrity that began with the pivot to youth culture by Hollywood and the music industry in the 1950s and 1960s before culminating in MTV throughout the 1980s. While

Desperately Seeking Susan is not a rock film proper, it is within the same film production tradition as *Jailhouse Rock* (1957) and *Viva Las Vegas* (1964) for their appeal to the youth market as a built-in audience by casting superstar Elvis Presley. Reflecting this change in media industry frameworks of stardom, Cyndi Lauper's fame would yield *Girls Just Want to Have Fun* (1985) and *Vibes* (1988), projects that owed credit to the breakout success of Prince in *Purple Rain* (1984). Contemporaneous with *Desperately Seeking Susan*, these films illustrate the impact of MTV's cable network on reorienting industry rubrics of celebrity and casting in film production.

In some sense, *Desperately Seeking Susan* mythologizes the new looking relations of this female celebrity by dramatizing how voyeurism with Madonna's star text functioned for young woman as a quasi-political exploration of their selves. In this view, *Desperately Seeking Susan* has substantively informed the mythology of Madonna, just as the singer came to imbue the film with a stronger feminist reading through her celebrity's explicit rejection of patriarchal norms. Part of the film's lore has been its status as an advertisement for Madonna's stardom at a time when her career was exploding. These performance-based aspects of her stardom reflected the demands of a new archetype of celebrity on MTV. In fact, her contemporaries were often treated as generic or interchangeable by some audiences. When production began in fall 1984, it was rumored that bystanders of the filming regularly mistook Madonna for Cyndi Lauper, another video music star who played with conceptions of girlhood in her promotional videos. Symbolic of this new mode of celebrity, Lauper's appeal was generated from an embrace of New Wave fashion. Reflecting this trend, the *Chicago Tribune* chronicled the new prosperity of Screaming Mimi's, a Manhattan vintage boutique where Lauper had once worked as a sales clerk.[19] The store's co-owners Biff Chandler and Laura Wills described how Lauper's fame owed credit to her fashion as an expression of her bold individuality, describing the performer's ability to turn a conservative dress into "something totally unexpected" with the addition of a dozen strands of colored pearls.[20] These stories speak to the paradoxical yet no less significant counter-cultural edge of performers whose consumerism and sartorial style served as vehicles for female individuality.

Moreover, *Desperately Seeking Susan* expanded on these fan-star dynamics by exploiting opportunities for fan merchandising. During the shoot, *Like A Virgin* (1984) was released by Sire Records and transformed Madonna into a video superstar, a circumstance that impacted the film's marketing considerably. In its release, Orion sought to position *Susan* within the context of MTV and its youth audience. In fact, post-production was rushed, reflecting the studio's desire for a March opening, due to industry speculation that Madonna's career might be over by the time of its release.[21] Towards the production's end, the set contended with Madonna's fame and its related frenzy, creating clear tensions that would lead to Rosanna Arquette expressing that she would not have made the film had she foreseen her co-star's meteoric rise.[22] Producer Sarah Pillsbury, a UCLA film school graduate known for *And the Band Played On* (1993), would recall the studio's initial difficulty to understand the film's market during its distribution meetings. Credited, however, was the success of the marketing team's Blaise Noto who came up with the idea of merchandising Madonna's lace gloves and rubber bracelets, a recognition of how fashion could be used to promote the film to young consumers.[23] Seeing opportunities for cross-promotion, the performer brokered a deal to include her single *Into the Groove* in the film, leading to the release of an official music video using *Desperately Seeking Susan*'s footage. The marketing poster included Madonna and Arquette together in matching pyramid jackets, as the Santo Loquasto design became a mass-marketed version to capitalize on the film's success. Elsewhere, licensing deals with Bakers and Leeds made Susan's studded boots available for purchase. Finding other markets for commercial success, these examples illustrate the synergistic strategies used to build on Madonna's celebrity for the film.

Further, *Desperately Seeking Susan* illustrates the cultural shifts posed by competing forms of television by cable and broadcast networks. The emergence of broadcast television marked a shift of media consumption into the home from the previous primacy of film. As Lynn Spiegel argues, the post-war moment featured the transference of "the primary site of exhibition for spectator amusements [. . .] from the public space of the movie theater to the private space of the home."[24] The 1950s saw television sets installed into nearly two-thirds of households, while the 1960s saw average consumption soar to almost five hours of television per day.[25] Spiegel's work interrogates how discourses on and about television both drew on and magnified what she describes as "the more general obsession with the reconstruction of family life and domestic ideals after World War II."[26] Writing at a time when the position of women as media consumers continued to be neglected, Spiegel surveyed middle-class home magazines to look at how television became situated within the forms of identity, belonging and place-making that characterized domestic life. In her analysis, pictorial advertisements sought to advise women "on ways to integrate the new medium into the traditional space of the family home."[27] It is these discourses around suburban domesticity and the family ideal that marks the subtext of Roberta's rebellion in the film, as in the case where we see Roberta's relationship to television marked by her domestic responsibilities of cooking for her husband. Television's historical status as a domestic medium underscores how the unsettled boundaries of urban and suburban space can be understood through the prism of cable television's arrival in the nation's homes, bringing with it new forms of female representation less easily situated within the confines of domestic life.

By 1985, MTV was well into its conquest of America's youth. Launched by Warner Cable, the cable network was described by its eventual CEO Bob Pittman as "much rougher, real, and more credible than TV."[28] In 1981, the network famously debuted with The Buggles' *Video Killed the Radio Star*, a prescient title that would reflect the network's influence on the music industry in the decade following. While academics frequently criticized its post-modern emptiness, MTV's programming was influential in the aesthetic style and cable revolutions of the 1980s and 1990s.[29] MTV's landscape came to be construed as a national battleground for the issue of racial segregation through critical frameworks of cultural representation, since the network's address of a rock (and subsequently white male) audience was accused of discriminating against Black musicians. As R. Serge Denisoff describes, the network's audience address through music formats and genres frequently worked as a bulwark for restricting Black culture on MTV's platform. For example, Rick James, excluded from industry definitions of rock music, struggled to find admission into the network's video rotations early in its history.[30] This criticism was not minimized on MTV's network itself, as David Bowie challenged VJ (video DJ) Mark Goodman about the lack of Black artists on the network, or about their videos being relegated to the earliest morning hours.[31] Goodman, rehearsing the same answer given by MTV executives, attempted to blame the prejudices of the national audience:

> Of course, also, we have to try and do what we think not only New York and Los Angles will appreciate, but also Poughkeepsie or Midwest – pick some town in the Midwest – that would be scared to death by Prince [. . .] or a string of other black faces and black music.[32]

These same types of concerns about racial mixing are seen in *Desperately Seeking Susan* through Gary and Leslie's conspiratorial fears about Roberta's disappearance in the city. Recalling this boundary-crossing into urban space, MTV, in fact, would become reliant on violating these industry imaginations of music format and cultural identity, as they came to rely on the super-stardom of Black artists for cultural relevance. While Michael Jackson's *Billie Jean* (1982) would initially struggle to find distribution on the channel, MTV publicist Dorene Lauer would later credit Jackson's blockbuster *Thriller* (1983) music video as a driver of the network's growth.[33] Moreover, the use of Black artists came to typify an ideology of cool that permeated the network as artists such as Michael Jackson, Run-DMC and MC Hammer came to serve as powerful commercial avatars for brands such as Pepsi and Adidas. These conditions, in particular, led to a number of Black artists entering the mainstream of youth culture at the latter end of the decade that spoke to how MTV's programming resettled national geographies of race through its youth culture address.

Understanding the history of domesticity is to understand the ways in which urban and suburban space are expressed through the language of race and gender. To this point, the cult of domesticity, finding popularity in the nineteenth century through women's treatises and home magazines, reflected the larger transition of the US from an agrarian society into an industrialized center of the world. In *A Treatise on Domestic Economy* (1841), Catharine Beecher argued for the standardization of domestic arts and practices as a science to be taught to young women.[34] Beecher's work fits into an emerging domestic ideology that elevated women's personal autonomy by privileging their moral authority over the home.[35] Within this ideological system, the late nineteenth century featured a growing emphasis on the suburban home as a haven from urban centers, afforded by the new network of rails that made morning commutes possible. These values were organized further by the increasing ornateness of the suburban home in magazine advertisements that sought a moral and spiritual remove from the growing labor unrest in the nation's cities. As Lynn Spiegel observes, the turn-of-twentieth-century United States saw the intensification of the Anglo-ethnocentrism and resistance to political activism that contributed to the ideological merger between suburbia and domestic bliss.[36] While cities gave middle-class women access to department stores, supplemental domestic labor and other luxuries, the influx of European immigrants and Black Southerners impacted the imagination of the American city over white fears of cultural and political impotency, long-running tropes in the history of white political backlash. In this way, the context of nineteenth-century industrialization ennobled the suburban home as a fixture of a new middle-class consciousness, but it did so, as well, by placing domestic life at the center of the moral retreat from the city, thus illustrating the role of racial, social and cultural hierarchies in mapping these national geographies.

These historical tensions around urbanization, immigration and industrialization help explain the peculiarities of the post-World War II moment. As Chad Heap describes, . . .

> Postwar suburbanization initially replicated many of the class and racial divisions that characterized turn-of-the-century cities. [. . .] Because a host of racially discriminatory practices prevented nearly all blacks from gaining access to suburban housing, residency in postwar suburbia became an undeniable marker of whiteness.[37]

As marriage rates rose sharply following World War II, American society experienced a revitalization of its suburban ideals, particularly as it came to articulate the new desire and dreams of post-war prosperity. These cultural ideals were structural at the legislative level, as they were made possible by the Housing Act of 1949, which created financial incentives for the building of single-family homes. Studying how white families were able to buy into manufactured communities such as Levittown, John A. Powell has argued that the Federal Housing Administration racialized "metropolitan space and home ownership," particularly through the Home Owners' Loan Corporation (HOLC) deeming of "ethnically diverse central city neighborhoods" as "too risky for investment."[38] Following Powell's argument, the suburbs, thus, were reconceived as an anchor of new forms of economic prosperity by using public policy to maintain racially segregated suburbs. These post-war suburbs were further marked by the re-emergence of domesticity in the shifts undergoing media consumption with the rise of television, thus illustrating how televisual domesticity in family sit-coms of the 1950s mirrored the re-enshrinement of racially exclusive suburban community in the post-war era.[39] Through these zoning practices, forms of racial segregation between urban and suburban space were codified into law, boundaries that were frequently resettled by the visual culture of MTV and post-feminist texts such as *Desperately Seeking Susan*.

To this point, MTV's female artists frequently employed a performative and symbolic take-over of urban space in their music videos to question gendered hierarchies and patriarchal sex roles. As Lisa A. Lewis observes, "female address emerged on MTV in the form of female-musician videos designed to speak to and resonate with female cultural experiences of adolescence and gender."[40] Lewis' work privileges four female musicians in particular – Tina Turner, Pat Benatar, Cyndi Lauper and Madonna – for how these artists resignified "the street" in their mid-1980s video work and, thus, challenged cultural anxieties over white middle-class women's sexuality as it became mapped onto the geographies of urban space from the late nineteenth century onward. In *What's Love Got To Do With It* (1984), Tina Turner offers an anthem to physical, not emotional, congregation with men and returns the sexual gazes of desiring men in public space. In *Girls Just Want to Have Fun* (1983), Lauper compares the generational freedoms of her on-screen persona with those of her mother (played by real-life mother Catrine Lauper) under the patriarchal authority of her controlling father. Lisa Lewis argues that, in Lauper's single, . . .

> . . .'fun' is articulated as an expansive and politicized concept for girls [. . .] visualized both in terms of doing what boys do – getting out of the house (and housework) and onto the street – and in terms of the kinds of activities and relationship girls devise in their attempts to create a contemporary order of female fun.[41]

In the video, latent fears of young girls and their own sexual autonomy are visualized in patriarchal terms, as the on-screen father (played by Lou Albano) is seen finger-wagging at his daughter, a theme also echoed in Pat Benatar's *Love Is a Battlefield* (1983). In *Girls Just Want to Have Fun*, Lauper's rebellion is rooted in ideas about bodily autonomy and everyday forms of surveillance that mark girls' gender as a lived experience. To this point, the video ends with a street parade entering Lauper's domestic bedroom, a counterpoint to how this space is traditionally imagined through patriarchal fears of the daughter's loss of innocence, signified by the father comically looking through her bedroom's keyhole to find writhing, dancing bodies. Here, Lauper's video articulates forms of pleasure as a critique of gendered norms that restrict the bodily autonomy and spatial mobility of young women. These themes are ones that would re-emerge in Lauper's visual work, most particularly in the music video for *She Bop* (1984), a single whose themes of self-pleasuring came under fire from the activist organization Parents' Music Resource Center in its crusade to bring a ratings system to the music industry.[42]

At the same time, Madonna's *Borderline* (1984) demonstrates more specifically for the context of *Desperately Seeking Susan* how this new wave of female artists unsettled tropes of domesticity that had defined earlier Victorian ideologies of young womanhood. Although not directed by Seidelman, *Borderline* and Madonna's other music videos embody an important extra-textual object for understanding how the solidification of Madonna's star image outside the film intensified second-wave feminist readings of *Desperately Seeking Susan* by its audience, many of whom were fans of the singer. Her star text has been notable for its attention to the social boundaries that women face, their sexuality and new modes of celebrity. Lisa Lewis has argued that *Borderline* raises "questions about how the code of prostitution is usually socially elaborated and about how representations of females on the street might be re-visioned."[43] In the first part of the video, Madonna is seen being discovered on the street as a model, a theme that echoes the discovery narratives of celebrity publicity. Depicting the performer's modelling and self-display throughout the city, the video illustrates how images of female sexuality were foundational to new systems of self-promotion in music video, while focusing how this lack of modesty – through such public self-display – intervenes in older ideas of female decorum and sexuality against urban space. Taken together, these female videos, thus, depict an image of girl culture that contests the construction of urban space as simply racialized, by showing how a countercultural embrace of these geographies intervenes in the everyday constraints on women's sexuality. Of course, this recognition does not sidestep the obvious ways in which such visual media construct and confirm new codes of decorum for women and the ways in which women's sexuality remains a core commodified element of capitalist culture. This recognition, however, reflects how new dynamics within white middle-class youth culture of the 1980s unsettled longer histories of gender, space and sexuality that are observable in cultural texts like *Desperately Seeking Susan*.

As female agency is juxtaposed against suburban domesticity in *Desperately Seeking Susan*, the film's narrative thematizes this relationship through the intimacy of the celebrity persona. Brandished for the film by the singular individuality of Madonna, the character Susan comes to operate as both a reflection and commentary on new models of female music stardom and its gendered address. MTV, like other cable networks of its day, split and resituated understandings of television's mass media address; in doing so, such cable networks not only offered new opportunities for branded promotional content for artists, but also expanded platforms for "activist" models of gender performance in popular culture, as new stars like Madonna created a visual body of work that explicitly thematized desires for female agency. These desires, phrased through metaphors of urban space, inform *Desperately Seeking Susan* and its working through of Roberta's "problem that has no name." These moments are interesting for how they point to the racial and gendered anxieties of urban space, as it came to be defined through domestic ideology of the late nineteenth century. These anxieties, about the racial and sexual mixing of the city, would come to define some of the very attitudes that informed the various "white flights" of the 1950s and 1960s following *Brown v. Board of Education* (1954). By satirizing old forms of traditionalism figured by suburban domesticity, *Desperately Seeking Susan* interrogates the very real issue of pleasure and sexual fulfillment for women through its screwball sendup of characters such as Gary and Leslie and thereby participates in reconfiguring the urban imaginary of the post-war era.

Evidenced in the abandoning of domestic respectability, *Desperately Seeking Susan*'s narrative constitutes a fight over Roberta's identity that marks a break in the presumption of her sexual innocence, as her disappearance comes to be defined through familiar ideas about urban difference. As Gary and Leslie worry about Roberta's jailing, Leslie frets about the tabloid story of a housewife who engaged in sex-work and extravagant shopping while hiding this double life from her husband for years. With a sense of paternalism about Roberta's sexuality, Gary responds: "That's impossible. She doesn't even like sex that much." Pointing to how fears of female sexuality are rooted, partly, in anxieties of male impotence, Leslie recalls reading that "four out of five prostitutes are lesbians," a remark that mixes sociological language with the classist and homophobic attitudes of the 1980s. Here, a version of racial and sexual difference is implicitly raised as a threat to Roberta's newfound sense of self. Moreover, it is this skewing of suburban sexual traditionalism that frames the housewife's emancipation from her husband. At the same time, Roberta's freedom is constituted alongside these cultural Others as a way of marking her own ability to exist outside dominant assumptions of white womanhood.

Importantly, *Desperately Seeking Susan* embodies how voyeurism of MTV celebrity functioned as an imagined form of sexual agency and cultural feminism for young women. In the film's climactic scene, Roberta pointedly asks why Gary wants her to come home, seeking to understand whether their relationship is romantically fulfilling. As Gary mocks her new clothes, Roberta pleads with him: "Look at me, Gary. Look at me." Next, one of the film's assertions of female subjectivity, desire and anti-domesticity is directly stated. Roberta declares: "I'm not coming home with you." Moments later, it is Susan who saves the housewife from an assailant, thereby taking up the mantle as the film's hero in a reversal of gendered expectations set by classical Hollywood narratives. Rekindling their romance in a projection booth, Roberta meets her lover Dez (Aidan Quinn) moments later as her true identity. They kiss as film stock starts to burn. Underscoring the sexual heat of their romance, the camera cuts to Susan in the audience, as Madonna's promotional single begins to play. The last image features Roberta and Susan together with the headline "What a Pair" in a copy of the *Mirror*, thereby visualizing how Roberta's voyeurism of Susan is celebrated by the conclusion's reference to tabloid journalism. Here, *Desperately Seeking Susan* offers an intriguing commentary on the fantasies of female empowerment engendered by media for women, a circumstance made more compelling by the post-second-wave context of the film and its use of Madonna as a representative star of a new kind of white womanhood.

While Lynn Stoever-Ackerman has argued that rock music created its own set of racialized erasures, it should be noted how the development of pop music through MTV's demographic address energized cultural imaginations of female representation through such urban and relatedly racial metaphors.[44] *Desperately Seeking Susan* visualizes these erasures and transforms its spatial operation in the city as the conditions for white women's desire and expressive agency. Here, the imitative structure of Roberta and Susan's relationship works to thematize the voyeuristic politics of female music celebrity as a system of meaning-making produced out of participation with a national consumer culture. Many of these issues are not entirely specific to *Desperately Seeking Susan*, but the film can be explicitly studied here as a representative text of the new forms of branding and synergy that MTV made possible, as crossover stardom became critical for meeting the new exigencies of an independent film system. Moreover, this valuation placed on female stardom as illustrative of shifting ideas about women's agency has a long history, observable through the figures of "starstruck girls" who moved to urban centers to pursue their dreams in the entertainment industry, a circumstance that, if anything, describes the origins and mythology of Madonna's career. Within this media history of female music celebrity, it becomes clear how developments in cable television participated in unsettling these earlier national geographies of the suburban domestic ideal for women by offering older promises of female empowerment through a voyeuristic embrace of MTV and consumer culture.

Although gendered and misogynistic music criticism downplayed the rebellious edge to these new female personas, *Desperately Seeking Susan* demonstrates how this music culture and its relationship to downtown New York rejected the racial and sexual underpinnings of suburban domesticity. These aspects of MTV are often overlooked in academic accounts of the period, precisely for how they marshal ambivalent tensions and oppositions around race, gender, sexuality and class. Yet, on MTV's airwaves, there came to be a radical redefinition of the image of women in youth culture using urban tableaus, shown in videos such as Madonna's *Borderline* or Lauper's *Girls Just Want to Have Fun*. These examples which illustrate how distinctions in generational address were phrased by attacking sexual traditionalism. These assertions of white female agency are made more interesting for how they draw on long-standing tropes in American culture around Blackness and sexual deviancy, which heterosexual white women have long used to solidify their own sense of agency within oppressive white patriarchal cultures. Continuing these tropes in critical ways, this new image of female representation, as embodied in *Desperately Seeking Susan*, intervened in older genealogies of female domesticity, anti-urbanism and white respectability that had been the hallmarks of national culture for much of the preceding century.

NOTES

1. Lisa Marie Hogeland, *Feminism and Its Fictions: The Consciousness-Raising Novel and Women's Liberation Movement* (Philadelphia: University of Pennsylvania Press, 1998), ix.
2. Ibid. p. 100.
3. For a discussion of television's relationship to feminism, see Bonnie J. Dow, "Prime-Time Divorce: The Emerging Woman' of *One Day at a Time*," in *Prime-Time Feminism: Television, Media Culture, and the Women's Movement Since 1970* (Philadelphia: University of Pennsylvania Press, 1996), 59–85.
4. See Susan Brady, "Seeking Madonna's Double," *Washington Post*, 31 May 1985, B2; Elizabeth Kastor and Chris Spolar, "Loading Up on Lace in Tribute to Their Idol's Material Whirl," *Washington Post*, 3 June 1985, C1.
5. Jackie Stacey, "Desperately Seeking Difference," *Screen*, 28, no. 1 (Winter 1987), 48–61.
6. Catherine Jurca, *White Diaspora: The Suburb and the Twentieth-Century American Novel* (Princeton: Princeton University Press, 2001), 5.
7. Michael London, "Strong-Willed Women Behind 'Seeking Susan'," *Los Angeles Times*, 2 April 1985.
8. London, "Strong-Willed Women."
9. Jeff Silverman, "Hottest Director in a Town Full of Directors Is – GASP – Female," *Chicago Tribune*, 7 April 1985, 5.
10. London, "Strong-Willed Women."
11. Lisa A. Lewis, *Gender Politics and MTV: Voicing the Difference* (Philadelphia: Temple University Press, 1990), 117.
12. Ellen Goodman, "Parents: Do Kids a Favor – Start Losing Your Cool," *Chicago Tribune*, 7 June 1985, D2.
13. *Desperately Seeking Susan*, DVD, directed by Susan Seidelman (Los Angeles: MGM, 2006).

14. Ibid.
15. Kathleen Rowe Karlyn, *Unruly Girls, Unrepentant Mothers: Redefining Feminism on Screen* (Austin: University of Texas Press, 2011), 11.
16. Betty Friedan, *The Feminine Mystique* (New York: W. W. Norton & Company, 2001), 57–79.
17. Silverman, "Hottest Director."
18. Janet Maslin, "At the Movies," *The New York Times*, 22 March 1985.
19. Melissa Sones, "Fans Scream for Lauper's Clothes Source," *Chicago Tribune*, 1 May 1985.
20. Ibid.
21. "'Desperately Seeking Susan' Turns 30: An Oral History of the Downtown Classic," *Yahoo! News*, 27 March 2015.
22. Lindsey Gruson, "'Susan' Draws Spirit from the Sidewalks of New York," *The New York Times*, 14 April 1985.
23. "'Desperately Seeking Susan' Turns 30."
24. Lynn Spiegel, *Make Room for TV: Television and the Family Ideal in Postwar America* (Chicago; London: University of Chicago Press, 1992), 1.
25. Ibid. p. 1.
26. Ibid. p. 2.
27. Ibid. p. 5.
28. Quoted in R. Serge Denisoff, *Inside MTV* (New Brunswick: Transaction, 1988), 60.
29. John Fiske, "MTV: Post-Structural Post-Modern," *Journal of Communication Inquiry*, 10, no. 1 (Winter 1986), 79. Quoted in Andrew Goodwin, "Fatal Distractions," in *Sound and Vision: The Music Video Reader*, edited by Simon Frith, Andrew Goodwin and Lawrence Grossberg (London; New York: Routledge, 2005), 52.
30. Denisoff, *Inside MTV*, 60.
31. "David Bowie Criticizes MTV for Not Playing Videos by Black Artists," *MTV News*, YouTube.com, 11 January 2016, 4:39.
32. Ibid.
33. Denisoff, *Inside MTV*, 211.
34. Catherine E. Beecher, *A Treatise on Domestic Economy* (New York: Harper & Bros, 1849), 5–6.
35. For a greater discussion of domesticity as what historians have called "the cult of true womanhood," see Barbara Welter, "The Cult of True Womanhood: 1820–1860," *American Quarterly*, 18, no. 2, Part 1 (Summer 1966), 151–74.
36. Spiegel, *Make Room for TV*, 17.
37. Chad Heap, *Slumming: Sexual and Racial Encounters in American Nightlife, 1885–1940* (Chicago; London: University of Chicago Press, 2009), 278.
38. John A. Powell, "How Government Tax and Housing Policies Have Racially Segregated America," in *Taxing America*, edited by Karen Brown and Mary Louise Fellowes (New York: New York University Press, 1997), 90–91.
39. See Megan Behrent, "Suburban Captivity Narratives: Feminism, Domesticity, and the Liberation of the American Housewife," *Journal of Narrative Theory*, 49, no. 2 (Summer 2019), 247–86.
40. Lewis, *Gender Politics and MTV*, 109.
41. Ibid. p. 117.
42. See Claude Chastagner, "The Parents' Music Resource Center: From Information to Censorship," *Popular Music*, 18, no. 2 (May 1999), 179–92.
43. Lisa A. Lewis, "Female Address on Music Television: Being Discovered," *Jump Cut: A Review of Contemporary Media*, 35 (April 1990), 2–15.
44. See Jennifer Stoever-Ackerman, "Reproducing U.S. Citizenship in *Blackboard Jungle*: Race, Cold War Liberalism, and the Tape Recorder," *American Quarterly*, 63, no. 3 (September 2011), 781–806.

CHAPTER 8

Directing a City: Susan Seidelman's New York

Josephine Maria Yanasak-Leszczynski

It is easy to say that director Susan Seidelman's projects in New York City feel like a cinematic time capsule. They keep the styles, attitudes and music of the era intact, but it may be more accurate to say that she was running a film world parallel to the *I Love New York* campaign beginning in 1977, which launched a period of renewed interest in tourism for the city. Just as that campaign defined the city's image to outsiders, Seidelman's movies reinvigorated an interest in New York as a locale with a particular personality and general appeal.

In 1974 Seidelman came to Manhattan to attend New York University for film school. She detailed what she loved about the idea of New York City and its individual identities in the 1992 documentary *Confessions of a Suburban Girl*. In it, she says that she liked the appeal of being "lost in a crowd." However, her films show anything but people becoming lost in the hordes of New York, instead providing insight into a variety of identities coming together for a relatable yet cinematic story. It was during her classes at New York University, with the access that being in the city afforded her, that she first came into contact with the French New Wave films that would inform her later work.[1] It also dropped her directly into the East Village neighborhoods where she would shoot some of her most famous films.

She was also introduced to stories by women about women living in the city.[2] This would be an ongoing theme in many of her works. During a discussion with the Indie Memphis Film Festival, she specifically cited another film shot in New York City, *Girlfriends* by Claudia Weill, as being one of her first memorable interactions with female friendship in cinema.[3] Seidelman was working alongside directors such as Lydia Lunch, Kathy Acker, Kathryn Bigelow, Nan Goldin, Lizzie Borden and myriad others of the 1970s through 1980s, cited by Maura Edmond in her overview of the post-punk No Wave world, which helped to shape a vision of New York that made room for a variety of personalities.[4]

Seidelman has crafted a fantastic version of New York for each production: "Moving to New York City, I felt I had finally come to a place where people played out in real life scenarios I had only played out in my imagination."[5] The effects of this authentic New Yorker vision have been long-standing and informed a generation of cinema set there. Most importantly, it was exciting, ripe with adventure and accessible.

New York is always on the cusp of change for Seidelman's projects, reflecting the change that her protagonists are experiencing in their lives. This is evident in *Sex and the City* as the women search for love, in *Smithereens* as Wren seeks a way out, in *Cookie* as her father is reintroduced to her life, in *She-Devil* as the women's lives are torn apart and in *Desperately Seeking Susan* when a housewife chafes against her stagnant life. Location is extremely important to Seidelman's curated vision of New York.[6] Often, the viewpoint is from the (wo)man on the street. She offers both an insider's knowledge and a spectacle to spectators who want to be wrapped up in the fantasy. There are many films set in New York and made by New Yorkers, but Seidelman's unique use of a mix of archetypes, such as the hip New Age girl and overly friendly cabbie, as well as real-life personas known mostly in then-underground subcultures of the city, creates a realism unique to her works. From pop stars to performance artists, her vision of the city is not limited to its architecture.

Speaking about her life in suburbia, which she found wildly boring during the 1960s, Seidelman says: "Bad Girls became my heroes."[7] Her high school years were framed by trying to get away with being bad in a clandestine way to fight against the mundane surroundings. While no characters quite hide themselves in bathroom stalls to sneak a cigarette or take on the full-on "B-movie bad girl" persona that she loved growing up, Seidelman repeatedly handles both wanting badly to be someone else and bad girls who are able to live openly in a place like New York.

The first day on set for *Desperately Seeking Susan*, publicist Reid Rosefelt remembered that "we removed the people on the street and replaced them with people who looked exactly like them."[8] In the same interview, they also recalled that "it's a record of Lower Manhattan that no longer exists." This speaks to not only the use of the city as an intentional setting, but also the thoughtful control enacted by the director over the city's presentation. Like Seidelman's other New York-based work, calling *Desperately Seeking Susan* a time capsule is too easy. Instead, she has created films that look and feel how the city felt at that time: they capture something of the emotion of being among New Yorkers in the presence of much older buildings that now had an unsure future. They crumble and become redecorated or are replaced, but the population marches ever onward in a constantly shifting array of people. At the conclusion of a composite interview about *Desperately Seeking Susan*, author Matthew Rettunmund perhaps says it best:

> I saw the city as a fantasy getaway, where people could be themselves. Now the only way to catch a glimpse of the downtown scene is to watch the movie. I'm still glad I moved here, but, man, I wish I'd moved there instead.⁹

PUNK, NO WAVE AND LATE 1900S NEW YORK

Seidelman's work, while often cited within Punk and New Wave, also aligns with the No Wave Feminist cinema being created in the city in the 1970s and 1980s. Encouraged by the rejection of avant-garde cinema, No Wave artists were taking punk a step further to create film with a "worldview from perspective the gutter."¹⁰ This was not just about the grit uplifted by the fleeing punk scene. It was also a deeply personal view of the city that de-personifies the city and instead makes it about the protagonist moving through it.

Seidelman's New York is part of a larger movement coming out of the period of New York's "decay" described by Mario Maffi as being directly related to the "city's bankruptcy."¹¹ It was a period of financial want that led directly to hard drugs and violence throughout the East Village, and the lack of the distribution of resources by "nouveau riches" born from a Wall Street renewed by the classist upheaval of what we now call Reaganomics.¹² Seidelman is often compared to other New Yorkers creating movies set in and ultimately about New York City, but as far as a fantastical, if not glamorized, vision of New York in this period, Seidelman's work acts on its own lexicon and visual symbols drawn from subcultures of the day. Her casting method included occasional street casting and faces from the local artistic and music communities. The characters that we see are uniquely New York, but even outside of archetypes are defined by their contemporary hair and threads. This fits within the look and feel of New York City cinema since the 1970s. Jon Savage has reminisced that at the time "filmmakers were in bands, and all of them starred as semi-fictional versions of themselves in each other's films."¹³

Seidelman's visual and fashion interests in the earlier films were heavily influenced by artists who opted for New York City as their base instead of the rapidly growing attraction of artistic communities in Los Angeles. These included the whirlpool of bands that began cycling in and out of the now-shuttered punk rock club CBGB. Also of interest was artist Andy Warhol, poet and musician Richard Hell, whom Seidelman cast in both *Smithereens* and *Desperately Seeking Susan*, and the Velvet Underground.¹⁴

In *Smithereens*, Wren's quick changes into parti-colored miniskirts and seemingly effortless cool style might paint her as a city girl used to the hip and decrepit surroundings of the East Village in the late 1970s, but Wren's family are relatively nearby in the safety of more residential surroundings. Reviewer Mas'ud Zavarzadeh described the film as "full of TV artifice, attracted and constructed by media hype."[15] Moving through this fantastically punk New York, Wren still does not face the implications that there is some faceless danger for her. In an interview, Seidelman revealed that she was not interested in implying any real, long-lasting danger for her leeching lead.[16] The audience in fact brings its own expectations of danger for a young woman wandering around the derelict neighborhoods of the East Village at the end of the 1970s. For all its gravel, it is still a vision of New York that requires some imagination to conjure. While the movie was filmed at possible legal peril to the crew, there is never quite the implied danger to its protagonist that we see in other films. "Grit" is the wrong term for such a city, as Wren's predicament is more complicated than the vision of the city painted by news coverage in the 1970s and 1980s as exceedingly violent and dangerous.[17]

The film that kicked off guerrilla-style productions depicts the lifestyle of wannabe band manager Wren from her point of view. Describing her experience filming *Smithereens*, Seidelman says she "never thought about getting permits" and that she saw New York as an "open city" that was free to film in.[18] Seidelman admits that her vision of the city was specifically curated for Wren's interactions within it. Mary Harron, also getting her start around the same time as Seidelman, said that "part of the feeling of living in New York at that time was this longing for oblivion, that you were about to disintegrate, go the way of the city. Yet that was something almost mystically wonderful."[19] Perhaps seeking that feeling, the crew that worked on *Smithereens* looked for sites that showed the crumbling nature of a late 1970s New York, but also encapsulated the abandoned feel of music and artistic scenes that were migrating.

Smithereens was shot from 1980 to 1981 and took a year and a half to complete. Seidelman says that the New York in the film is one that "no longer exists."[20] She describes New York, at that time, as "falling apart."[21] *Smithereens* offers us the feeling of being left behind, as Wren has been, while the punks move to LA. That does not mean that the city itself was empty. People were still everywhere, and the police were still patrolling the streets. The neighborhoods that the transient Wren traverses are not ones where she could afford to sign a lease in 2022, but in 1982 they were dilapidated and cheap in a way that was not quite hip. The team filmed in an extended past tense: the story being told was really about the New York of the 1970s drifting away, being hit with recession in the 1980s and being replaced by the proto-gentrification and de-punkifying that would occur into the 1990s.[22]

The production was truly as punk as its subject-matter. Its budget was miniscule for a film: $20,000 from an inheritance that Seidelman had set aside for a wedding that never took place.[23] The film was shot in SoHo (where Eric's loft is located), Hell's Kitchen (Paul's van in the deserted lot), by the Westside Highway (specifically 48th and 49th Street) and in the East Village.[24] The section of Hell's Kitchen used as backdrop is the now popular Highline. While shooting, the neighborhood was in clear transition. Seidelman calls the locations they chose "a little bit magical."[25] In choosing them, she paid special attention to the graffiti backdrops and specifics of the surrounding buildings.[26] In comparison, the world of *Desperately Seeking Susan*, occurring just a few years later, appears downright glossy. The sheen of punk-infused boutiques that would later give way to various flavors of hipster had already taken hold. This is played up to full effect, undoubtedly with the help of their budget, which at five million dollars was many times that of *Smithereens'* $20,000.[27]

Despite the bigger budgets, "guerrilla filming" is not something that Seidelman abandoned after her jump into more produced features and television shows. Her unique framing of outside spaces, such as using panning shots at odd upward angles to show the exit of a gala in *Sex and the City*, or an aerial shot of a gay run across the street by the two lovers in *She-Devil* was certainly informed by the confidence built on shoots that were illegal or hampered by open foot and street traffic. She did not stop shooting in public without a permit, either. In 1993 she produced an hour-long documentary on her life outside of Philadelphia, *Confessions of a Suburban Girl*, that features her driving by and shooting her own childhood home, claiming that she will be back "with a long lens" to "sneak some shots" without the current owners' awareness.

While in other stories directed by Seidelman the boroughs are localized and familiar, New York expands into unknown territory in *Desperately Seeking Susan* where a housewife with amnesia can be lost as easily as a musician heading across town. Suburban housewife Roberta (Rosanna Arquette) reads about the happenings elsewhere through the personals section of her newspaper. This includes following the back-and-forth of two lovers, Susan (Madonna) and Jim (Robert Joy), but when Susan moves to meet up near her, the focus shifts to the city of New York itself. Roberta is not far away from her home in New Jersey when she goes to spy on them, but the city itself is presented in its full mass only once the events of the film turn it into the location of an adventure. Miriam Bale calls it a "persona swap" film.[28] This swap includes their respective geographic and cultural territory.

Desperately Seeking Susan provides two New Yorks: the city perhaps dreamed about by suburban Roberta, in direct contrast to the one well-trod by the eponymous Susan. Roberta is not unaware of the city itself, demonstrated by her successful stalking of Susan and her admirer. However, after her amnesia, the city becomes a complete unknown. Susan's pieces of narrative are knowledgeable and even smug: she walks into a store and already plans to make off with a jacket just as she did with the earrings at the beginning of the plot. This city is one that she can take from because it is her right. Alternatively, Roberta is following both Susan's movements and the rhythms of New York. Roberta has to buy the jacket, place an ad and eventually accept the help of Dez (Aidan Quinn), because her lack of insider knowledge, both before and after her amnesia, makes New York mysterious to her.

Speaking about the movie in 2015, screenwriter Leora Barish describes the women as coming from "two different realms."[29] These planes are geographic as well as societal. Seidelman, originally brought on due to her "clear visual style," explains that she was attracted to the script because it let her explore the process of living as someone whom one wishes to emulate. In this case, Roberta's transition from homemaker to urban adventurer includes a transition from her physical surroundings in the New York suburbs to the much more varied surrounding of Manhattan in the 1980s. In this way, is she the same Susan, desperately sought, as in New York? Or does she take on a persona for this particular place and the inner workings she interacts with so easily? Is the Susan running through the streets of the East Village the same Susan being kept in a hotel, sharing a mobster's bed? Or is the city itself as it is depicted another machination of New York, an idea of it projected by a protagonist who assumes that she knows best but is still bound by her surroundings?

Desperately Seeking Susan is the ultimate tale of having a fantasy from afar. But it also reveals some of the artifice in Susan's character that Zavarzadeh saw in Wren from *Smithereens*. It is clear why Roberta would want to swap places with the cool, calm and courageous Susan, but the same interiority is not immediately apparent in the character played by Madonna. Instead, audiences who saw something of themselves in Roberta can cast their idealized vision of what they would like to be on Susan as she moves through this fantasy New York.

In the construction of this Manhattan, the cast of characters also included many underground artists. Besides Richard Hell in a named role (Bruce Meeker), John Lurie plays his saxophone, and Annie Golden and Gary Ray form a band with main character Jim. Other alternative and punk cameos are brief, and while they may or may not have lines, they are treated as set dressing. Many of these cameo characters are from when "New York was a shithole," but the New York of *Desperately Seeking Susan* and other Seidelman productions is never quite presented this way.[30] Instead, they revel in its decay, its "exhilarating combination of cheap apartments, abundant squats and affordable living on the fringes of the city," while building up stories around the setting.[31] With *Smithereens* we see a New York at the beginning of the 1980s. It is in deep transition from the decline of New York's economy to the movement of artists from the downtown neighborhoods of the city and into boroughs such as Brooklyn and Harlem. It also tracks the movement of the punk scene toward LA. *Desperately Seeking Susan* is a definitive 1980s film that establishes the look and feel of the renewed hip of Manhattan. *Cookie* is another New York, but at the end of the decade.

Unlike Seidelman's earlier work, *Cookie* was shot in a wide variety of neighborhoods and focused on a family dynamic over one girl's explorations in the city. It was released before the now-classic mobster movie *Goodfellas*, but firmly inside the *The Godfather* era established in the early 1970s. The Italian-American and, in turn, mafia cultures are a staple in New York and were brought into Seidelman's view of the city in *Cookie*. She personalizes characters belonging to them by placing them firmly in a community and without the obfuscating monologues of earlier mafioso films. The story had a wide-ranging view of the city and took the film crew from Queens to Little Italy, Chinatown and even Coney Island and Atlantic City.[32] The vehicle for these travels is the limo of Cookie's father (Peter Falk), which she drives through the neighborhoods with the finesse of a teenager who jumps turnstiles for fun.

How characters move through the city is as important as where they live in these versions of New York City. *Sex and the City* includes shots and tension built around trying to grab a taxi because public transportation could never be considered. The use of the iconic yellow New York taxicab heightens the vision of the show's four protagonists as successful and elegant New Yorkers. The question of transportation also defined the experience of capturing a work: *Smithereens* was shot on location without permission, even though it was shot during an era where New York was welcoming filmmakers into the city.[33] Years after its release, Seidelman admits that they were thrown off the subway.[34]

Transportation in Seidelman's work is rarely the impetus for introducing lengthy narrative scenes or locales. *Smithereens* features only the New York subway, which is iconic unto itself, but none of the grandeur of a sweeping New York horizon. While *Sex and the City* opens on an overhead view of the city, this view of New York serves only as prologue. Transportation may also, however, become a narrative focus. The events in *Cookie* are kicked off when she attempts to board New York's subway without paying her fare; Susan in *Desperately Seeking Susan* is arrested, and her place is switched with Roberta's after she refuses to pay her cab fare. In *Musical Chairs*, Mia (Leah Pipes) is hit by a yellow taxicab.

Beyond those interactions with the major ways to get around New York (driving or by cab and the public transit system), much of our interaction with the city is done via walking. There are no lovers staring out the back of cab windows in these works. Instead, we overhear conversations and see action as a bystander in a cozy shopfront or on the street.

SUBURBAN GIRL, SUBURBAN DREAMS

She-Devil provided a new age group of leading ladies, but also new class, culture and gender role interactions. Interpreted from Fay Weldon's British novel *The Life and Loves of a She-Devil*, the film is an elaborate suburban revenge fantasy that takes place mainly on the outskirts of New York City. Seidelman's vision of the film highlights the tensions between the urban and suburban in a way that could not have taken place in the vicinity of any other metropolis. The generational wealth of the communities built up around New York have created a unique blend of classic New England vibes thriving on commerce from "the city": just as Bob Patchett (Ed Begley Jr.) primarily maintains his business by having an office downtown, the central love affair of the story is flavored with adventure and romance through the inclusion of New York City proper, while creating a rich fantasy with the tools provided by the spacious estates made famous on Long Island.

The palatial estate that served as the set of Mary's (Meryl Streep) fantasy life is famous in the real-life community of Belle Terre. With thirty bedrooms and acres of land, its bright pink design has garnered much attention, despite its apparent seclusion. A neighbor reported in 2017 that "being parked right in front of it you couldn't see it at all between the bushes and the gates."[35] Even with miles of space, in typical Seidelman style, audiences are wisely limited to a few key areas. These become a quick lexicon into the immensity of Mary's wealth without expansive shots. For instance, the interior is limited to a living room area, a bedroom and a massive pool, which is reused as the location for a cocktail party. On the exterior, the front drive leading up to the easily recognizable pink façade is used both for narrative scenes and for the television spot introduction to Mary's glamorous life as a successful author. The same terrace is used outside for Mary's conflict with Bob's children, as well as interviews with the media on her career. Whether the limitations are based on the agreements with the house's owner or simply a judicious use of resources, we do not need to see more of the house to understand that it is gigantic.

Interiors also define the city in the film and its characters' relationships to it at various points: against the stark white of the Guggenheim's spiraling staircase and balconies, Ruth (Roseanne Barr) is clearly out of place among the elegant people, and Mary looks like something out of one of her own novels. Standing out in a building that caused such an uproar upon its construction is quite a feat. It is also an ironically fitting location for a first meeting between the two women and the man who will kick off the drama. After slipping out of the dreamworld that she manifested and into the chore-filled realities of a work-from-home partner, Mary names her failed book *Love in the Rinse Cycle*. In a piece of historical parallelism, architect Frank Lloyd Wright told interviewer

Mike Wallace in 1957 that critics accused the Guggenheim of looking "like a washing machine."[36]

In the second half of the film, the plot moves into the city, not only as a place of opportunity, but also as a place to live out one's darker fantasies. The affair of Bob and Mary moves all over the city: we see them going shopping together and running across taxi-filled streets toward New York institutions. The city remains a place of freedom while the outer communities turn into a cage. Just as Ruth was relegated to the grocery store and kitchen while Bob worked downtown, Mary is now forced to do the laundry while her lover begins an affair in his office. These definitions mirror the themes of mundane boredom felt by Roberta in *Desperately Seeking Susan* and Wren's reaction to her family's on-the-outskirts abode in *Smithereens*. In these stories, New York City is a place to let the audience's imagination roam while the suburbs represent the known archetypes and safe assumptions of these films based on their genres.

THE GENTRIFIED CITY

Gentrification has likely begun occurring in the neighborhood where Ruth sets up shop under the guise of improving it. The building was clearly not used as an employment office, and in recent history was not used for anything besides graffiti practice. This is the view of gentrification that the audience receives: *Smithereens* is in a transitional period between two potentially shifting populations, and in *She-Devil*, gentrification is actively occurring. In both cases, gentrification is on the ground and directed from the point of view of self-involved citizens following the path that best serves them. There are no evil, overarching developers in these narratives; instead, individuals take advantage of the resources of a neighborhood without connecting themselves to the community to which it belongs.

Ruth's recruits are various women walking through Times Square in Manhattan. They are unwanted in myriad ways, being newly single mothers, apparently homeless or painfully earnest as well as naive. Rather than the savvy and stylish New York women whom audiences see painted in Carrie's streets in *Sex and the City*, Ruth's fantasy New York is full of women whom one might describe as losers. Luckily, redemption is near. These recruits introduce the disposability of people in New York City who are not our protagonists. While they may have screen time and be the focal point of entire scenes, they are a sort of cast of characters that one might expect in the city but for whom one might lack compassion. This makes it even more of a flat fantasyland. For instance, actress Lori Tan Chinn's character in *She-Devil* exactly mirrors Ruth (who is now going by "Rose"), but she is not even granted a name in the script.

In a plot-perfect twist, Chinn's character has found a job as a clerk at the courts. Ruth uses that placement to remove the final "freedom" point on her agenda against her husband: she phones in to the "Vesta Rose Woman" and has her swap judges from the presumably white and male one on whom her husband's defense banked and puts the much less empathetic Judge Brown (Rosanna Carter) on the bench. He is made an example of, as a stand-in for all men who under-value their wives, and his freedom is removed. But Ruth's triumph is using communities and people who were already living and interacting in the city while also taking up space in a community to which she has no ties. While she provides a service to women who are perhaps underserved overall, the end goal of her business is revealed to be hitting back at her husband, more so than at the structures that keep his lifestyle ideal after their divorce.

She-Devil, like the later *Sex and the City* pilot, presents New York financial men as the pinnacle of manly prowess. Perhaps emblematic of New York itself where Wall Street continues to be the symbol of wealth and success, men in the financial fields continue to have their pick of the best of New York. Bob the accountant is unlikely to be a protagonist normally found in one of Mary's bestsellers, but he is who she falls for, and their torrid affair is clearly the source of much inspiration for her. A finance guy is the first prospective mate suggested in *Sex and the City*, although he is equally callous toward his female lovers.

In *Landscape and Gentrification*, Johan Andersson suggests that, by "romanticizing" the city's subcultures into the "accessible form" of romantic comedy, Seidelman's earlier film in the genre was assisting in gentrifying it.[37] This gentrification continues with *Sex and the City*. Yohana Desta, writing for *Vanity Fair*, describes the city portrayed in the show as a "fantastical version" that enticed Seidelman into directing the titular episode.[38] It had been sixteen years since she directed the view-from-the-street boroughs of *Smithereens*. Seidelman directed the initial episode and two later episodes in the series' first season: "The Power of Female Sex" and "The Baby Shower." The series begins with a temporary protagonist introduced by voiceover from Carrie (Sarah Jessica Parker). She is on her way over the bridge into Manhattan, the iconic twin towers of the World Trade Center in view out the left window of her taxi. Instead of opting for an epic fly-over of the city, the audience sees it as a new arrival would. In this way, the city is presented at an intimate as opposed to monumental scale.

This is also a departure from Seidelman's earlier depictions of New York City, which more closely matched up with contemporary films from the 1980s. Andersson describes these stereotyped skyline introductions as "awe-inspiring aerial shots of Manhattan's skyline, panoramic vistas from luxury apartments and offices, crowded sidewalks and traffic-congested avenues."[39] In this case, there is no "parallel iconography of desolation and urban decay [. . .] emblematic of early 1980s New York cinema." A decade later, Manhattan has been wholly gentrified, and in this new, prolonged romantic comedy format, the city's "emerging yuppie culture" has burst into full flight.

Vying for the same feeling of wonder as the young woman looking to make her new life here, shots are taken from the viewpoint of the taxi's windows. After hearing her story, viewers are inducted into a rapid-shot tour of the scenes in New York: Carrie has a cute breakfast date with her English journalist friend, followed by a twist on a gym montage, and then a series of restaurants and club excursions all flavored by the city. The initial episode shows us the intimate interiors of clubs and white-table restaurants where you may recognize anyone. Instead of a surprise recurrence of a character in the background of the shot, another character notices them, and the audience is left in suspense until Carrie interacts by looking at them or pretending to accidentally bump into them. The shot then switches to another camera, another part of the interior, making each cozy locale feel like a world of drama contained within itself. From diners to hip clubs, each interior is cropped to only the characters' conversations.

Even the streets feel cozy in their familiarity. Like a true New Yorker living the glamorous lifestyle, Carrie gets her news from a newspaper box, she takes cabs and not the subway, and she walks everywhere in four-hundred-dollar heels among crowds of women doing the same. When it does come time to revel in the grandeur of the city, the audience is still treated to cropped locales. For instance, when Charlotte attends her black-tie gala, she is arrayed in floor-length finery on the instantly recognizable concrete steps of a New York institution. But again, audiences are brought in close to witness her not-quite-successful goodbye rather than to gawk at the jewels and bolts of fabric dressing those around her.

Main character Carrie is wise to the ways of New York, and while her financial status will be explored briefly in future episodes, the messy and tiny apartment lit by a neon café sign disappears after the pilot. It is replaced by a spacious, multi-room affair with a walk-in closet that a single writer in New York could not even afford to attend the open house for nowadays. This updated apartment will be used more fully in crafting Seidelman's New York fantasy in the *Sex and the City* vein in future episodes.

"The Power of Female Sex" is initially set against the backdrop of the impossible-to-get-into Balzac, a high-class restaurant where the hostess wields true power over who gets to show their face among the who's-who of New York. The upscale dining scene in New York City is legendarily difficult to get into. At least, episodes in popular shows in New York City certainly present it that way. Viewed from the unseated side of the hostess stand, Balzac is solidified as an exclusive and desired part of the city. Just like the clubs and restaurants of the pilot episode, you can run into just about anyone. Whom you meet may also adjust your prospects of getting into the more exclusive side of the city: in this case, an old friend brings Carrie back to Balzac after buying her shoes. Just like these locations, New York City itself becomes the place where all things end up. When Charlotte runs into a hero artist of hers and visits his studio out in the country, it is a New York gallery opening where all of the characters, back from their individual adventures, reconvene.

While it is absent of the nostalgia of the city that Seidelman presented in previous flicks (there is no punk and certainly no No Wave in *Sex and The City*), the series provides a little contemporary New York, presenting it as a big small town. It also cast real-life New Yorkers to fill out its characters, such as Rudy Guiliani's then-wife Donna Hanover.[40] While not street-casting, it infuses the real-life, high-end New York being crafted in the series with a glamorous faux cinema verité.

The characters are brought off their island again for Seidelman's third and final episode, "The Baby Shower." On a drive to Connecticut – "Can anyone drive?" Samantha asks the cab-savvy foursome – each character is offered a possible future in the distinctly suburban fate of their old party girl friend Laney. As they exit to a full lawn, a two-story house and a properly pure-bred dog fit beside plots of suburbia much the same, Carrie declares: "Oh, Toto, I don't think we're in Manhattan anymore." This plotline flips the dynamic of suburban to urban as played out in *Desperately Seeking Susan*, where we see a suburban housewife much like our baby shower honoree adventuring into Manhattan, or Wren returning from the city to her less-than-glamorous origins. In *Sex and the City*, the suburbs provide a vision into what might have been for its cosmopolitan heroines.

Seidelman's films and television work explore the tensions between the urban and suburban for its female protagonists, while also providing a constructed New York City for them and the audience to redefine themselves within. In Seidelman's New York, the landscape becomes a playground, even as it is actively changed by gentrification. Her presentation of the cast of characters into whom one could run within that landscape created a kind of small-town dynamic that pulls audiences into the city, as much as the stories being played out on-screen. How audiences view the city and whose view they look at it with was certainly influenced by Seidelman as a director. Afterall, she in many ways discovered Madonna as a film star just as Madonna's music took off with her second album; she directed and co-wrote the first American independent movie to be invited to Cannes, introducing the unique New York cinema flavor to the world; and she helped launch one of the most successful television series of all time.

NOTES

1. Indie Memphis Film Festival, "Virtual Discussion with Susan Seidelman (Desperately Seeking Susan)," *YouTube.com*, 2 June 2020.
2. Christine Lemire, "Susan Seidelman: Survivor," *Rogerebert.com*, 12 July 2013.

3. Indie Memphis Film Festival, "Virtual Discussion."
4. Maura Edmond, "Deracination, Disembowelling and Scorched Earth Aesthetics: Feminist Cinemas, No Wave and the Punk Avant Garde," *Senses of Cinema*, 80 (September 2016).
5. Susan Seidelman, dir., *Confessions of a Suburban Girl* (1992, BBC Scotland), *YouTube.com*.
6. Susan Seidelman, 'How I Made *Smithereens*, the Cult 80s NYC Punk Film', interview by Laura Jacobs, *Dazed*, 21 August 2018.
7. Seidelman, *Confessions of a Suburban Girl*.
8. "'Desperately Seeking Susan' Turns 30: An Oral History of the Downtown Classic," *Yahoo Entertainment*, 27 March 2015.
9. "'Desperately Seeking Susan' Turns 30."
10. Edmond, "Deracination, Disembowelling and Scorched Earth Aesthetics."
11. Mario Maffi, *Gateway to the Promised Land: Ethnicity and Culture in New York's Lower East Side* (New York: New York University Press, 1995), 40.
12. Maffi, *Gateway to the Promised Land*, 40.
13. Jon Savage, "Cinema of Punk: The Filth and the Fury," *Sight & Sound*, 26 (2016), 22.
14. Seidelman, "How I Made *Smithereens*"; "'Desperately Seeking Susan' Turns 30."
15. Mas'ud Zavarzadeh, "Review: Smithereens," Film Quarterly, 37, no. 2 (Winter 1983–84), 58.
16. Rich Juzwiak, "Susan Seidelman on How the 'Woman Director' Label Went from Pejorative to Political," *Jezebel*, 24 August 2018.
17. Edmund White, "Why Can't We Stop Talking About New York in the Late 1970s?" *New York Times*, 10 September 2015.
18. Susan Seidelman and Susan Berman, "Inside the Making of Post Punk Classic Smithereens," *Little White Lies*, *YouTube.com*, 25 August 2018.
19. Savage, "Cinema of Punk," 22.
20. Susan Seidelman, "Smithereens Q&A with director Susan Seidelman," interview by Lars Nilsen, *Austin Film Society*, *YouTube.com*, February 2020.
21. Seidelman, "How I Made *Smithereens*'."
22. Alanna Schubach, "Stop Blaming the Hipsters: Here's How Gentrification Really Happens (and What You Can Do about It)," Brick Underground, 15 February 2018.
23. Seidelman, "How I Made *Smithereens*."
24. Rebecca Bengal, "Famous for Being Famous in Downtown '80s New York: Susan Seidelman on Smithereens," *Vogue*, 27 July 2016; Juzwiak, "Susan Seidelman on How the 'Woman Director' Label Went from Pejorative to Political."
25. Seidelman, "How I Made *Smithereens*'."
26. Ibid.
27. "'Desperately Seeking Susan' Turns 30"; Seidelman, "How I Made *Smithereens*."
28. Indie Memphis Film Festival, "Virtual Discussion"; Bale, "Persona Swap pt. 1: Past," *Joan's Digest: A Film Quarterly* (Spring 2012).
29. "'Desperately Seeking Susan' Turns 30."
30. Cammila Collar, "Can You Spot All the Underground Music Cameos in Desperately Seeking Susan?" *Medium.com*, 30 June 2017.
31. Edmond, "Deracination, Disembowelling and Scorched Earth Aesthetics."
32. Myra Forsburg, "Susan Seidelman's Recipe for 'Cookie'," *The New York Times*, 29 May 1988.
33. Johan Andersson, "Landscape and Gentrification: The Picturesque and Pastoral in 1980s New York Cinema," *Antipode*, 49, no. 3 (2017), 1.
34. Susan Seidelman and Susan Berman, "The Making of Post Punk Classic *Smithereens*," *Little White Lies*, *YouTube.com*, 25 August 2018.
35. Alex Petroski, "'Pink House' in Belle Terre Village Torn Down," *TBR News Media*, 13 December 2017.

36. Frank Lloyd Wright, "Frank Lloyd Wright Interview," interview by Mike Wallace, *The Mike Wallace Interview*, 1957, *YouTube.com*, [n. d.].
37. Andersson, "Landscape and Gentrification," 10.
38. Yohana Desta, "Meet the Women Who Molded 'Sex and the City's' Very First Season," *Vanity Fair*, 6 June 2018.
39. Andersson, "Landscape and Gentrification," 1.
40. Kelly Conaboy, "Being a Male Jerk in the Sex and the City Pilot: An Oral History," *The Cut*, 7 June 2018.

CHAPTER 9

Making Frankie Stone: Feminism, Post-Romance and *Making Mr. Right*

Vanessa Cambier

INTRODUCTION

Susan Seidelman's 1987 film *Making Mr. Right* is, on its surface, a science-fiction-infused romantic comedy that plays with tropes made popular in other 1980s films such as *Weird Science* (1985) and *Mannequin* (1987). Namely, a human being falls in love with an android (or android-like) almost human. One of the critical differences between *Making Mr. Right* and other films in this genre is that Seidelman flips the expected gender dynamics of the central couple. Instead of depicting a man (or men) who successfully create a fantasy woman, through science or magic, only to fall in love with her, here a female publicist, Frankie Stone (played by Ann Magnuson) falls in love with an android, Ulysses (played by John Malkovich in a dual role, also playing Dr. Jeff Peters, the scientist who created Ulysses). Frankie, originally hired as a publicist by the Chemtec corporation to boost publicity and funding for Dr. Peters, ultimately teaches Ulysses how to behave and how to interact with people (especially women), and she basically raises him to be her perfect partner.

Rather than focusing on Malkovich (arguably the bigger star at the time) as Dr. Peters/Ulysses or the romantic, science-fiction center that ends with Ulysses and Frankie together, I investigate Frankie Stone's character. I argue that Stone, and *Making Mr. Right* overall, are exciting additions to feminist film and media studies' focus on expanded representations of women in 1980s cinema. This time-period is critical because it follows feminism's second wave which gave rise to new versions and visions of women's lives on film and also helped to construct a new idea of women's cinema.[1] *Making Mr. Right* offers a brilliant portrayal of a female character, Frankie Stone, both embracing and challenging the shifting norms for women in the mid- to late 1980s. Notably, this film builds on Seidelman's two previous films, *Desperately Seeking Susan*

(1985) and *Smithereens* (1982). In each earlier film, women venture alone through city spaces that are undergoing massive transformations – think early 1980s New York City – while also negotiating public and domestic space in new ways. In both *Desperately Seeking Susan* and *Smithereens*, the concepts of public and domestic spaces are filtered through ideas of belonging to post-punk music scenes that help triangulate shifting notions of identities available to women in the films. Frankie Stone, however, has a new and different point of identification that assists her navigation through space: her job as publicist.

While this piece will use small points of comparison with *Smithereens* and *Desperately Seeking Susan*, it will focus on key scenes and elements in *Making Mr. Right* in order to argue the complicated feminist politics of Seidelman's representation of Frankie Stone. I am particularly interested in Frankie's mobility through the world and the ways in which her domestic space goes with her through her own automobile, a red convertible. Frankie's mobile domestic sphere allows her aimless approach to her job and life (and, perhaps, also her love story) to intertwine with a concept of home that she is constantly producing and reproducing in various situations throughout the film. Frankie's aimlessness does not translate into an illumination of a New York City scene, through post-punk and new wave women such as Wren and Susan, but rather into the disjuncture between the promises of feminist freedoms past and the somewhat new terrain of exploitation centered on "women's work" in the late 1980s. *Making Mr. Right* is, at least spatially, organized by Frankie and Frankie's movement, and this challenges the textual organization and logics of a normative "romantic comedy." This analysis of *Making Mr. Right* is structured on relationships, to be sure. However, I argue that the important relationship is not necessarily the romance. Rather, I structure this argument around two key concepts: Frankie Stone's relationship to work and media. Both hinge on the visual elements that Seidelman employs, including the use of color and the use of mass media especially targeted towards women (magazines, advertising and soap operas especially). Most notably, however, it is Frankie's spatial aimlessness that is held in tension with her high-powered job as media publicist that drives the film and creates a female character that gestures towards feminist ideals of second-wave politics while also inhabiting the emergent "post-feminist" woman in popular media.[2] This tension is unresolved at the end of the film, ironically, through the resolution of the romantic coupling of Frankie and Ulysses.

FRANKIE STONE: CINEMATIC REPRESENTATION, SECOND-WAVE FEMINISM AND POST-FEMINIST REPRESENTATION

Frankie Stone is played by Ann Magnuson who, around this time, was establishing herself in the underground art music scene.[3] Similar to the casting of

Madonna in *Desperately Seeking Susan*, there is a radiating "coolness" from Magnuson's Frankie that transcends the world of the film, even though the film follows, in some sense, the formula of the romantic comedy. However, where *Desperately Seeking Susan* played with, among other things, the split between Roberta as housewife and Susan as a free spirit (and Roberta's desire and mimicry) capitalizing on Madonna's coolness to especially highlight the constraining aspects of Roberta's suburban "wife life," Frankie has to "do it all" but does not ever fully buy into the concept of "having it all." In other words, she is constantly challenged to be both Roberta and Susan, but without the longing of Roberta's character or the effortless ease of Susan's character. Each time we see Frankie ride around in her red convertible, carelessly applying make-up or shaving her legs in her car, it is countered with some sort of constraining run-in usually related to her job or a possible romantic partner. She is never fully free nor fully contained; thus, the concept of the romantic couple in this film does not quite work in the conventional sense (android partner aside).

Rather than distilling Frankie's ambitions at work through the concept of finding love or romantic coupling, she consistently has to be convinced of the benefits of "settling down," both by her sister (played by Susan Berman who was the lead, Wren, in *Smithereens*, who shows up here looking far more "punk" than Frankie and who seems far more invested in marriage than Frankie will ever be) and by her best friend, Trish (Glenne Headly). Trish spends most of the movie separated from her cheating boyfriend, only to return in the end because he is "better than nothing," or, in other words, better than being alone. But Frankie has something that Trish and her sister do not, at least obviously, and this is a job. Frankie's work creates a tension around romance, something she is typically ready to escape, by continually placing her near and around potential romantic partners. As both Trish and Frankie's sister provide a sort of chorus in the background, maintaining the benefits of "better than nothing," the viewer is quickly introduced to Frankie's three potential suitors. These men include her on/off slimy politician boyfriend, Steve Marcus; the completely off-putting and antisocial Dr. Jeff Peters of the Chemtec organization, the scientist who creates Ulysses; and Ulysses, an incredibly child-like android designed in Peters' image. Her PR firm represents Marcus' campaign as well as the Dr. Peters/Ulysses project. Frankie's work is often the focus of the film's reviews which also note the difficulty in pinning *Making Mr. Right* firmly into the romantic comedy genre.

Despite multiple reviews in publications such as *The New York Times* or by the likes of famous critics such as Roger Ebert praising the film's uniqueness and offbeat humor, there is not a concentrated focus on Frankie's character, aside from her quirks. Much is made of Frankie as upbeat and stylish, wading through what is often considered to be an awkward blending of genres on Seidelman's part (romantic comedy and science fiction, primarily). For instance, Ebert notes that Magnuson infuses Frankie with "fun" via her "high heels and designer outfits, clipboards and speculative looks."[4] Another states that "Frankie Stone is not your average dressed-for-success career woman [...]. With her brisk, gamin style, she is irresistible, particularly to Ulysses."[5] Some reviews gesture towards a critique of gender relations and roles, but none of the literature available on the film goes as far as thinking about how the film is shaped by feminism. Frankie Stone is a figure who embodies, especially through her mobility, the dynamic qualities and multidimensional aspects of media ideology about women and feminism in the 1980s.

The mid-1980s saw the emergence, within media studies especially, of the concept of "post-feminism." Early forms of scholarship on this term characterized post-feminism as temporally located in the shift from second-wave ideals to the contemporary 1980s.[6] However, later scholarship, especially by Angela McRobbie and Rosalind Gill, located the concept of post-feminism within neoliberal ideals of successful, individual women. Often surfacing in popular film and television, these women were productive and worked hard to "have it all" as wives, mothers and consumers set against the backdrop of powerful careers. A slew of sexy career women hit the movie and television screens, especially in the late 1980s, garnering much debate between feminist media and film scholars about what constitutes images of women's empowerment as well as providing extremely contradictory representations of supposedly empowered women. Films such as *Broadcast News* (1987), *Baby Boom* (1987) and *Working Girl* (1988), as well as network television shows such as *Designing Women* (1986–93) and *Murphy Brown* (1988–98) reinforced these ideals.

However, some feminist scholars also point out the blatant non-reality of such images by noting that, in contrast to media depictions, women's labor outside the home is often cast as "cheaper" and more easily made part-time. Women are generally thought of as homemakers and mothers first and workers in the world second.[7] Often used to "fill in the gaps" in public while maintaining and reproducing the family in private, the realities of the gendered labor in public space should interrupt the smooth, neoliberal media texts which insisted on a covering up of such a contradiction.[8]

Frankie Stone is a playful depiction of shifting social norms and a critique of post-feminism: her character is built on these contradictions but never fully inhabits either a feminist or post-feminist position. This is largely because Frankie is a boundary figure who walks in both worlds, the career woman and the under-appreciated, part-time female worker who must care for and constantly attend to others. This is especially encapsulated in the child-like Ulysses android who is dependent on Frankie and, also, where she finds love and eventually partnership. It makes her character an extremely unique representation, to be sure. It also marks the transformation happening for women outside the world of the film, which goes beyond the concept of shifting "scenes" (musical, post-punk, or otherwise). This film actually opens with the contradictory position in which Frankie is, while also illuminating the critical importance of mass media for the film. Images, values and discourse around romantic relationships and femininity are constantly swirling through television and presented on screens. Frankie is fully involved in the world of circulating media through her job as a publicist but also through her everyday existence which is saturated with television soap operas, tabloid newspapers, women's magazines and advertising. In fact, the entire film opens not on Frankie, but rather on the importance of Frankie's television for relaying critical information to her, and to the viewer, about her personal life.

COLOR/TELEVISION

Television along with color, and especially red, are both remarkably important storytelling components in *Making Mr. Right*. Televisions are much more than just screens showing sitcoms or movies in the background. TV emerges as an important communication tool for women: this is how they all learn of men's infidelities. In fact, televised infidelity starts the narrative, framing both the importance of TV and Frankie's relationship to romance. The film opens with a slow pan across a room full of campaigning materials for Steve Marcus' (Frankie's slimy boyfriend) run for Congress. The camera eventually settles on her television which is playing the end of a news segment about the local Little Miss Havana beauty pageant. Steve Marcus appears, pictured here for the first time on a screen, kissing and groping beauty pageant contestants. Notably, the campaign materials strewn about the apartment prominently feature the color red, and the dominance of red bleeds also into the television scene: Marcus' campaign hat, his polo shirt, the beauty contestant's bathing suit and the news anchor's blazer are all bright red. The next shock of red, however, is Frankie Stone's hair. The camera cuts to her waking up to the news of Steve's behavior the night before. Of course, this sequence sets up all we need to know about Frankie and Steve: she works for him and with him, while he cheats on her. In the following scene, he tries to bring flowers and to apologize for last night's "indiscretions," but Frankie shuts him out, believing the media reports rather than Steve's stories. More important, however, is the role of the television, or form of media, in shuttling information to and from Frankie about intimacy. The rest of the film uses an expansive network of media, including magazines and newspapers, not only as storytelling devices for the viewer, but also for Frankie and her best friend Trish.

Shortly after this breaking apart of Frankie and Steve, Trish comes to stay with Frankie because her own boyfriend has also cheated on her. The star of popular soap opera *New Jersey*, Donald (Hart Bochner), Trish's estranged partner has not only cheated on Trish but has done so with his female co-star.

Frankie and Trish watch his fictional character seduce the woman with whom he had the affair outside the world of the soap story. This strange blending of and bleeding through of life events and television are typical of the film, beginning with Frankie and Steve and then moving on to Trish and Don. Not only does the film elevate the role of television (and perhaps even soap opera) to great importance for women, but the blurring of TV and life also gestures towards the importance of representation in media for women and of women.

This opening sequence also introduces the importance of color, especially red, within the world of the film. Red is Frankie's color, from hair or nail polish to her slick retro convertible. In her article on the film for *Monthly Film Bulletin*, Pam Cook notes the extraordinary use of color more generally in *Making Mr. Right*. Cook states:

> Color is put to meaningful use (a la 50s Technicolor, or 70s Godard) with Frankie's tacky Miami Beach setting alive with vibrant color clashes (Frankie herself is coded predominantly red), creating a highly charged ambience which is the antithesis of Michael Mann's color coordinated designer cool [. . .] Frankie's "feminine" world, chaotic and heterogenous, contrasts sharply with muted blue-green orderliness of the Chemtec building where science and reason prevail.[9]

One of the things that the creative treatment of color does in this film is to enable and reinforce representing a somewhat "new woman" with Frankie's character. It is true, as Cook notes, that the Chemtec building, which houses Dr. Peters and Ulysses, is predominantly blue. Other scenes in the film really push the color pink. Pink shows up in accents around Frankie's office and even the main entrance to her home (although this quickly bleeds into red). Thus, while other color coding in the film falls into a sort of blue/masculine and pink/feminine dichotomy, Frankie is a striking figure represented by red.

Notably, Cook also speaks of Frankie's chaotic, feminine world. Stone is sort of a career woman and kind of a free spirit. In one sense, Frankie neatly fits into the romantic comedy genre through this style of chaos with the potential promise of order restored when (not if) she finds love and a romantic partnership. In another sense, however, Frankie also demonstrates a totally different kind of feminine chaos by falling in love, and presumably making a life, with a robot who cannot reproduce or even have sex successfully without short-circuiting (something unfortunately confirmed by Trish). Biological reproduction is out of the question, as is Ulysses' ability to age. The choices that Frankie makes represent an atypical femininity that is also linked, through the color red, to Frankie's mobility.

For example, and returning to the start of the film, as Frankie recovers somewhat from her run-in with Steve, she gets ready for work. Rather than sitting in front of a vanity or even applying make-up in front of a bathroom mirror, Frankie gets ready for her day in her bright red convertible. The car's style clashes with Frankie in its temporal associations with the past (vintage, retro, and so on), but blends with her style of contemporary black-and-white clothing based on color. The color red marks Frankie's involvement in Steve's political campaign as well as her own sense of agency (car, scarf, make-up) associated with gender.

Red, the color of passion and love, is not only associated with a kind of freedom to dabble in normative romance (Steve and the campaign materials), but also with feminine escape and self-fulfilling movement, using the convertible like a rolling vanity. While the story itself is a love story, albeit with some science-fiction reimagining of partnership (for better and worse), Frankie's primary relationship is truly with herself.

WORKING WOMAN, MODERN WRESTLER

Romance is not the only thing that Frankie negotiates by escaping in her convertible; she is also very much associated with work and, like her romantic prospects, always seems to be in some sort of tense relationship with her own labor, in need of escape. Described as a "shady publicist," the "barefoot heroine" and "an overachieving woman who is constantly stressed and late for appointments," Frankie is generally cast as someone obsessed with her job and working herself to the brink of a breakdown, all the while employing under-handed or "shady" methods to get the work done.[10] Frankie is not over-achieving at all. Rather, Frankie marks the contradictory position of being a career woman in the middle of a media landscape pointed directly at supposedly conventional female consumers. This is evident immediately as Frankie enters her offices.

Upon stepping into her building at work, Frankie stops at a news and snacks stand and asks for several magazines: "*Cosmopolitan*, a *Glamour*, a *New Woman*, a *Complete Woman*, a *Working Woman* and *Modern Wrestler*." Not only does her entrance into work necessitate passing through a place in which magazine media are prominent, her selection underscores all the things she must potentially be and all of the identities towards which she must also market. In the background, a sign bears the company name: Stone and Cohn. This is the only real marker of her authority at work and the only sequence of her doing an official form of work, albeit performative, in her office space. Frankie primarily functions individually through the film, and often the thread of labor slips out of her work scenarios as they fill with relationships and personal crises mediated by her rolling second home in the convertible.

As she continues to rush through the halls getting updates from her staff, the background interior is revealed to be pink, signaling the more appropriate version of "Working Woman" than Frankie's general energy which is arguably a bit more "Modern Wrestler." She brushes past a life-sized figure of

Marcus used for his campaign, lingering, as an image, in both her work and personal life. As she enters a meeting, Frankie answers the earlier criticism of lateness with stating "I am always late but always worth it" to a boardroom full of cookie-cutter, and alarmingly silent, businessmen. She takes a seat just in time to view a Chemtec promotional film for the Ulysses android. Here, introduced via a screen, Dr. Peters appears for the first time to explain the project of designing an android who will spend seven years alone in space.

Chemtec's promotional film is fully steeped in the imagery and iconography of the post-war American suburban 1950s, boasting a desire to "bring space into the American home" and "revolutionize the American way of life." An animated figure of the astronaut android is inserted into a suburban home, settled at a dinner table with the perfect (white) American family. The nostalgia for a time when gender roles were, at least in terms of media images, separate, "clear" and based on representations of home and family that mimicked the private/women and public/men divide are aligned with science. Frankie, without missing a beat, takes it further by suggesting a sales and marketing technique also aligned with this traditional gender divide and nostalgia for the 1950s obsession with Atomic Age design.

Frankie rises from her chair and says: "Do you know who controls the majority of America's TV dials and buys 72% of all magazines? Women." At this point, Frankie walks to the front of the meeting room and pulls down her own mini-presentation poster, clearly at the ready for any and all marketing meetings, decorated with retro graphics and illustrations of women, declaring them "decision-makers." Just as Frankie entered the sequence purchasing her own stash of magazines, this moment underscores an important point inside and outside of the film: while women are certainly implicated in the discourse of media representations, they are also consumers of media. The anachronistic representation of home and family, the 1950s suburb used to sell the 1980s space android, is also part of Frankie's vision. Not only do her presentation materials look incredibly similar to Chemtec's ad, but her pitch also emphasizes the role of TV, with women being primary consumers.

Furthermore, the addition of Frankie as media publicist to this discourse complicates this dualism of being produced by media (as sexy, housewives, mothers and so on) and consuming media (magazines and TV) to also shaping and controlling aspects of media representation and dissemination, as she is constantly watching television and reading several magazines. Frankie goes on to say that she must publicize the project her way and describes this as "full media saturation." Somehow, there is a link between activating women as a consumer base and target demographic and gaining funding from Congress for Chemtec's deep space exploration project, but it is never fully explained how that might work.

Frankie furthers her media saturation argument by claiming to promote "people" – politicians, businessmen, the occasional rock star. In other words, Frankie generally represents men. The film holds a tension between marketing men to women by using iconography and ideologies from a time-period before second-wave feminism and using Frankie Stone, 1980s working woman, to do so. Frankie Stone simultaneously critiques the shifting nature of work along gendered lines, while also participating in new forms of mass media directed at women, both as consumers and as a potentially liberating force in the way in which women are able to seize the means of representation and also receive information. Media is not passive, and although Frankie is ready to sell to women, she does not script them as apathetic consumers. Again, she calls them "decision-makers." But what are they deciding? If television is a communicator of intimacy and infidelity, and if it takes a somewhat free agent, such as Frankie Stone, to market men "her way," then the choice seems to fall in the blending of terms in Frankie's workplace and life: gender relations and public relations. There is something in the tricky relationship between these two phrases in terms of what Frankie is performing as well as what she is selling.

To be sure, both Wren in *Smithereens* and Susan in *Desperately Seeking Susan* are performers. They both have auras of cool (especially Susan) that exist within the films and outside of them, centering a sort of knowingness about their relationships with New York City scenes at the time as also cool, and this definitely expanded beyond the scope of each film's diegesis. And, of course, Magnuson herself was a fixture of the 1980s downtown club scene and founding member of the avant-garde psychedelic band Bongwater. Like Madonna, Magnuson would go on to star in several bigger budget films such as *Clear and Present Danger* (1994) and *Panic Room* (2002).

Seidelman's film leverages Magnuson's extratextual coolness here, with Frankie representing the straining of a kind of aimlessness of 'cool' into a job that creates aura, publicity and celebrity. Further, shifting labor and work landscapes also hold stakes for shifts in the social expectations around gender. As Kathi Weeks argues, work creates more than income and capital; it creates "disciplined individuals, governable subjects, worthy citizens, and responsible family members."[III] Frankie's job is a site of gendered discipline that she at once both utilizes (marketing to women in a fairly sexist way) and resists (putting women in the driver's seat of choice and capability), all while moving through media as a kind of language that women understand.

Unlike Wren and Susan, Frankie's job is a site of gendered reinforcement that is neither wholly liberatory nor utterly awful. It is, however, as Weeks also states,

> a particularly important site of interpellation into a range of subjectivities [. . .]. To say that work is organized by gender is to observe that it is a site where, at minimum, we can find gender enforced, performed, and recreated [. . .]. Gender is put to work when, for example, workers draw upon

gendered codes and scripts as a way to negotiate relationships with bosses and co-workers, to personalize impersonal interactions, or to communicate courtesy, care, professionalism, or authority to clients [. . .].[12]

The shift to working women is not only a media studies concern, but also a subjectivity concern. The range of options available to Frankie at work, where she most definitely draws on gendered codes to negotiate business dealings, is slightly more open to inhabiting both conventional and unconventional forms of femininity. This meeting sequence, with its reliance on outdated imagery and American Dream ideology, is both funny (especially because of Frankie's ultra-modern appearance) and a point at which it is clear that Frankie Stone is a figure negotiating multiple female subjectivities, from Modern Woman to Modern Wrestler.

SPACE EXPLORATION

Frankie lands her job with Chemtec and now has to go and meet Ulysses (Malkovich), an android that Dr. Peters (also Malkovich) has designed both in his own image and for the purposes of spending isolated time in deep space for seven years. The end of her business meeting at Stone and Cohn immediately cuts to a scene of Frankie driving her red convertible. Shown in a medium shot, the red of the car and the black of Frankie's dress and glasses provide a sharp contrast to the green, rolling hills in the background.

As Frankie changes her focus to look at something out of frame, the camera does not immediately tell us what she is seeing. Rather, we linger on a shot of her, green hills behind her, looking for a little longer than average before we are let in on the look. The shot cuts to the Chemtech plant behind fences and barbed wire. The color focus shifts, too, from the bright reds and greens to cool steely blue and institutional grey. In a film with a focus on sending an android into deep space, the imagery, especially at Chemtec, mimics that idea as much of the film is closed in and shot in tight interiors.

Frankie's convertible, however, provides a sense of openness, air and light, while also serving as a kind of mobile domestic space for her character. Frankie seems to live in a sort of blending of the public and private spheres through her car. Traveling as she does, she produces a new type of space which oddly fits the discourse associated with Chemtec's rhetoric around deep space exploration and isolation. Aside from Ulysses, Frankie's mobile world is largely experienced in isolation.

Frankie's interaction with the spatial is a constant building and undoing of the space around her, with not only tension (all the need for escape) but also an ease that the male characters in the film do not possess. Perhaps more potent in terms of a film such as *Smithereens*, in which the cityscape of 1980s New York

City is always in tension with Wren's movements, here the semi-predictability of a romantic comedy film coupled with the spatial unpredictability of a new type of working woman clash in Frankie. The result is her "chaotic feminine" world which is now perhaps less about the color red and more about disorganizing the spatial arrangements typical of where the rest of the film takes her: a wedding reception, a robotics lab or even a shopping mall.

As Frankie drives through the Chemtec lot, her convertible, appearing in a long shot, moves through the grey spaces and dome-shaped buildings. Upon entry to the building, Frankie is given a visitor's pass and taken to robotics. Here, the interior, saturated in blue, looks like an underground bunker. The space and freedom that opens the sequence, with Frankie in her convertible, rolling hills in the background, is now shut into this claustrophobic interior. Frankie is then led to further containment, left to wait for Dr. Peters in a small room.

Frankie's introduction to Ulysses the android comes with confusion, as he looks identical to Dr. Peters but, unfortunately, has not been socialized and grabs Frankie's chest, causing her to push him away. He falls and malfunctions. From here, the dialogue about gender takes a fairly predictable turn, as Dr. Peters exclaims: "I knew it! One minute with a woman, and he short circuits!" And, as he disassembles Ulysses to repair him by removing his head, he snorts, in Frankie's direction: "What's the matter? No man ever lose his head over you before?" The jokey and stereotypical rhetoric around Frankie and her "chaotic feminine" energy is, on the one hand, expected. Women, at least in terms of the way in which they are discussed in Frankie's marketing meeting, are decision-makers at home but not necessarily so at work (especially science labs). On the other hand, Frankie takes her unconventional home space with her via her convertible actively disrupting the tight and careful organization of interiors which are mostly inhabited by men with a sense of spatial and social reorganization. This plays out in Ulysses' malfunctioning, which also highlights the stiffness of Dr. Peters, who is generally in the tight confines of the robotics building, and Steve, primarily shown on the confining television screen or inside at campaigning events. Even Trish's cheating boyfriend exists primarily in the world of a soap opera, also screened in and, in a sense, stuck.

Although Frankie solidifies her job with Chemtec by agreeing to improve Ulysses' "social graces," she gives him much more. In terms of training Ulysses, Frankie seems to actually teach the android about escape and mobility outside the confines of the Chemtec robotics lab. When Frankie leaves Ulysses alone with her purse, he ends up finding her lipstick, smearing it all over his face, and the shock of red changes his narrative flow. From the point of his "makeover," he figures out a method of escape, finding his way to Frankie's convertible and hiding himself underneath her backseat pile of trash and clothing. Here, "a woman's influence" involves a sense of mobility rather than being stuck (in the space of the lab, office or television screen). Ulysses might look like Dr. Peters, but he clearly wants to be like (and be liked by) Frankie.

Questions of social space usually evoke notions of stasis rather than motion, however.¹³ Often painted as the opposite of movement and time, or even the container in which events happen, space, as a concept, is easily ignored as an active producer of events. Doreen Massey argues that space must be considered with time (space-time) as distinct but intertwined entities. Massey also argues that space and the spatial are implicated in the production of gender, in the way in which we understand it, and that spaces are "gendered through and through."¹⁴ Thinking about the spaces of the film in this way allows Frankie's character to emerge as a constant disruptor and rebuilder of the spaces around her, through her role as this contradictory representation of part worker, part chaotic feminine. Her figure reorganizes and rearranges both the spatial and the gendered dynamics in the film, allowing Ulysses more access to her world and less need for a performance of masculinity. Where female figures such as Wren and Susan were obviously part of a cool downtown or music scene that helped structure their characters, Frankie has no external structure; she builds her own framework out of existing pieces and from parts of the old and the new.

This is most evident in her aesthetic style, which collides a classic convertible with 1980s-inspired career attire, as well as her marketing style, which still scripts women as home-makers as well as decision-makers. Frankie's "look" reinforces this idea, as she is not only semi-postpunk but also semi-1980s professional. Her aesthetic is a combination of Seidelman's earlier characters, Susan and Wren, for example, Patrick Nagel's 1980s illustrations and a touch of classic Hollywood reminiscent of Mildred Pierce. It also explains her exhaustion with normative romance; Frankie does not fit into the claustrophobic spaces of the men in this film, nor does she sink into a particular time-period in a smooth fashion. Frankie's eventual decision to partner with an android who looks like a man is also about choosing freedom, with another being willing to escape the tensions of constraining spaces (and relationships).

POST-FEMINIST, POST-ROMANCE

The culmination of Frankie's work tensions, mobility, spatial rearrangement and romantic prospects happens at her sister's wedding. Notably, Frankie is out of her element and instead of her usual tight dress with red accessories, she is forced to wear a stereotypical bridesmaid dress: lacy, frilly, lavender and huge. Frankie attends with Dr. Peters, at the insistence of her mother that she should not go alone, and she has to suffer being in the wedding party with Steve who follows her in a constant state of jealousy (even though he is now in a relationship with his new campaign manager, Frankie's former assistant). Ulysses eventually shows up having figured out how to use a credit card and computer for shopping, as well as how to hitchhike, to let Frankie know that he loves her.

Even Trish's ex-boyfriend, Donald, shows up, determined to win Trish back. Once all of the men are there, chaos breaks loose around Frankie, as she moves from dancing with Dr. Peters, to an interruption by Steve, another interruption by Ulysses and a fight with Donald.

Frankie's mobility is the disturbing factor to any sense of order around gender and romance. Her blatant refusal to choose any of these competing men, complete with their various worlds of containment, brings them all together in a way that ends up in most of the aggression, at least from Donald and Steve, being taken out on Ulysses. While narratively the cause of Donald's anger is the discovery of Ulysses' tryst with Trish (which ended in malfunction), Frankie attempts to shield Ulysses, intervening and telling Donald to hit her instead. In this sequence, Frankie and Ulysses are united, but not by romance, although Ulysses tells Frankie that he loves her. Rather, they spark chaos because the choice for either of them to be together is to not be contained: Frankie does not have to settle into a normative relationship, and Ulysses does not have to spend years in isolation in space.

When Frankie and Ulysses finally do kiss at her sister's wedding reception, a cameraman passes, recording the moment and setting off a wave of newspaper reports on the subject of a human woman and an android as romantic couple. Media as conveyer of intimacy returns to record, announce and denounce Frankie's relationship with Ulysses. The film presents a montage of newspaper headlines: "Splashdown! Lovesick Android Crashes Wedding!"; "Stone Quits over Rumored Romance"; "Ulysses Rivals Men – 10 Single Women Share Their Views." The next sequence features a set of well-manicured hands grabbing a copy of *The Sun*, and as the camera pulls back, the full shot reveals a beauty salon. Female clients under dome-hairdryers are reading *The Examiner* and *The Sun*, which boasts the headline "Man or Machine?"

Media again plays a role in announcing romantic relationships by reporting on her sister's wedding. The reports center on Frankie and Ulysses, and newspapers now announce the relationship to the world. Ulysses is both constructed as a would-be lover and child, bringing together all components of the "other" work that we almost never see Frankie engage in or talk about; family life does not seem to be her priority. And yet, her draw to Ulysses is immediate.

It is Ulysses who gifts Frankie another version of the convertible. Still red, although a darker shade, it implies a shared sense of mobility, for use together. Through attachment to each other, they will both also remain paradoxically free, as it is revealed that Dr. Peters goes to space, leaving Ulysses on earth for Frankie.

Frankie's position as a character in the middle of second-wave ideologies and political proclivities, as well as the supposed "post-feminist" time-period, open the text itself up to a range of readings, including feminist. However, even with the brief treatment, or often dismissal, of the film's politics in popular reviews, it still gets coded as "post-feminist." Of the film, Pam Cook notes that "*Making Mr. Right*'s futurism resides mainly in being post-just about everything from feminism to punk."[15] Returning then to the debated feminist media studies notion of "post-feminism," is it truly the case that Frankie embodies the neoliberal ideals of an individual woman's success and disdain for the ideologies and political purposes of second-wave feminism? *Making Mr. Right* is more complex than that, precisely because Frankie's relationship with mobility and media makes her a threat to spatial structures of control, while promoting a certain brand of "new working woman," and all under the umbrella of a decidedly non-normative partnership. In a sense, the film is more post-romance than it is post-feminist.

It is not, however, post-media as Frankie's TV gets the final word. Mimicking the opening shot portraying Steve Marcus, this closing shot features Dr. Peters from space, declaring that being isolated is "truly the most exciting thing in the world." Ultimately, this appears to be the film's moment of closure. Instead of ending with the coupling of Frankie and Ulysses, the film ends with Dr. Peters and the concept of isolation as the most perfect example of happiness in a post-romance economy.

CONCLUSION

A review in *The New York Times* notes that *Making Mr. Right* should have been as, or possibly even more, successful than its predecessor *Desperately Seeking Susan*. Published in 1988, it states of Seidelman that

> It may simply be that she is not quite at home with this slightly less effervescent story idea, or with finding satirical potential in high-tech settings, or even with the principal characters here, than she was last time. In any case, *Making Mr. Right* aims for the carefree style of Ms. Seidelman's last film and has much the same sense of whimsy and the same distinctive touch. But it's a little more labored and a little less fun.[16]

Yes, the film does labor. It specifically labors because Frankie works. And that role is both full of contradictions and does indeed form the center of her actions and movements. Mass media is the language of women in this film, especially forms largely disregarded as non-critical and lacking seriousness or legitimacy. Soap operas and television, women's magazines and tabloids all frame narratives of intimacy that begin with Frankie's cheating boyfriend and end with isolation. The film is not as "whimsical" as *Desperately Seeking Susan* because it cannot be. Too many things have changed for "modern, working women," although Frankie Stone still has echoes of aimlessness and coolness. But this is also the trouble of expecting films made by women to be "effervescent" in the first place. And, arguably, *Smithereens* was not a whimsical narrative at all, finding main character Wren very much involved in much less fun and a lot more isolation (without any of the high-tech settings, so the review notes, as hindering the fun). Seidelman's next film, *She-Devil* (1989), is an even darker comedic take on the nature of women, work and the power of being alone.

Notes and writing on the film since 1987 are limited. However, a more recent write-up about the film for Turner Movie Classics does call Frankie Stone a feminist character and also points out the importance of *Making Mr. Right* for providing key critical commentary on heteronormative relationships and male/female gender roles.[7] Choosing Ulysses is ultimately choosing to be alone, and there is a power in this for women, in a new way that ultimately also affects the narrative, disrupting the normative and organized ending of a romantic comedy while opening space for a different representation of women in 1980s popular cinema.

Media, space, mobility and work all come together in the rich and contradictory character that is Frankie Stone. Frankie embraces and challenges the shifting roles for women in the late 1980s, marking important changes to representing women, careers and domestic space in film and television. Rather than coding Frankie as merely a sum of many quirks, this essay has argued for her importance in feminist film and media history, as well as for Susan Seidelman's notable role in representing difficult contradictions for women both on and off screen. *Making Mr. Right* is definitely a science-fiction romantic comedy, but it is also a critical film about gender identity, spatial configurations and labor.

NOTES

1. For more on this, see Annette Kuhn, *Women's Pictures: Feminism and Cinema* (New York: Verso, [1982] 1994); E. Ann Kaplan, *Feminism and Film* (Oxford: Oxford University Press, 2000); Judith Mayne, *The Woman at the Keyhole: Feminism and Women's Cinema* (Bloomington: Indiana University Press, 1990).
2. See Angela McRobbie, *The Aftermath of Feminism: Gender, Culture, and Social Change* (London: Sage Publishing, 2008); Rosalind Gill, "Postfeminist Media Culture: Elements of a Sensibility," *European Journal of Cultural Studies*, 10, no. 2 (2007), 147–66.
3. Frosty, "Interview with Ann Magnuson: The Actor, Musician and Performance Artist on Club 57, Bongwater and New York's Downtown New Wave Scene," *Red Bull Music Academy*, 10 October 2017.
4. Roger Ebert, "Making Mr. Right," *Rogerebert.com*, 10 April 1987.
5. Constance Rosenblum, "Making Mr. Right," *New York Times*, 3 January 1988.
6. McRobbie, *The Aftermath of Feminism*; Gill, "Postfeminist Media Culture."

7. See Doreen Massey, *Space, Place, and Gender* (Minneapolis: University of Minnesota, 1994); Silvia Federici, *Revolution at Point Zero: Housework, Reproduction, and Feminist Struggle* (Oakland: PM Press, 2012); Robin Truth Goodman, *Gender Work: Feminism After Neoliberalism* (New York: Palgrave MacMillan, 2013).
8. See Robin Truth Goodman's reading of Hardt and Negri in her chapter "Gender Work: Feminism after Neoliberalism," 139–74.
9. Pam Cook, "Making Mr. Right," *Monthly Film Bulletin*, 1 May 1988.
10. Ebert, "Making Mr. Right."
11. Kathi Weeks, *The Problem with Work: Feminism, Marxism, Antiwork Politics, and Postwork Imaginaries* (Durham: Duke University Press, 2011).
12. Ibid. p. 7–9.
13. See Doreen Massey in *Space, Place and Gender*: "This is the view of space which, in one way or another, defines it as stasis, and as utterly opposed to time" (251); "This does not mean that such a 'spatial' structure cannot change-it may do-but the essential characteristic is that all the causes of any change which may take place are internal to the structure itself [. . .]. The spatial, because it lacks dislocation, is devoid of the possibility of politics" (252).
14. Doreen Massey, *Space Place and Gender*, 186–88.
15. Cook, "Making Mr. Right."
16. Janet Maslin, "John Malkovich in *Making Mr. Right*," *New York Times*, 10 April 1987.
17. "Making Mr. Right (1987)," *Turner Classic Movies*, 23 October 2019.

PART 3

Making Room

CHAPTER 10

Electric Melodrama: Susan Seidelman, Childhood and the Girl Next Door

Debbie Olson

In *Melodrama Unbound*, Christine Gledhill suggests that "melodrama's expressive rhetoric mediates the tension between supposedly gratuitous sensation and the critical search for meaning."[1] Susan Seidelman's work featuring young girls also finds itself negotiating melodrama's oscillation between emotional highs and lows and the search for meaning. While melodrama has historically been associated with "women's pictures," melodrama as a form has taken a prominent place in everything from soap operas and crime shows to horror, science fiction and even big action blockbuster films. According to Lyn Joyrich, the melodramatic form "orchestrates the emotional ups and downs and underscores a particular rhythm of experience [. . .] that expresses] ideological and social conflicts in emotional terms."[2] The emotional highs and lows attributed to the melodramatic form are also part of the experience of childhood. Children and teens experience and perform emotional excess in their everyday existence; for instance, the dramatic temper tantrum, the emotional high gained by listening to a popular song or the effusive hugging and kissing of excited youngsters. For them, emotions are experienced raw and pure, before they are taught to restrain themselves, or to control their emotional excesses. Children's television programming often mimics a child's emotional swings in its characters, sound, visuals and dialogue in such a way as to nurture both a camaraderie between children in the emotional experience itself and to reaffirm the normalcy of such emotions. The use of melodrama in children's television and film works to underscore the validity of emotional excess in childhood and to emphasize relationships between disparate elements. Indeed, melodrama in children and for children is expected, an integral part of the childhood experience. Those who produce children's media are regularly engaged in producing melodramas that reinforce modern conceptions of family and society, even while they omit the actual word "melodrama."

While the majority of Susan Seidelman's work has been directed at adult audiences, she has on occasion ventured into the realm of childhood. Seidelman's *Confessions of a Suburban Girl* (1992) is a visual memoir of her own childhood, a delightfully nostalgic romp through childhood in 1960s Philadelphia, an era energized with innocence, hope and dramatic social change. And while *Confessions of a Suburban Girl* is an adult look back at childhood, Seidelman focuses her commentary on female independence and her admiration for the agency of the "bad girls," themes that permeate many of her later works. But it is in her work directed at children that Seidelman's expertise with melodrama aesthetics finds its apex, as she keenly captures the emotional excesses of childhood in ways that extend into cultural norms more broadly. In this chapter, I will argue that Seidelman's use of melodrama in the four *Electric Company* episodes she directed privileges female agency in ways that underscore the broader connections between childhood, girlhood, womanhood and American culture.

BRIEF HISTORY OF *THE ELECTRIC COMPANY*

In 1969, James E. Allen Jr, then President Richard Nixon's Commissioner of Education, gave a speech to the National Association of State Boards of Education, where he declared the 1970s as the "right to read" decade. Allen believed that education was a "concept which honors the dignity and worth of an individual" and that all children should able to have access to good education, including the right to learn to read. When Nixon outlined his educational policies in a radio address in 1972, he echoed Allen's words and set up a "Right to Read" program in order to further those educational goals.[3] The cultural focus on education for children at this time worked in tandem with groups who sought to harness television as an educational tool. The Children's Television Workshop (PBS), the company that developed *Sesame Street*, was just such a group. The Children's Television Network, awash in the success of its award-winning show *Sesame Street*, developed a second show designed to build on the content of *Sesame Street*, which was targeted to children two to six years old. This new show would teach reading to a target audience of children six to ten years old; thus, using some of the effective style elements of *Sesame Street*, *The Electric Company* was born.

Although never as wildly popular as its sister show, *Sesame Street*, *The Electric Company* boasted six seasons (780 episodes) and ended production in April 1977, with reruns continuing on PBS until 1985. Since the advent of cable television, and later the Internet, episodes of the original *Electric Company* are today easily available across multiple streaming platforms. The original show's twenty-eight-minute episodes focused on grammar, reading, sounding out words, putting words together into sentences and combining words. The show was made up of short skits that focused on a particular skill, musical numbers and new colorful computer animation. *The Electric Company* generally received favorable reviews and, although it never became the money-maker that *Sesame Street* did, it still resonated with audiences and has become a childhood classic for those who grew up in the 1970s and early 1980s.

In 2009, PBS and Sesame Workshop (formerly Children's Television Workshop) revived *The Electric Company* for modern audiences. The new show borrowed some elements from the original – for instance, the show's classic silhouette segments – but it was mostly a new vision of the show for modern, tech-savvy children. While it attempted to contain the same educational elements, the addition of a singular story narrative, rather than a collection of smartly developed skits about words and sentences, changed the focus of the show in ways that some critics claimed were disloyal to the educational project of the original show.[4] While the single narrative does highlight reading concepts, it is weighted more in favor of traditional sitcom elements of plot and character. Unlike the original show, the new *Electric Company* only ran for three seasons (fifty-two episodes), but it boasted three consecutive Emmy Awards for Outstanding Children's Program, among other honors. And while the new *Electric Company* moved away from content that strictly adhered to promoting reading, it nevertheless spotlighted important social lessons for its child audience.

SEIDELMAN'S ELECTRIC GIRLS

We get a glimpse of the way in which Seidelman views childhood in her 1992 biopic docudrama, *Confessions of a Suburban Girl*. Commissioned by BBC Scotland, the light-hearted film is a nostalgic look back at girlhood in 1960s Philadelphia, mixing archival footage with recreations and present-day interviews.[5] The film explores both girlhood dreams and adult disillusion; as Seidelman describes, they lived in a "glass bubble," in a "world without drama, without adventure, where everything was the same" and where their only real goal was to find a husband. Seidelman adroitly examines the almost fairy-tale-like innocence that framed childhood in the 1960s. As teenage girls in the 1960s, Seidelman and her friends existed in the interstice between traditional values and the rise of new beliefs in feminism and civil rights. Seidelman and her childhood friends – Debbie, Ivy, Ellen and Brenda – discuss their mother's and father's limited expectations for them: find a good husband. Seidelman in the film makes a point of exploring the double-standard inherent in gendered cultural expectations for children in the 1960s. She and her friends complain that "suburban life was boring" and that they spent much of their time in the pursuit of boys – potential husbands. As Ellen states later in the film,

"I wanted to feel safe and being married meant to me being safe – I wanted to be safe." Seidelman talks about the king and queen sculptures that her parents put on the front lawn of her childhood home. She "hated that king and queen and all they represented," as the queen was placed slightly behind the king, her eyes downcast and demure, while the king sported a "smug look" and faced straight ahead. Seidelman was encased in the "dos and don'ts of being a good girl" in the 1960s and was taught that "it was a woman's job to be beautiful; after all, she was defined by the way she looked." But these traditional lessons conflicted with the younger generation's counterculture messages of female agency and feminism. As Seidelman and her friends half-heartedly complained about the lack of excitement in their upper middle-class existence, they developed a deep admiration for the "real" bad girls, the Italian girls who lived on the "other side of the shopping center. I [Seidelman] thought they were the coolest girls in the world [. . .] it was at this time that bad girls became my heroes." And while Seidelman and her friends were "good girls" wanting to be "bad girls," they "never [had] the nerve to do anything about it." So when Seidelman began making films, she created the "bad girl" characters that she had so admired as a youth. Her female protagonists, such as Wren in *Smithereens* (1982) and Madonna in *Desperately Seeking Susan* (1985), embrace a "badness" that is sometimes punished, sometimes rewarded, reflecting Seidelman's internal grappling with the good girl/bad girl duality.

In 2009, and again in 2010, Seidelman was hired to direct a total of four episodes for the new *Electric Company*: "The Flube Whisperer" and "Mighty Bright Fright" in 2009, followed by "Jules Quest" and "Revolutionary Donuts" in 2010. Each of the episodes feature strong, young girls who merge the melodramatic with agency. And while Seidelman had little involvement in the development and pre-production of these four episodes, her desire for "bad girl" agency coupled with "good girl" intentions, I argue, does inform her directorial approach to these child characters.

"THE FLUBE WHISPERER"

In this episode, young Keith (Ricky Smith) has a "flube egg" in a biosphere and is carrying it around with him, so that he does not miss it hatching. There are hints of the masculine as nurturer here, particularly for an "egg" which is often associated with femaleness. When Lisa (Jenni Barber) stops by to say hello, she asks Keith about the flube egg. As Keith tells her about the biosphere and the egg, she notices that the biosphere is not very warm, which puts the flube egg in danger of dying, setting in motion the plot-quest to fix the biosphere. Seidelman and cinematographer Bill Berner utilize specific camera movements in this episode to highlight the girls as the voices of reason amidst

Keith's heightened emotional state. The girls are often shot in center-frame, or with low angles to emphasize their role as the authority.

While it is Keith's biosphere and flube egg, it is the girls, Lisa and Jessica (Priscilla Star Diaz), who throughout the episode discover the problem, offer solutions to the problem and ultimately provide the means (the portable Shrinkinator 3002) to solve the problem. As is common in television for children, problems – no matter how large or small – are met with a rush of emotional outbursts from the child characters. According to Peter Brooks, melodrama is a mode of "high emotionalism and stark ethical conflict."[6] Keith is visibly shaken and in crisis mode over the potential death of the egg and the biosphere, displayed in his panicked speech, his wide eyes and his voice's rise in pitch. Jessica and Lisa use the Shrinkinator to send Keith into the biosphere to fix the thermostat. But Keith discovers a page missing from the manual and cannot fix it on his own. The ethical conflict of this melodrama lies in the girl's debating whether to ask Manny Spamboni (Dominic Colon) to help because he is knowledgeable about electronics. Manny, however, has a reputation as a "bad" boy and causes trouble by playing pranks on the others, so that they are not sure whether they can trust him. But he is also the perfect person for the job. The girls, along with Hector (Josh Segarra), convince Manny to help by appealing to his softer nature (protecting something vulnerable and small) and his love of pets, furthering the theme of the male nurturer. They use the Shrinkinator on Manny, and he joins Keith in the biosphere to fix the thermostat. When Jessica blows a word message to Keith that help is coming, the girls are foregrounded as the source of knowledge and help. The visual contrast of small Keith looking up at a giant Jessica also suggests affective awe as a visceral response to the crisis of the egg, underscoring the legitimacy of the heightened emotions and the girls' maternal authority. The biosphere malfunction frames the "melodramatic transformation of scientific causality into a narrative of responsibility," as the boys work together to save the egg under the girls' direction.[7] The biosphere warms up, the flube egg hatches, the crisis is averted, and they learn that Manny can be trusted. And while the girls do not necessarily push the boundaries of traditional roles, they do come up with the solution of using the Shrinkinator 3002 and asking Manny for help.

It is also important to note that this episode explores the notion of motherhood in the sense that an "egg" needs nurturing, with the biosphere effectively functioning as the "womb." Moving beyond the stereotypical melodramatic female motherhood image, Seidelman highlights male nurturing in the character of Kevin, who protects the egg within its womb, while the knowledge about mothering resides with Jessica and Lisa, who solve the problems inherent in the "production" of the egg to full term. This unique twist on parenthood roles offers to the child viewer a modern, less rigid gender role structure, as anyone – even Manny – can birth/hatch and nurture another life. Such fluid gender role images play an important part in the normalization of alternate cultural forms of domesticity and family for the youth audience, as well as foregrounding female agency.

"MIGHTY BRIGHT FIGHT"

Being safe was a theme throughout Seidelman's childhood, as it was throughout *Confessions of a Suburban Girl*, and so a character that chooses not to take the safe route challenges the traditional ideals with which Seidelman grew up. In this episode, Jessica and Harper (Tessa Faye) reluctantly team up with Manny to perform a skit in a competition at the Mighty Bright Knight-i-con where the creator of the popular comic books (*The Mighty Bright Knight*), Stan Flea (John Pankow), will be in attendance. The particular melodrama in this episode is the heightened emotional response to celebrity in form of the Mighty Knight and his creator, Stan Flea. As Brooks argues, "melodrama represents both the urge toward resacralization and the impossibility of conceiving sacralization."[8] While Jessica and Harper are hesitant to team up with Manny, who has a reputation for being unreliable, Jessica chooses to trust him and allows him into the skit anyway. She connects his love (his sacralization) of the Mighty Knight to his desire to win the competition and relies on that love to keep him loyal to their skit, allowing her to make the "unsafe" decision to let Manny work with them. She meets resistance from her other friends who do not understand Jessica's decision. But Jessica defends Manny, praising his handiwork in making the costumes, re-emphasizing her desire to work on this skit with him.

As Jessica, Manny and Harper are practicing their skit, Jessica spies her brother Hector watching. She confronts him about why he is "spying" on her, and he claims that he is protecting her. Despite Hector's attempt at the traditional protector role (through voyeurism), Jessica resists his belief that she cannot make her own decisions, and the segment veers off into a song and dance number. The visual style of the performance is reminiscent of 1980s big production numbers, as "the aesthetic means of melodrama – the orchestration of music, sound, color, space, dynamic movement, and so on – have a functional and a thematic use, both evocatively marking emotional intensities."[9] Jessica's costume is suggestive of Madonna, with huge, wide shoulder pads, a cape and boots, as she dances and sings "No, nobody's perfect" – a passionate argument for giving Manny a chance. Seidelman showcases child agency here, as Jessica makes her decision, stands by that decision in the face of opposition and successfully supports her reasoning. But, just before the competition, Stan Flea asks for volunteers to become his temporary assistant, and Manny immediately volunteers, abandoning the girls and leaving them without a key player for their skit. Manny's abandonment would seem to suggest that Jessica should have chosen the "safe" route, but there is no denying that Manny contributed a great deal to the skit despite his eventual leaving. And Jessica took responsibility for her decision, despite how it ended. She accepted Hector's offer to help, and they were able to complete the competition, even though they got last place.

After the competition is over, Manny tries to make it up to the girls by offering them autographed comic books, but they emphatically decline. In the end, Jessica is rewarded by Stan Flea who, before he leaves, shows the gang a new character that he created for his comics: the Electric Empress, and it is Jessica drawn as a super-hero. Stan Flea praises her for her loyalty to her friends, emphasizing that the Mighty Bright Knight's motto is "friendship is the best reward," while Manny dramatically groans in the background. Earl F. Bargainnier argues that "the world of melodrama [is] an ideal world in which the good [are] very, very good, and rewarded for being so, and the bad [are] very, very bad and punished accordingly."[10] Jessica and Manny both received the reward that their behavior dictated, with Jessica being the clear winner. But even more important is the subtext of the family breakup that is suggested when Manny "abandons" his skit "family" and the family is then left to carry on alone. It is "how" Jessica and Harper deal with Manny's desertion, and the fact that they continue the skit anyway is the significant lesson here. While the abandonment is hurtful, it did not deter the girls from their ultimate goal – to perform in the competition.

"JULES QUEST"

In the "Jules Quest" episode, Seidelman utilizes nature as a special style of melodramatic aesthetics. This episode contains aerial omniscient shots as well as strategic long takes that position the characters against a backdrop of forest, open green space and a waterfall. In fact, in this episode the earth and nature figure prominently, as Seidelman uses such imagery to underscore melodrama's "search for moral value through story and character."[11] The episode opens with a close-up of a shovel full of dirt, then the shovel digging, then cuts to an omniscient view of a man's body digging, then back to the close-up of the shovel; the series of cuts repeats one more time before a final close-up of hands lifting a small wooden chest then depositing it in the hole. The next cut is a low-angle shot from the hole, as we see Hector's (Josh Segarra) face hovering, then he shovels dirt over the camera, ending the shot. Next is a long shot of Hector and Jessica walking to the spot where the chest is buried, discussing their conservation mission to plant trees. Danny (William Jackson Harper) is sitting on a bench reading a magazine, as Hector and Jessica each take a side to start digging.

The moment Jessica "finds" the chest, dramatic music plays, highlighting both the mystery and the emotional thrill of finding something unexpected. The contents of the chest, a set of scrolls, send Jessica on a scavenger hunt through the neighborhood. The episode has a subplot involving Danny, who feels left out of the scavenger hunt and decides to follow the hunt on his own to capture the jewels before Jessica finds them. When Jessica hands out the scrolls to Lisa and Hector to read, Lisa's scroll "curses her tongue," and she begins to talk gibberish. Hector reads the last scroll, which says that they must go on a quest in order to reverse the curse and find the jewels. Jessica then goes in search of the next chest, although Danny gets to it first, and they find the chest empty. The next segment opens with Hector, Jessica and Lisa positioned center-frame in a tracking shot, with the expanse of green woods and paved walkway leading into the distance behind them. Seidelman here underscores the connection between the quest and nature.

All of the "clues" lead them to places that highlight the natural world – a bear statue under a rock and by a waterfall. In this episode focused on friendship and belonging, nature serves to suggest nurturing and security amidst the uncertainty of the quest. At the bear statue, Hector intercepts Danny and explains that the "jewels" which the scroll says are at the end of the quest really consist of Jessica's best friend "Jules," who had moved away and is back to visit for Jessica's birthday. According to Gledhill, "Melodrama's protagonists embody and enact – rather than represent – socioethical values."[12] Here Hector does not get angry at Danny, but rather understands his feelings of being excluded and exhibits compassion and kindness to him. Hector explains to Danny that the scavenger hunt is made up and leads to a surprise birthday party for Jessica. Danny then offers to help with the surprise party for Jessica. For Gledhill, melodrama aesthetics provide a new perspective, as "dramatic emphasis shifts from cause to consequence."[13] This shift takes place specifically when Hector confronts Danny about the quest and its purpose. When Danny assumes that he has been excluded (the cause) from the quest and the party, his emotional reaction, and his motivation for action, is to try and sabotage the quest. But once Hector explains that the "jewels" are not real, Danny pivots emotionally in order to help Hector and the others surprise Jessica at the end of the quest (the consequence as motivation). Gledhill explains that the melodramatic aesthetic of cause to consequence in a character's motivation "opens up areas of feeling unanticipated by character or audience."[14] Rather than elicit anger or disappointment from the child viewer over Danny ruining the quest, the child viewer can now comfortably accept Danny's changed motivation.

At the end of the quest, Jules appears from behind a large chest, and the two friends are happily reunited, beginning a musical number with everyone singing "Good Friends Are as Good as Gold." As Charles Burnetts suggests, musical numbers in melodramas "provide relief from the tense events of their plots" and "often [serve] a pedagogical purpose, bringing characters together romantically or socially despite their initial disagreements or conflicts."[15] Jessica is reunited with her friend Jules, and Danny was able to participate in the quest and the surprise party, helping him to feel part of the group. The episode ends with a low medium shot of the children at the picnic table, then a slow dolly backwards until the camera launches skyward for an omniscient shot of all the cast members singing "Happy Birthday" to Jessica in front of the waterfall.

"REVOLUTIONARY DONUTS"

In the last episode that Seidelman directed, Lisa discovers some uncomfortable information about one of her ancestors; thus, she, along with Hector and Keith, go in search of the truth. Of all the episodes that Seidelman directed for *The Electric Company*, it is this episode about generations of women and the value of domesticity that highlights her use of a melodramatic aesthetic imbued with the underpinnings of relationships between girlhood, womanhood and national culture.

While in the library, Lisa runs into Annie (Sandie Rosa), who brags that she is writing an article for the newspaper about Lisa's ancestor, Cordelia Heffenbacher, who was rumored to be a traitor. When asked, Lisa's mother confirms that Cordelia was indeed a traitor during the Revolutionary War. Cordelia was a baker who disappeared for some days. When a Red Coat soldier was later captured, he had Cordelia's famous donuts in his possession. She was then labelled a traitor. Lisa's aunt directs them to an old trunk full of Cordelia's possessions, and when Keith discovers letters to Cordelia from the British general, thanking her for the donuts, Lisa is distraught. But then they find a different series of letters by none other than George Washington, who had asked Cordelia to use her famous (turnip-flavored) donuts to distract the Red Coats and slow them down. Lisa discovers that, instead of being a traitor, her ancestor was actually a hero. Lisa then writes a story about Cordelia for the newspaper, usurping Annie's fabricated story and setting the record straight about Cordelia Heffenbacher.

Scott Loren and Jörg Metelmann suggest that melodrama has become . . .

> . . .a pervasive cultural mode, with distinct signifying practices and interpretative codes for meaning-making that assist in determining parameters for identification throughout a variety of discourses and mediated spaces [. . . such as] the sentimentalization of national politics.[16]

For Lisa, the connection to her ancestor was important for her own identity construction: "I thought she was just like me." That emotional connection to the ancestor "just like me" not only fueled her desire to prove that Cordelia was not a traitor, but also suggests the importance to her own identity. When Lisa first opens the trunk, she finds one of Cordelia's hats and puts it on. Then she finds a painting of Cordelia, who looks exactly like Lisa, and she is wearing that same hat, cementing the generational connection between them. Lisa closes her eyes and "imagines" what Cordelia would say, transitioning to a musical number where Lisa and Cordelia communicate with each other across the void of time through song. This pairing of living girl and her ancestor together in music "affects the audience and provides an emotional connection beyond language, identifications of a shared situation that exceed identifications based on identity." For melodrama's impact "exceeds the immediate and the historical,"[17] effectively merging the impenetrableness of time and space with emotion, the singular human constant.

The beauty of the visual elements of the Lisa-singing-with-Cordelia scene highlights the emphasis on femininity, family and the domestic. The music is soft and intimate; Lisa's voice is clear and soulful; and the warm, gently moving, rosy-beige paisley-inspired background reinforces the timeless moment between niece and aunt. The episode features maternal generations via mother, daughter, aunt and great-aunt, suggesting a transcendent connection beyond the physical in which you can "close your eyes" and imagine what your ancestor would say. Such an example of historical feminine narrative works to suture the individual viewer with the cultural imaginary (in this case, the Revolutionary War), in ways that emphasize a classic melodramatic approach to "woman's time, a movement which has been described as both cyclical and bound up with the monumental time of the regeneration of the species."[18] Cordelia's message to Lisa (however imagined) helps Lisa to solve the mystery and clear her ancestor's name, thus reinscribing her ancestor's identity as well as revitalizing her own.

CONCLUSION

As Seidelman and her friends observed in *Confessions of a Suburban Girl*, . . .

> We grew up with a certain set of rules: you acted a certain way, you looked a certain way. Then all of a sudden everything changed – all of the rules changed [. . .]. And life was much harder, much harder, than I ever imagined it would be.

Seidelman's work often presents itself in the interstice between tradition and the post-modern, suggesting a clever project of foregrounding and then complicating and interrogating socio-cultural gender norms and beliefs. The use of the melodramatic mode in the new *Electric Company* episodes lends itself to Seidelman's unique ability to peel back the layers of gender expectations and question their limitations, in this case within the framework of childhood.

According to E. Deidre Pribram, . . .

> Melodrama represents a pervasive narrative mode in which emotions are recognized and accepted as fundamental to its aesthetic functions. Yet melodrama's emotionality also rankles and disturbs, a discomfort that continues to the present day, too often resulting in accusations of excess or dismissive disinterest.[19]

Conversely, in programming for children, such emotional excess does not disturb or rankle; rather, it underscores the essential childhood experience. Innocence in children is reflected in their emotional honesty, which is often exaggerated and unfiltered. Such exaggerated emotions in adults are viewed quite negatively, but "through their myriad inappropriate gestures [and emotions], children's innocence is celebrated."[20] We expect children to display heightened emotion, and adults often become suspicious if a child does not display "correct" emotional abandon. Adults tend to view a child who is too emotionally controlled as adultified, having clearly lost their innocence and losing the protections that innocence provides. Seidelman's work is often framed by the tenets of melodrama, from the screwball-comedy tradition, and subtly infused with a cautious idealism rooted in her own childhood experiences. As her work on *The Electric Company* episodes reveals, Seidelman's merging of melodrama and idealism privileges both female agency and female domesticity in ways that are not limited to traditional gender roles, but more fluid and diverse gender dynamics: Keith can hatch an egg, Jessica and Harper successfully work through the loss of Manny, friendships of any gender take work and are as beautiful as "jewels," and the bonds of family transcend time and space. For Seidelman, "the melodramatic mode [. . .] offers a way to navigate the tension between our awareness of the conditions of human life and our very human desire for overcoming or countering those conditions," no matter what your age or gender.[21] As Robert Lang observes, melodramatic structures are composed of "clearly legible differences on all levels. It is a world of binary structures: men and women, masculine and feminine, the 'right' side and the 'wrong' side [. . .] brother and sister, work and love, material wealth and poverty."[22] But in her *Electric Company* episodes, Seidelman's use of the melodramatic style discombobulates those binaries; instead, such normative binaries are refracted and rearticulated in ways that celebrate the richly textured conditions of childhood, girlhood and the human condition.

NOTES

1. Christine Gledhill, "Prologue: The Reach of Melodrama," in *Melodrama Unbound: Across History, Media, and National Cultures*, edited by Christine Gledhill and Linda Williams (New York: Columbia University Press, 2018), xxii.
2. Lynne Joyrich, "All that Television Allows: TV Melodrama, Postmodernism, and Consumer Culture," in *Private Screenings*, edited by Lynn Spigel and Denise Mann (Minneapolis: University of Minnesota Press, 1992), 226–51.
3. Richard Nixon, "Radio Address on the Federal Responsibility to Education (25 October 1972)," *The American Presidency Project*, by Gerhard Peters and John T. Woolley, University of California Santa Barbara, [n. d.].
4. See Monica Hesse, "'Electric' Is Rewired For the '00s," *The Washington Post*, 23 January 2009; see also Joan Anderman, "Wordplay's the Name of the Game on New Electric Company," *The Boston Globe*, 19 January 2009; Neil Genzlinger, "Back From the '70s, without the Zaniness," *The New York Times*, 19 January 2009.
5. Derek Elley, "Confessions of a Suburban Girl," *Variety*, 3 September 1992.
6. Peter Brooks, "The Uses of Melodrama," in *Imitation of Life: A Reader on Film and Television Melodrama*, edited by Marcia Landy (Detroit: Wayne State University Press, 1991), 58.
7. Despina Kakoudaki, "Melodrama and Apocalypse: Politics and the Melodramatic Mode in Contagion," in *Melodrama Unbound*, edited by Christine Gledhill and Linda Williams (New York: Columbia University Press, 2018), 321.
8. Brooks, "The Uses of Melodrama," 61.
9. Jörg Metelmann and Scott Loren, *Melodrama after the Tears: New Perspectives on the Politics of Victimhood* (Amsterdam: Amsterdam University Press, 2015), 11.
10. Earl. F. Bargainier, "Hissing the Villain, Cheering the Hero: The Social Function of Melodrama," *Studies in Popular Culture*, 3 (1980), 50.
11. Charles Burnetts, "Sentiment and the 'Smart' Melodrama," in *Improving Passions: Sentimental Aesthetics and American Film* (Edinburgh: Edinburgh University Press, 2017), 153.
12. Gledhill, "Prologue," xxi.
13. Ibid.
14. Ibid.
15. Burnetts, "Sentiment and the 'Smart' Melodrama," 148–49.
16. Metelmann and Loren, *Melodrama after the Tears*, 9.
17. Jonathan Goldberg, *Melodrama: An Aesthetics of Impossibility* (Durham: Duke University Press, 2016), 39.
18. Rachel Thomson and Lisa Baraitser, "Thinking Through Childhood and Maternal Studies: A Feminist Encounter," in *Feminism and the Politics of Childhood: Friends or Foes?* edited by Rachel Rosen and Katherine Twamley (London: University College London, 2018), 68.
19. E. Deidre Pribram, "Melodrama and the Aesthetics of Emotion," in *Melodrama Unbound*, edited by Christine Gledhill and Linda Williams (New York: Columbia University Press, 2018), 244.
20. Joanne Faulkner, *The Importance of Being Innocent* (Cambridge: Cambridge University Press, 2011), 54.
21. Despina Kakoudaki, "Melodrama and Apocalypse: Politics and the Melodramatic Code in Contagion," in *Melodrama Unbound*, edited by Christine Gledhill and Linda Williams (New York: Columbia University Press, 2018), 315.
22. Robert Lang, *American Film Melodrama* (Princeton: Princeton University Press, 1989), 163.

CHAPTER 11

Age, Disability and Agency in the Late-Period Films of Susan Seidelman

Cole Bradley

Susan Seidelman began her career with films about outsiders. Early works such as *Smithereens* or *Desperately Seeking Susan* focused on women who found themselves rejecting traditional societal norms in favor of carving their own way through the world. Upon returning to feature filmmaking in the twenty-first century (after spending much of the 1990s working in television), Seidelman found herself once again exploring stories of people not traditionally depicted in mainstream culture, only now her concerns were less with behavior and more with bodies. Rosemarie Garland-Thomson has defined the normate as "the constructed identity of those who, by way of the bodily configurations and cultural capital they assume, can step into a position of authority and wield the power it grants them"; a position that, despite its centrality to culture, only describes "a minority of actual people."[1] Seidelman's final three films (2005's *Boynton Beach Club*, 2011's *Musical Chairs* and 2013's *The Hot Flashes*) are light comedies, frothy on the surface, yet all three focus on protagonists with nonnormate bodies navigating interactions with a society that chooses to other them and deny them agency. Looking at them in sequence reveals a clear intent to expand the types of bodies that films can cover beyond the paradoxically small yet centered normate standard.

Boynton Beach Club is, on the surface, a standard ensemble romantic comedy, concerned as it is with paring off its central group of friends and watching them go through the upsides and downsides of falling in love. What sets the film apart is its focus on a group of seniors; as Roger Ebert put it, it is "an indie teen sex comedy of the sort with which [Seidelman] began her career [. . .] only now the teens are in their 60s and 70s [and] live in Florida instead of SoHo."[2] The film centers on the titular Boynton Beach Bereavement Club, a support group for local seniors dealing with the loss of a loved one. The audience is first introduced to Marilyn (Brenda Vaccaro), who recently lost her husband in an accident and must figure out how to live the rest of her life. She befriends Lois (Dyan Cannon), the social butterfly of the group. Finally, there's Jack (Len Cariou), some months removed from the death of his wife Phyllis and being aggressively pursued by Sandy (Sally Kellerman). Although these interlocking narratives are often light-hearted and carefree, Seidelman uses them to explore the radical notion of seniors moving forward in a world that expects them to be in their final acts.

What immediately separates *Boynton Beach Club* from Seidelman's final two films is that it lacks the competition narrative around which the other films center. Yet, despite not focusing on physical movement to the same degree, it is instructive to view these love stories, knowing where Seidelman would go, in the context of non-normate bodily politics and, in a way, disability. After all, aging is, as Garland-Thomson puts it, "a gradually disabling process" that affects all who live long enough.[3] Returning to the concept of the normate's ability to navigate society with authority, we can see that despite the film's emphasis on social, rather than physical, behaviors, the implicit and explicit denial of agency depicted relies on the limits placed on non-normate bodies.

Timothy Shary and Nancy McVittie have argued that cinema often features "the perception of romance among the aged as an unorthodox and ultimately aberrant phenomenon."[4] Much of *Boynton Beach Club* focuses on the characters grappling with their internalized fears that to be romantically and sexually active at their age is an aberration, an idea directly tackled in Jack's plotline. Upon attending his first meeting, he befriends Harry (Joseph Bologna), one of the only other men in the support group. Harry relishes the attention he receives from women at the meetings and offers support and encouragement to Jack to get on with his life. At a later meeting, Jack meets Sandy, who quickly takes a liking to him, asking him to a local dance that very day. While initially apprehensive, he quickly gathers up the nerve, and they begin seeing each other.

The surface-level issues with Jack and Sandy's relationship revolve around the lingering memory of Phyllis, but this is merely a vehicle for Seidelman to get at his discomfort with being a sexual and romantic being at his advanced age. The issue of sex first comes up at one of the meetings, where a woman mentions her partner having issues getting an erection. It is treated as a joke, as group leader Elaine lets them laugh and then moves on. Yet, Seidelman lingers on Elaine's uncomfortable face, and the awkward tension that can only be diffused by the group laughing. A tossed off response from the crowd – "Get yourself a boy toy, honey!" – shows that these seniors, as a group, cannot see themselves having sex as anything other than ridiculous. Even Harry, who carries himself as a swinging single and actively goes looking for women on the Internet, freezes in the moment. Upon meeting Florence, a beautiful woman his age who shares all his interests, he is beaming, until he finds a shelf of sex toys and a willing Florence lying in bed, propositioning him. He is so thrown by the idea of a woman his age having a sexual appetite that he can only assume she is a prostitute. Raquel Medina Bañón and Barbara Zecchi note that overly sexualized elder women are traditionally depicted as "wrong, out of place, and punishable,"[5] and *Boynton Beach Club* is not free of these conventions, as both of these scenes do rely on the ostensible outlandishness of a sexually active elder woman as a sight gag. Yet, the joke is ultimately not on these two women, but on their peers who have so internalized the shame that society signifies onto their bodies that they cannot conceive of someone thinking otherwise.

This sense of shame is literalized later in the film when Harry, upon realizing that Jack and Sandy might have sex, decides that he needs to warn Jack about what he calls "the weird part." He describes getting naked with a woman for the first time and taking in her body: "Then it hits you. You're about to have sex with an old lady." For all his braggadocio, Harry finds himself inherently repulsed by women his age. Indeed, when Jack and Sandy are preparing to get intimate, he walks in on her wrapped in a sheet. She drops the sheet, exposing her naked body both to him and to the spectator. The film quickly cuts away as Jack turns in discomfort and Sandy covers herself. While this scene had centered Jack's perspective, the resulting conversation alternates between a wide shot of him and a close-up on her, grounding us in her discomfort and pain while he tries to extricate himself from the situation. Her nudity is not played as a joke, nor is it something to be horrified by, but rather an honest depiction of an elderly woman as a sexual being.

In fact, the camera lingers on Jack's nude form far more than Sandy's. Immediately preceding this scene, Jack is in the bathroom, psyching himself up for the sex he is about to have. He is wearing only boxers, and the camera pans up his body, mirroring his eyes in the mirror, taking in his doughy, wrinkled form. He is as discomforted with his own elderly body as he will soon be with hers and forces down Viagra with a weary resignation – there is none of the joyful anticipation from a man about to have sex. With both Jack's extended semi-nude scene and Sandy's brief topless shot, the film invites the viewer to consider how these bodies differ from the younger nude forms traditionally seen in romantic comedies. Furthermore, in removing any glamor from these shots, the film centers what Josephine Dolan calls the "biological changes associated with ageing [. . .] written on bodies that fall short of the Hollywood ideal" that is traditionally hidden in depictions of celebrities of their generation.[6]

Certainly, there could be something grotesque about the film suggesting that their bodies are shameful, an issue exacerbated by the brevity of Sandy's nudity. However, the film seems to be in conversation with Laura Mulvey's famous argument that women function "as erotic object for the characters within the screen story, and as erotic object for the spectator within the auditorium, with a shifting tension between the looks on either side of screen."[7] Here, the tension lies is Sandy's presentation of herself as erotic spectacle to the camera, and Jack's resulting discomfort; the spectator is not invited to share in Jack's gaze, but is rather challenged to reflect on the erotic potential of these elderly bodies. The scene resolves with them cuddling in bed, the shame and embarrassment evoked by the speed of the cut dissipating into comfort and tenderness as Jack grows content with these two bodies in tandem. Dolan has critiqued elder romantic comedies of the era in which "heterosexual activity is configured as therapeutic for men with women operating as sexualized carers" who exist to restore virility,[8] and to be sure, while the critique of Jack's self-loathing is commendable, Sandy's embarrassment and erotic fulfillment is discarded in favor of Jack's growth. Still, this is an honest portrait of elderly sexuality, especially for a romantic comedy of the time, and only recently have mainstream films such as *Good Luck to You, Leo Grande* been willing to expand on *Boynton Beach Club* and broach the subject with the frankness and sensuality that it deserves.

While the other narratives in the film do not address bodily discomfort to such a degree, when taken in juxtaposition with Jack and Sandy's struggles, they indicate a running theme. When characters are introduced, viewers see snapshots of the actors playing them from the 1960s – a constant reminder that these characters were young once, that the bodies they have onscreen are not the ones that they always had. The juxtaposition of the faces is most compelling with Marilyn, unique to the film in that she never pursues a romantic relationship. Rather, she is left adrift after the loss of her husband, having to adjust to life as a sole person rather than part of a duo (fittingly, the image of her younger self is of her and her husband together). Early on, her daughter tries to get Marilyn to move in with her, saying: "Daddy did everything for you. You don't even know how to balance a checkbook." This inspires a fire in Marilyn; rather than pursue a new relationship, she will prove to the younger generation that she can manage on her own, primarily through a quest, with Lois' guidance, to learn how to drive. At the DMV, she gets in the wrong line, prompting a clerk to wonder if she might be having memory issues. Defiantly, she asserts: "I may be sixty-five, but I'm not a friggin' idiot." Sally Chivers has written that in film "[l]ooking old means being old, which, in this discourse, means being ill. To age visibly means to admit ill health."[9] By associating Marilyn's young face with her current, older face, Seidelman conditions viewers to assume that Marilyn is frail and in need of assistance from the normate world. Yet, over the course of the film, she asserts control over her life, learning how to drive, building a new friendship with Lois and confronting the woman who killed her husband. Christina Lane has praised this subplot as one that "prioritizes female friendship even within a heterosexual romantic comedy framework,"[10] and indeed it is a refreshing contrast to the rest of the film, asserting that bodily agency is not solely reliant on sexual or romantic pleasure. Fittingly, the movie ends with one final snapshot: Marilyn and her dog in the present day, her body no longer existing in contrast to what was, but rather her elderly form presented in and of itself as a body worthy of admiration.

Much like Marilyn is left at a crossroads following her husband's death, the protagonist of Seidelman's follow-up effort, *Musical Chairs*, is similarly faced with a choice of how to proceed after a life-altering event. The focus here is Mia (Leah Pipes), a young dance instructor left paralyzed after an accident who sees a new opportunity in wheelchair ballroom dancing and must decide if dancing is still for her. Again, Seidelman engages with non-normate bodies, in this case with a narrative emphasizing the physical to a much greater degree. Yet, while *Boynton Beach Club* feels authentic and true, *Musical Chairs* is much more saccharine for several reasons, not the least of which is the interplay between Mia and her able-bodied love interest Armando (E. J. Bonilla).

Armando is the true protagonist of *Musical Chairs*. He is introduced dodging his mother's attempts to set him up with a neighborhood girl and juggling his responsibilities at his family's restaurant with his passion of dance. It is quickly made clear that he devotes so much of his time to a local dance studio because it allows him to be around Mia, as shown through a series of scenes where he watches her dance, transfixed by her beauty. The attraction is mutual. Although she is dating Daniel (Phillip Willingham), the cold owner of the studio, she similarly watches Armando dance by himself, making a crack that she was "enjoying the show." It seems as if the film is setting up a traditional love triangle between Armando, Mia and Daniel – until Mia exits the studio and is hit by a car. Although the accident is shot from a neutral angle, framing Mia's full body in the center of the frame as the car speeds in from offscreen, the film quickly cuts to a series of shots that favor not Mia's pain, but Armando's reaction to it, either shots of his horrified face, or shots looking down on the accident from his vantage point, peering out of an above window.

This edit to Armando is a small choice, but one that reveals much about the film's relationship to Mia's body. Garland-Thomson has argued that the representation of disability often "gains its rhetorical effectiveness from the powerful, often mixed responses that real disabled people elicit from readers who consider themselves normates."[11] By situating the response to the accident in a combination of Armando's reaction and gaze, the film invites the spectator to identify with the act of spectatorship itself; Mia's injury is thus not something to be directly empathized with, but something to be perceived and reflected upon. This framing is indicative of the film to follow, one in which the non-normate position is reduced to an object to be observed. Immediately after the accident the audience observes a brief scene of a despondent Mia lying in a hospital bed, the camera showing but not lingering on a surgical scar along her spine, resituating her experience as the center of the narrative. Yet, the film quickly cuts back to Armando coming to visit Mia, encouraging her to engage in hospital activities and take her therapy seriously. Seidelman further centers Armando, as on the way to Mia's room he is shown flirting with sassy receptionist Erma (Capathia Jenkins). This strange tonal shift immediately discards Mia's pain in favor of Armando's lady killer antics. Yet, as awkward as it is in the moment, it indicates the film's ultimate relationship to disability.

Writing on the broader depiction of disabled pain in cinema, Martin F. Norden notes that "filmmakers posed the unsubtle suggestion that death inevitably follows despair, that no alternative to the misery exists."[12] *Musical Chairs* is not a quite a melodrama, and the film wants to show Mia finding new avenues to continue on with her life with her new, changed body, and so it counters these conventions by not wallowing in her suffering. Yet, by having Armando be both our point-of-view character and the assertive, positive force in Mia's life, the film strips her of the very agency that the narrative grants her. Armando, insistent upon returning passion to Mia's life, goes so far as to organize a wheelchair dance class for paraplegic patients in the hospital. When Mia does not show, he goes to her room at night and, over her protests, carries her out of bed and to the hospital swimming pool, where he dances with her in the water. The film portrays this as a tender, lovely moment – Armando coaxing Mia out of her depressed state, culminating in a kiss. Norden notes that disability melodramas often position women "not as erotic objects but as bearers of symptoms" for the spectator's gaze, such that their "physical/sexual restoration, if it occurs at all, is rigorously monitored and controlled by patriarchal authorities."[13] Norden is specifically referring to male doctors, but Armando functions similarly here, making decisions for and enacting his will upon a helpless Mia for her own good, only to be rewarded when she is transformed into the romantic object of his dreams. Just as Mia's disability had been positioned as something to be observed, the film has further reduced her to a body that must be directly acted upon by her normate, masculine betters.

The film proceeds in its second half to grant Mia more narrative agency. When her parents come to visit and try to get her to move home so that they can act as her caretakers, she refuses, insisting: "I just like my apartment, my independence, my own life." In a way, she is like Marilyn – refusing to be pitied in favor of carving out her own path, despite the circumstances thrust in her way. When the time comes to leave the hospital, she asks Armando to help her back to her apartment, and upon discovering that the elevator is out of order, she is the first to turn to look at the staircase. The film then cuts to Armando, once again, carrying Mia, but her giggly demeanor and her behavior in the previous shot suggests that this is, in fact, how she is choosing to approach her disability, that his help is wanted and appreciated. Yet if disability is, as Garland-Thomson puts it, "the ways that bodies interact with the socially engineered environment and conform to social expectations,"[14] then it is telling that the film denies Mia the opportunity to directly engage with the barriers presented in front of her, instead assuming that it is her place to be assisted by Armando and, thusly, skipping directly to the result of her in his arms.

Upon reaching her apartment, Armando briefly leaves Mia alone, at which point she falls onto the floor. Viewers are transported into a fantasy sequence of Mia standing and walking around the apartment, suggesting that she has not fully accepted that her life has changed. Yet, when Armando returns, she snaps out of the daydream and rejects his help, successfully pulling herself back on the couch. It is a striking and complicated sequence, the transition into the daydream legitimately jolting and fantastical, and it culminates in the film finally exploring the capabilities of Mia's transformed body. Yet, it also ultimately underscores the film's portrayal of Mia through a normate gaze. Sharon L. Snyder and David T. Mitchell have argued that film often uses disability to invoke fear in the audience, noting that "the production of disability serves as a site of visceral sensation where abject fantasies of loss and dysfunction (maimed capacity) are made to destabilize the viewer's own investments in ability."[15] In emphasizing the capabilities that Mia had before her accident, it ultimately serves as an assertion that she has lost something. Thus, rather than position her disability as a new path moving forward, the film contextualizes everything that follows as growth in spite, not regardless, of, suffering and of a violent removal that invites the presumed normate spectator to reflect on the privileges they may have taken for granted.

The film climaxes with a wheelchair ballroom dancing competition, in which Mia and Armando are finally given the opportunity to dance together in public. In this scene, the tension between the narrative's designs for Mia and the gaze that has been inflicted on her is most striking. As the competition begins, Mia sees Daniel in the audience with a new woman. Losing confidence, she flees the dance floor, insisting that she does not want to embarrass herself. A lesser movie would have her receive a pep talk and go back out on the floor and dance. Seidelman, however, chooses not to have one character comfort her, but three: first Armando, then fellow disabled dancer Chantelle (Laverne Cox) and finally Armando's mother Isabel (Priscilla Lopez). Notably, this procession rejects Armando's paternalistic narrative influence in favor of a tender, if rebuffed, act of disabled solidarity – although the film undercuts this with Isabel's profession of Armando's love being the deciding factor. When Mia does make her decision, she bluntly tells Armando that it is time to dance, a reversal of their earlier dynamic: much like in *Boynton Beach Club*, the film has built to the feel-good moment of Mia choosing to assert an authority over her own life that normate power structures would want to deny her.

Armando and Mia's final dance should be the ultimate culmination of her journey, a triumphant assertion of her validity as a disabled body, yet the framing undermines the moves made by the script. While the other disabled dancers are filmed largely in full-body shots, allowing viewers to see how they are manipulating their wheelchairs into a dance, Mia and Armando are almost entirely framed in tight shots of them as a duo. To achieve this without Armando's head being out of frame means that Mia must be shot from the torso up, resulting in her wheelchair almost never being in the frame. Helen Polson has praised the wheelchair dance for . . .

> . . .the way it pushes its viewer to see human movement as dependent on more than just the human body [. . .] something which exists always at the intersection of our bodies and the technologies and environments we move with and through.[16]

Rather than showcase the radical potential of wheelchair dance and ask the audience to reflect on their existing notions of movement and the value of Mia's body, the film instead literally hides what is unique about her performance to emphasize the romance.

Only two shots clearly show Mia's wheelchair. One is a breath-taking bird's eye view of Mia spinning in her chair which, in a few seconds, shows the grace and unique beauty of wheelchair dance. The other shot, however, shows Mia crashing into another wheelchair and falling onto the floor. The film does not take this climactic dance as an opportunity to show the unique choreography of which Mia's new body is capable, nor does it emphasize the wheelchair's status as, in Polson's words, an instrument "which can be practiced and mastered by the dancer to beautiful and radical effect."[17] Instead, her disability is inherently clumsy and awkward, and the wheelchair is an impediment that ruins, rather than evolves, her dance. It is fitting, then, that Armando swoops in and picks her up, holding her in his arms and dancing with her sans wheelchair. Martin F. Norden has codified films of this type as "Civilian Superstar" narratives and notes that, while intended as inspirational, they ultimately center disabled people ostensibly overcoming limitations, while "any disabled person who doesn't stage a dramatic personal comeback – including a virtually mandatory attempt to pass – is a failure."[18] By isolating her wheelchair out of the frame and ultimately placing her in Armando's arms, the film isolates Mia from the primary visual signifier of her disability and thus, in a way, allows her to pass as normate in her moment of triumph. For all the work done in the back half to center Mia and make this a story about a non-normate body asserting control and authority in a world that wants to box her in, the ending takes viewers back to where we started: the able-bodied man graciously carrying the disabled woman who does not even need a wheelchair to be a stunning dancer. Paul Darke has identified a normate cultural dichotomy between the "good cripple" who "does his/her best to overcome the abnormality of his/her body" and the "'bad cripple' who is happy to be a cripple."[19] The ending of the film reveals its strained relationship with this very dichotomy: ostensibly, *Musical Chairs* is a story about a disabled woman growing to understand the value and authority that she can claim with her new body, but it visually centers the normate to the degree that it codes disability as something that can and should be overcome.

Susan Seidelman's final feature film, as of this writing, is 2013's *The Hot Flashes*. Fittingly, the film strikes a middle ground between her two previous efforts, as it is both about a group of older women trying to assert control over themselves beyond the identity that society wants for them, and a group of differently abled athletes insisting that their bodies are just as valid as the younger and more traditionally fit. Here, the focus is on Beth (Brooke Shields), a middle-aged housewife in a small Texas town who decides to raise money for a local breast cancer clinic by putting together a basketball team of women her age and challenging the local state-champion high school girls' team. On paper it seems like a slam dunk, a chance for Seidelman to integrate all the themes of her later career in an inherently feminist package. Yet, as with *Musical Chairs* the depiction of non-normate bodies falters.

The film begins with a striking close-up on Beth's face, sweating and breathing heavily, patting herself with a napkin. The title of the film literally flashes onscreen, making it evident that these are menopausal symptoms. She swallows a pill, and the camera suddenly zooms out to reveal that she is in the crowd at her daughter's basketball game, the sounds of the roaring crowd a stark contract to the ambient breathing before the zoom. In a 2018 editorial, columnist Suzanne Moore notes that menopause is largely absent in mainstream film, writing that "the actual process by which women age remains largely taboo [. . .]. The onscreen invisibility of the menopause is a form of denial."[20] Here, viewers see the film directly engaging with this denial, as it were – Beth suffering in silence, surrounded by her community who does not even notice. It is a powerful opening, immediately suggesting a narrative about a woman adjusting to her changing body, directionless as her daughter grows into an adult and needing to, once again, claim her agency rather than fade way.

Unfortunately, the movie does not explore menopause in depth beyond those opening moments. Aside from a couple of gags about middle-aged women overheating, which are mostly discarded by the second act, the only remaining element of the setup is the title – which is also the name of their basketball team, cleverly proposed by Beth once the line-up is complete. The film does integrate the concept of the non-normate in ways beyond age. Roxie (Camryn Manheim) is concerned that she cannot play at the level she did in high school because she has gained a significant amount of weight, but aside from some crass jokes in early practice scenes this never impacts her performance on the court. We also have Florine (Wanda Sykes), the town's Black mayor who fears that, if she plays basketball, her largely white constituency will view her as a stereotype, remembering a time when "the fans called me 'Jumpin Jigaboo' throughout the entire game." This is another fascinating narrative thread that the film brings up and abandons; once Florine sees the assembled team, her competitive spirit takes over. The film's disinterest in actively exploring the bodies of its stars is made most clear during one team practice where their coach Paul (Mark Povinelli), referring to the high schoolers whom they will be playing, says: "Those girls, they are younger and they are faster [. . .] so we need to use our innate abilities." Then, he asks them to name what they have that the girls do not. Erin Harrington has argued that "barren bodies are not the binary 'other' to the actively or successfully reproductive, fecund body, but instead have different capacities [. . .] that are perhaps denied to actively reproductive bodies."[21] As the movie has centered menopause as a defining trait of these women's bodies, it has an opportunity for the women to further delve into the specifics of their non-normate identities and the values of their bodies. Instead, they crack jokes about "lazy husbands" or "a welding license." It is taken as fact that the teenagers have inherent advantages due to their bodies, yet the film refuses to consider whether the adult woman might have advantages of their own.

It should be noted that Paul is a little person. This is largely ignored throughout the movie, much like the other non-normate bodies are ultimately treated as no different than any other. However, in his introductory scene, Beth says that she wants him to coach the team "because you're a little person and a felon, and lots of people are scared of you for one of those reasons." If Seidelman's previous two films dealt with individuals claiming their agency in a normate society, then this moment hints at *The Hot Flashes* extending the idea to a radical conclusion: the team weaponizing the supposed deviance of their bodies to destabilize their normate opponents and neighbors. Yet, this is tossed off in his introduction, only to not factor into the rest of the film. Paul's body, like all the highlighted bodies in the film, exists in a strange liminal space. It is not a complete non-entity, nor is it something with which the film is willing to engage. Instead, the characters' positions as non-normate are emphasized briefly and then ignored.

Perhaps the movie is not willing to engage with these bodies because ultimately it is meant to be a feel-good comedy, something to raise awareness about the importance of breast cancer screenings (in a late film cameo, Robin Roberts shows up, playing herself, giving the team and, by extension, the film, the affirmation that they are doing good in the world). Acknowledging that the women might have difficulty on the court would be too harsh for the film's tone, so instead, in the words of critic Mike D'Angelo, it "just lazily works its way through the standard underdog-sports clichés."[22] The Hot Flashes lose the first game (although not to such a degree that they feel defeated), but once they decide to play a little dirty, they dominate the younger generation to such a degree that the opposing coach tries to get the final bout cancelled rather than see his star team embarrassed. Whatever potential the film had as a portrait of women entering a third act in their lives, instead, by the final game, it becomes wish fulfillment. Near the end, Florine sings along to Donna Summers' *Hot Stuff*, making it clear that *The Hot Flashes* is, to a degree, supposed to be a gender-flipped, across-the-pond riff on *The Full Monty*. But whereas that film used bare, doughy male flesh to explore the emasculating effects of poverty, *The Hot Flashes* is content to acknowledge that they are old and have the heroic underdog narrative play out much as it would at any age.

An exception to this is the halftime performance during the final game. Beth has arranged for the wives of the school board, all former cheerleaders, to perform one last time. The audience is fittingly treated to a group of octogenarian women dancing to the Commodores' *Brick House*, a song about an extremely attractive woman. Given the comedy of *The Hot Flashes* up to this point, one would assume this juxtaposition would be played for uncomfortable laughs. The film, however, does not just portray these women with dignity, it sexualizes them, delivering close-ups of their breasts and hips as they gyrate to the song. Additionally, Seidelman gives most of them a close-up of their face, emphasizing each as an individual person, showing a variety of ways in which a woman can grow old. Sally Chivers has discussed how turn-of-the-century Jack Nicholson films would use the nudity of his older female stars for shock or humor, even though no one of that age would be that surprised by a naked elder form.[23] Seidelman, now in her sixties, appears to be directly rebuking these depictions of older female sexuality, even rebuking the troublesome elements of Jack and Sandy's sex scene from *Boynton Beach Club*. Here, there is no male protagonist to function, as Mulvey describes, as "the bearer of the look of the spectator" who is then given "a satisfying sense of omnipotence."[24] Rather, here we see her celebrating older women as inherently sexual beings, not eroticized by their value to men but by the natural ways in which their bodies have aged. It is the most powerful and legitimately progressive moment in the film, celebrating non-normate bodies in a way in which the rest of film only pretends to do.

The closest the film comes to truly reclaiming agency on the level of Seidelman's other works is the very end. Throughout the film, it is clear to the audience, if not to Beth, that her husband Laurence (Eric Roberts) has grown tired of her and is having an affair with the evangelical Kayla (Andrea Frankle). Beth discovers the two of them together and ends their marriage. "Beth, face it. You can't make it all alone," Laurence says, making sure to dig the knife in deeper: "At your age?" Yet, in the film's coda, she is single and writing a profitable blog about being single after fifty. Here, at the very end, viewers get a narrative similar to *Boynton Beach Club* and *Musical Chairs*: a woman starting over after a life-changing event, reclaiming herself as the center of her narrative. Indeed, had the movie fully explored its titular menopausal theme, it would be extra poignant: a woman, previously defined as a mother, having become infertile both literally and metaphorically (as her daughter has gone to college), accepting that the absence of fertility, as Harrington writes, "is not a negative category but another form of expression."[25] Yet, the film is ultimately disinterested in examining the dynamics of these women and their bodies in a town that has little use for them.

Timothy Shary and Nancy McVittie have observed that "we have seen roles for aging characters since the earliest twentieth century become more nuanced and diverse, if not more mature."[26] Seidelman's work, if we allow for age and disability to be grouped together, covers all three of those adjectives. *Boynton Beach Club* blends a series of teen movie narratives with a tender portrait of old age, allowing for nuance and both maturity and lack thereof. *Musical Chairs* reaches for a nuance that it never quite grasps, but in its untraditional subject matter certainly adds a diversity to the romantic melodrama. *The Hot Flashes*, finally, features a diverse array of bodies, but is not very nuanced, nor does it aspire to maturity.

What ultimately unites these three films is, of course, the types of bodies centered in the narrative. If disability is, as Garland-Thomson defines it, "a product of cultural rules about what bodies should be or do,"[27] then a clear pattern in these films emerges of people attempting to negotiate the limits of these cultural rules. Whatever their success or failures on this front, all three films explore the ways in which a normate society ignores and minimizes the experiences of the othered body, and the way in which the marginalized can reclaim authority and dignity, whether through explicit domination in a contest, or through smaller, personal victories. Most strikingly, the generic demands of all three films, two romantic comedies and a sports film, make all three feel refreshingly casual – familiar stories, but with central figures whom Hollywood traditionally ignores. Christina Lane has argued that these three films, reliant as they were on independent and crowd-sourced and grassroots distribution and marketing, are examples of how female filmmakers can "take advantage of the cracks that have inevitably opened up within a marketplace system that has been at least temporarily upset by digital and emergent technologies."[28] While Seidelman is certainly making space for female filmmakers of her generation and younger, she is additionally using her capital as a filmmaker to expand notions of what bodies viewers see onscreen. Even her earlier films from the twenty-first century flirt with similar ideas: *Gaudi Afternoon* features multiple differing types of gender non-conformity, and both *Power and Beauty* and *The Ranch* are built on the notion that women are inherently othered and lead towards transactional relationships with the men in their lives. It is outside the scope of this essay, but knowing the context of where her career would go, these earlier films' structure dynamics of how the non-normate position factors in gender and sexuality. However, even these movies often feature young, attractive performers, as in much Hollywood product of the time. Her three final films all radically expand assumptions about whose stories are told, whether aging actors getting to once again be the stars they were in their youth, or disabled dancers getting a bigger platform than ever to show off their talents. We can only hope that *The Hot Flashes* does not end up being Seidelman's final film; regardless of their stumbles, her late-period films, in the bodies they depict, broaden the narrative and representational possibilities of independent cinema.

NOTES

1. Rosemarie Garland-Thomson, *Extraordinary Bodies: Figuring Physical Disability in American Culture and Literature* (New York: Columbia University Press, 2017), 8.
2. Roger Ebert, "Aches on a Pain," *RogerEbert.com*, 17 August 2006.
3. Garland-Thomson, *Extraordinary Bodies*, 13–14.
4. Timothy Shary and Nancy McVittie, *Fade to Gray: Aging in American Cinema* (Austin: University of Texas Press, 2016), 139.
5. Raquel Medina Bañón and Barbara Zecchi, "Technologies of Age: The Intersection of Feminist Film Theory and Aging Studies," *Investigaciones Feministas (Feminist Research)* 112 (2020), 256.
6. Josephine Dolan, *Contemporary Cinema and "Old Age": Gender and the Silvering of Stardom* (London: Palgrave Macmillan UK, 2018), 81.
7. Laura Mulvey, "Visual Pleasure and Narrative Cinema," *Screen*, 16, no. 3 (Autumn 1975), 11–12.
8. Dolan, *Contemporary Cinema and "Old Age,"* 208.
9. Sally Chivers, *The Silvering Screen* (Toronto: University of Toronto Press, 2011), 26.
10. Christina Lane, "Susan Seidelman's Contemporary Films: The Feminist Art of Self-Reinvention in a Changing Technological Landscape," in *Indie Reframed: Women's Filmmaking and Contemporary American Independent Cinema*, edited by Linda Badley, Claire Perkins and Michelle Schreiber (Edinburgh: Edinburgh University Press, 2016), 84.
11. Garland-Thomson, *Extraordinary Bodies*, 11.
12. Martin F. Norden, *The Cinema of Isolation: A History of Physical Disabilities in the Movies* (New Brunswick: Rutgers University Press, 1994), 28.
13. Norden, *The Cinema of Isolation*, 321.
14. Garland-Thomson, *Extraordinary Bodies*, 7.
15. Sharon L. Snyder and David T. Mitchell, "Body Genres: An Anatomy of Disability in Film," in *The Problem Body: Projecting Disability on Film*, edited by Sally Chivers and Nicole Markotić (Columbus: Ohio State University Press, 2010), 177.
16. Helen Polson, "'The Dance is in Your Body and Not in Your Crutches': Technique, Technology, and Agency in Disability Movement Performance" (PhD diss., New York University, 2013), 313.
17. Polson, "The Dance is in Your Body," 278.
18. Norden, *The Cinema of Isolation*, 221.
19. Paul Darke, "No Life Anyway: Pathologizing Disability on Film," in *The Problem Body: Projecting Disability on Film*, edited by Sally Chivers and Nicole Markotić (Columbus: Ohio State University Press, 2010), 103.
20. Suzanne Moore, "Let's See Menopausal Women on Screen – In All Their Glory," *The Guardian*, 15 March 2018.

21. Erin Harrington, *Women, Monstrosity and Horror Film: Gynaehorror* (London: Taylor & Francis Group, 2017), 226.
22. Mike D'Angelo, "The Hot Flashes," *The AV Club*, 11 July 2013.
23. Chivers, *The Silvering Screen*, 140.
24. Mulvey, "Visual Pleasure and Narrative Cinema," 12.
25. Harrington, *Women, Monstrosity and Horror Film*, 225.
26. Shary and McVittie, *Fade to Gray*, 214.
27. Garland-Thomson, *Extraordinary Bodies*, 6.
28. Lane, "Susan Seidelman's Contemporary Films," 83.

CHAPTER 12

And You Can Dance! Movement, Mobility and Magic in *Musical Chairs*

Warren Holmes

If *Desperately Seeking Susan* (1985) remains Susan Seidelman's most familiar work, *Musical Chairs* (2011) occupies a diametrically opposed position in her filmography. Compared to the vehicle crucial to Madonna's ascent to superstardom, *Musical Chairs* has received scant attention. A forty-six-percent rating on Metacritic is emblematic of the indifference to the film and its failure to find a wide audience. Although the New York setting is just one of the similarities between *Desperately Seeking Susan* and *Musical Chairs*, the focus of this chapter will be the latter film. The continued fondness for Seidelman's films such as *Desperately Seeking Susan*, *She-Devil* (1989) and others have, arguably, resulted in her later work being overlooked. If part of this disparity can be attributed to the seismic changes in the filmic landscape since Seidelman's most productive studio-based period, she has, nonetheless, continued to helm uniquely singular and innovative projects. According to Seidelman, "[i]t's all about timing,"[1] in consideration of the possibility that some of her films have been under-appreciated. Recognizing *Musical Chairs* as an overlooked but noteworthy later Seidelman film, then, this chapter endeavors to counter the imbalance and to respond to the rather belittling charge that the film is, according to Roger Ebert, merely "an escapist fantasy [that] uses a group of identikit stereotypes in a formula story."[2]

Musical Chairs is the story of celebrated dancer Mia (Leah Pipes) whose prospects are seemingly curtailed when she is involved in a car accident that leaves her a quadriplegic. As a fulltime wheelchair user, Leah must now adapt to her drastic change in circumstances, reassessing possibilities, including her relationship with movement and dance. Romantic admirer Armando (E. J. Bonilla) is a constant source of encouragement, and, together with a troupe of trained patients from the rehabilitation facility, the couple enter the New York Wheelchair Dancing Ballroom Championships.

Musical Chairs is presented here as both a significant film in terms of the comparatively radical handling of subject themes and its progressive nature. Seidelman acknowledges that the distribution and marketing of the film contributed to its disappointing box office performance. "It died a quick death in the mainstream cinemas,"[3] she says. "The Times Square crowd are not going to see it."[4] For a project modelled in tone on *My Big Fat Greek Wedding* and, at one stage, imagined as an offering presented by the Lifetime Network, Seidelman's directorial sensibilities render the film accessible as a romance, despite deeper themes, while also twisting genre. "All the stuff with magic, that was Susan," says screenwriter Marty Madden, who remembers that the director "wanted some rewrites" to help develop certain aspects of the script.[5] Composer Mario Grigorov also recalls Seidelman being "brilliant at" sharing her vision of the film's soundtrack, stating that working on *Musical Chairs* "was one of my happiest experiences."[6] Such sentiments from her collaborators identify Seidelman's involvement as key to elevating the material.

If, for example, the numerous pleasures offered by *Musical Chairs* are, in part, derived from the jettisoning of negative stereotypes, these are indisputably accented by what Seidelman terms "a voice"[7] unique to her being imprinted upon the text. Examining *Musical Chairs* in the context of her long association with New York, this chapter contends that Seidelman's assured, exuberant, often funky sensibility provides a conduit for a committed filmic treatise on the social model of disability. Moreover, the synergy of themes juxtaposed in the film aligns *Musical Chairs* simultaneously as accessible and as alert to wider discourses as her esteemed earlier work. Like Seidelman's description of *Desperately Seeking Susan* as "a feminist tract disguised as a screwball comedy,"[8] *Musical Chairs* can be considered a stylistically mainstream romantic text exploring issues usually ignored by mainstream cinema.

In recognition of the frequency with which specific concepts and terminology will be used here, it is necessary to provide clarification. When the notion of "impairment" is discussed, it refers to an immutable physical characteristic used to refer to a semiotically signaled difference between characters in the narrative. Following the car accident, for example, Leah becomes a quadriplegic on account of her limbs no longer functioning as they once did. Conversely, "disability" is understood as a socially constructed phenomenon encompassing a plethora of external structures that impact people in routinely limiting ways.

Correspondingly, then, the social model of disability identifies the origins of the oppression experienced by disabled people as located within the broader societal context. According to Michael Oliver, individuals can have or develop impairments but are disabled by barriers including "inaccessible education systems, working environments [. . .] through negative images in the media – films, television, and newspapers."[9]

Within *Musical Chairs*, the emphasis on society's complicity in the oppression of disabled people is clearly reflected in the character of Mia and others. While a collision physically impairs her, she is ultimately forced to renegotiate her identity, encountering challenges borne out of both material reality and the attitudes of those around her. As Armando's mother exclaims: "A girl in a wheelchair! How can he have children with a girl like that?"

Musical Chairs was a passion project for philanthropist Janet Carrus, who "was able to pull together the financing"[10] with the intention of creating a narrative about "everything a person is, no matter how severely disabled you are."[11] Reviewing current trends, Maria San Filippo suggests that contemporary romantic comedies are particularly "likely to have their initial release online."[12] Despite a limited cinema presence and some exposure through the festival circuit, *Musical Chairs* can, therefore, be considered a precursor of sorts to the emerging pattern of films having what has been termed "a post theatrical release."[13] In other words, a film is unveiled on a streaming platform and, thus, bypasses the traditional means of exhibition.

The challenges associated with production and distribution were likely further compounded by the prospect of wheelchair dancing, whether choreographed or not, emerging as an apparent paradox within the public imagination. As the film's choreographer Aubree Marchione remarks, "[i]f you've never seen it before or experienced it, it's hard to imagine somebody in a wheelchair dancing."[14] Based on the output of the ableist mainstream American film system, it is credible to assume that audiences have not seen wheelchair dancing or had the opportunity to confront what Marchione calls "the biggest misconception"[15] of the practice. Said misconception typically translates into equating impairment with the automatic exclusion of individuals from activities requiring a degree of physical effort. In essence, using a wheelchair and full engagement in society are incompatible. The prevalence of this dissonance is acknowledged by wheelchair ballet dancer Joe Powell-Main. As Powell-Main comments, "I've had people make snap decisions and be like: 'You're in a wheelchair. . . so how are you going to be able to dance?'"[16]

Seidelman herself admits that the project immediately piqued her curiosity, but she "had never heard of wheelchair ballroom dancing."[17] Seidelman was, however, able to locate more familiar terrain, seeing the film as "about the meeting of these two very different worlds."[18] She says, "You have this Latino man [. . .] who lives in the Bronx [. . .] and this Waspy young woman who is a dance instructor, both love to dance."[19]

Charged with the incumbent task of having to essentially explain wheelchair dancing in a manner that eschews didactic posturing was also likely to restrict the commercial appeal of the project. A cursory summary of the film is sufficient to acknowledge that *Musical Chairs* represents a pointed departure from the established and narratively linear triumph-over-tragedy trope that is often synonymous with depictions of disability. On a thematic level, the film is engaged in the active disruption of the established paradigm, being inflected with notions of explicit empowerment and transformation.

Reflecting on the development of the film, screenwriter Madden remembers: "I think a lot of producers were scared away."[20] Assuming that there is substance to Madden's assertion, producers' ambivalence is perhaps understandable. There is a clear sense of disability pride informing the film; a force that is amplified through its visual style and other equally powerful elements including costume and music. Emerging from the fusion, then, *Musical Chairs* is an anomaly amongst other disability related narratives. If this marked difference derives from the film being an independent feature, it is consolidated by a sustained subversion of certain generic components and Seidelman's direction.

In a mixed review, critic Roger Ebert comments on the film's compressed timescale: "It's unlikely that anybody paralyzed from the waist down is going to be ballroom dancing in a few weeks. The physical and mental trauma would make it impossible."[21] Although in agreement with Ebert, this chapter reframes his perceived weakness of the narrative as a strength. Nobody would indeed be dancing, in whatever form, so soon after an accident as the time in which Leah returns to the floor. Nonetheless, Seidelman and Madden are, seemingly, fully aware of this, wanting to move beyond a straightforward narrative of adaptation to an acceptance of disability. Rather than charting the process of recovery and witnessing a character become acquainted with their impairment, *Musical Chairs* invites participation in a fittingly more accessible journey that remains aligned to Carrus' original vision for the film. In the absence of a familiar tonal earnestness that colors many disability narratives, we are treated to vivacity and optimism. The comparative brevity of the text also functions to mitigate against the potential pitfalls that Seidelman was anxious to avoid. "I didn't want to be saccharine, sentimental or condescending," she asserts.[22]

A consideration of the use of music in *Musical Chairs* illustrates how accomplished she was in achieving her objectives. The soundtrack is certainly aurally vibrant, immediately providing a point of entry into the film, but it is also more muted at times to proportionally anchor the emotional beats of the text. In a significant narrative moment dubbed by both composer Grigorov and Seidelman as "the swimming pool scene,"[23] for example, the music is restrained to not over-announce the evident significance of Leah discovering that she can dance in the water and of the lovers' first kiss. A similar approach is taken with the last scene where we see the couple dancing in the final heat of the championships. As if to reinforce the narrative's rejection of anticipated generic conventions, the music does not trumpet the outcome. While visual codes signal success, the true accomplishment is the union of Mia and Armando, literally center stage in full view, rather than being named winners. The accompanying score has a delicacy that is, in Grigorov's words, "not too on the nose."

The avoidance of an obvious, more familiar narrative structure also subverts the often deficit-hued, pitying stance of more mainstream fictions of disability that display ambivalence towards characters with impairments. What, for instance, is the function of a text such as *I Am Sam* (dir. Jessie Nelson, 2001) in which the learning disabilities of the title character are reduced to a child-like camp, Oscar-nominated persona? What cultural tensions are being explored, and ultimately perpetuated by *Adam* (dir. Max Mayer, 2009), as we follow the lead character return to singlehood when the impact of his autism spectrum disorder prevents lasting romantic intimacy?

By contrast, in *Musical Chairs*, Mia does not initially recognize the power that she eventually claims, but the film posits that a major physical loss does not equate to the disappearance of possibilities. The adoring gaze, for example, with which Armando looks at Mia in the opening section of the narrative's first act is not replaced with sympathy following the change in circumstances, nor is passion lost as the reality created by such changes becomes more apparent to both partners. In a pivotal scene prior to Leah's accident, *Musical Chairs* most closely mirrors myriad dance-themed narratives to which a generic debt is owed. Impressed by his moves, Leah praises Armando, and the pair fall into a dance sequence backed by Cuban sounds and rhythmic editing flourishes. Poignantly, this is the first and only occasion the couple are both standing dancers. The energy generated between them dissipates with the sudden arrival of Mia's oblivious boyfriend who, shortly thereafter, makes a swift departure once she becomes disabled. Realizing that Mia has left a scarf in the dance studio, Armando's calls to alert her, and her attempts to retrieve the garment frame a sequence that culminates in Mia's impairment. The moment is, indisputably, affecting, with the image of the scarf carried away in the breeze evoking a palpable, almost melodramatic pathos. At a point where the narrative could, however, descend into typically somber territory on account of what has happened, a comparatively upbeat mood is maintained. We see, for example, few ensuing scenes to substantiate Leah's claim that, since the accident, "My days suck!" We are spared a montage mapping her progress in therapy.

Musical Chairs can be received as a film advocating for greater understanding of disability. Yet, the film surpasses this objective precisely because of its commitment to explore a panoply of issues that is not enacted at the expense of a narrative restricted by a single note of focus. Just as Seidelman's *Boynton Beach Club* (2006) is not exclusively about aging and *The Hot Flashes* (2013) is not solely concerned with menopause, *Musical Chairs* is equally polysemic and cannot be reduced to being a text singularly about impairment. Several characters obviously have physical limitations, but they also have their own backstories; thus, the suggestion that disability is a uniform experience for all is not accommodated.

Based on this premise, then, *Musical Chairs* cannot be easily reconciled with the historic largely myopic representations of disability in film. Such myopia is, inevitably, the product of interlocking systems of oppression. Katharine Quarmby argues that, while society does not "hate disabled people," there is an "underlying feeling that disabled people have not earned the equality they enjoy in name."[24] Discussing the number of disability-related hate crimes in the United Kingdom alone, Quarmby suggests that many incidents are motivated by the belief that disabled people "should still be shut away."[25] Mainstream film may not be exactly "infuriated by disabled people demanding they too should have the freedoms non-disabled people take for granted,"[26] yet solidarity-signaling gestures have not been forthcoming. Couple this reticence with a desire to achieve authenticity by including as many disabled performers as possible, the commercial viability of *Musical Chairs* would have, inevitably, been lessened further. According to Seidelman, the filmmakers did "go out of our way to find disabled performers."[27] While both lead actors E. J. Bonilla and Leah Pipes are not disabled, there is a significant number of supporting artists with physical impairments. Choreographer Aubree Marchione remembers that there was the division "about fifty/fifty"[28] when it came to the ballroom dancers. "I told everyone I knew about the audition and said to them 'You better show up'," she laughs.[29]

For a film about wheelchair ballroom dancing, Marchione was well-placed to call on potential participants. As the artistic director of *The American Dance Wheels Foundation*, Marchione has extensive experience preparing and performing in pieces that routinely pair standing and wheelchair dancers. Marchione considers *Musical Chairs* to have broken barriers but concedes that there is "still a long way to go" before wheelchair ballroom dancing is viewed as comparable to other forms of movement.[30] Marchione says that interest from programs such as *Dancing with the Stars* has not yet materialized into a combination of dancers being invited to perform. The considerable distance, therefore, still to be travelled cannot be traversed by a single film. Nonetheless, *Musical Chairs'* celebration of the collaboration between disabled and non-disabled people is a lesson from which the industry could take heed. For filmmakers wanting to create narratives that navigate the subject of disability, there should at least be an authoritative dialogue between both parties, with an emphasis on achieving a synchronicity that is, at least hopefully, more satisfying than some previous representations.

Despite this, the prospect of the system suddenly becoming receptive to disability remains unlikely. It can also be argued that another obstacle in presenting disability on screen is the almost immediate dismissal of texts that attempt to challenge the status quo. In a negative review of *Musical Chairs*, for instance, Nathan Rabin argues that the film "wants to speak eloquently and powerfully for the disabled."[31] Instead, Rabin accuses the text of "speaking down to them in the vernacular of bad television comedies, cheeseball underdog dance movies and abysmal soap operas."[32] Rabin's derision of the film is echoed by hostile online reactions. "The fact they decided to call a movie about disabled people dancing *Musical Chairs* says everything I need to know,"[33] writes one commentator. "Cannot wait for the sequel," jokes another, "Paraplegic Boogaloo."[34]

The continued absence of disability-related themes in major texts is, at once, both surprising and predictable. The mixed results of Hollywood's long delayed efforts to begin to tackle representational issues pertaining to gender and race have provided few equivalent opportunities for the stories of other minority groups to be told. When, for example, a film like *The Help* is described as "a missed opportunity" by its lead actor, Viola Davis,[35] and when the streaming generation recognizes the extent to which the handling of identity politics in sitcoms produced in the previous decades are now problematic, the topic of disability is unlikely to feature high on the agenda for redress. At the time of writing, for instance, the feature directorial debut of singer Sia, *Music* (2021), centering on a young protagonist with autism, has been met with near universal derision for its representation of the condition. Riz Ahmed's Oscar nomination for lead actor in *Sound of Metal* (2019) sees a non-disabled performer being venerated for playing a character who acquires a disability through hearing loss. If the Barack and Michelle Obama-produced *Crip Camp* (2020) had won the Best Documentary Feature, co-director James Lebrecht would have made history and been the first wheelchair user on stage collecting an Oscar statue. On one hand, the best picture win for *CODA* (2021) and the best supporting actor prize for deaf performer Troy Kotsur could be interpreted as evidence that Hollywood is at least beginning to reconceptualize potential ways in which disabilities can be presented on screen. Yet, when compared with *Musical Chairs*, *CODA* can be viewed as a significantly more palatable film – not least because the main protagonist Ruby (Emilia Jones) is a hearing teenager in a household of deaf adults. As the chief point of identification for the audience, we are encouraged to share Ruby's perception of the hearing impairments of her parents and brother that have always been part of her life. If *CODA* effectively strives to normalize disability, this is achieved by drawing on notions of sameness beyond hearing loss. Ruby is indeed a child of deaf adults, but she is ultimately a young female coming of age in unusual circumstances. By virtue of its characters, tone and direction, *Musical Chairs* is, arguably, more political in its insistence on spotlighting disability, as opposed to endeavoring to mitigate its existence. The film thus strikes a provocative, unapologetic pose that serves to emphasize its transgressive nature.

WHAT HAVE WE SEEN? REPRESENTATIONS OF DISABILITY ON SCREEN

Prefacing an extensive overview of disability in film and literature, for instance, Nicole Markotić claims that "depictions of disability are conveyed by way of narratives of heartbreak, misfortune or tragedy."[36] Consider, for example, the preferred readings championed in texts including *The Theory of Everything* and *Me Before You*. Both films utilize the established triumph-over-tragedy trope and function partly as "message movies" intended for an assumed prejudiced audience. If the prestige afforded to *The Theory of Everything* was partly assured because of being a biopic of scientist Stephen Hawking, *Me Before You* registers as an equally well-acted extended plea for its suddenly disabled male protagonist Will Traynor (Sam Claflin) to exercise the right to end his life through assisted suicide. In the penultimate scene that takes place in a Swiss clinic, the message – reappropriated by activists in protest upon the film's release – is clear: "Better Dead Than Disabled!"[37]

Limited depictions of disability are also matched with a concurrent commentary about often non-disabled performers playing the roles and how much was personally invested in preparation for the part. Daniel Day Lewis appears to have set a symbolic precedent for the process when he reportedly spent weeks living in a wheelchair to find the character of Irish artist Christy Brown in *My Left Foot*. Subsequent acknowledgement of this practice has seen actors being praised for the perceived dedication to their craft and the performance configured as likely to be added to the roster for the awards season.

The cast of *Musical Chairs* did engage in similarly immersive preparation, which included the non-disabled actors being required to travel around New York City using a wheelchair. In pursuit of the authenticity sought by Seidelman, Auti Angel provided invaluable guidance. An acclaimed performer whose own personal experience of impairment resulted in becoming a full-time wheelchair user, like the character Nicky whom she plays, "Auti was very helpful in terms of authenticity."[38] Angel recalls that she was able to assist the actors in achieving an appropriate physicality for their performance. The significance of the collaboration described above can thus be considered indicative of the innovative spirit that powers the film.

Aside from one scene where Mia returns to her home following the accident, little screen time is given to opportunities to illicit sympathy. Instead, Mia is almost immediately in the company of the heroines of Seidelman's other films. Striving for self-realization in unforeseen and often unpredictable circumstances, Mia resembles Roberta from *Desperately Seeking Susan*, Ruth of *She-Devil* and the eponymous *Cookie*. Like those protagonists, Mia's situation is necessary as a catalyst for her own agency which moves at a dramatically accelerated pace. Even more refreshing is the non-endowment of Mia with an exceptional skillset offered as a form of exchange for giving primacy to her vantage point as a disabled person. There is, for instance, no mathematical genius, as shown in *A Beautiful Mind*, to soften the disability so crucial to the narrative. As Tom Shakespeare points out, the character of the "Super-Crip" is not uncommon in respect of representations of disability.[39] In this incarnation, the disabled character has a special talent that neutralizes the significance of their impairment. Whether it be *Rain Man* or *Forrest Gump*, amongst others, characters have triumphed over the perceived stigma of having a disability.

In the aftermath of reinvigorated debates concerning representational diversity, *Musical Chairs*, released almost a decade earlier, has, for example, disabled actors in roles with a commitment to capturing a sense of authenticity in respect to how life can be for individuals living with impairments. Such factors are crucial in positioning Seidelman as a filmmaker of commendable range and a director who is often ahead of her time.

SEIDELMAN AND THE CITY: SUSAN IN NEW YORK

Surveying romantic comedy's love affair with New York, Deborah Jermyn argues that the city provides immeasurable opportunities to filmmakers.[40] Consideration of films directed by Woody Allen, Nora Ephron and Mike Nichols does indeed highlight the prevalence of holding the location as synonymous with romance. In an extensive discussion, Jermyn considers the potential mismatch between the "reel" New York and the "real" city. If the "reel" New York on film is often signaled by references to established landmarks, the "real" New York as a place of lived experience functions in direct contrast to the filmic projections. In Seidelman's New York, the romantic possibilities offered by the city are certainly exploited, but typically, these remain in the tangible realities of the setting. Whether these realities are the impact of economic disparities, the marginalization of groups or other issues, they can always be detected. Seidelman's films can, therefore, be seen to inhabit the space in which the "reel" and the "real" New York converge: "I like grittiness. But I also like magic and hyperreality."[41]

Introducing her examination of American culture and ethnic female stardom, Diane Negra writes how the US "prides itself on the coherence and orderliness of its internal differences."[42] According to Negra, this emergent portrait has various individuals and different ethnic groups coexisting across texts in the oft-imagined melting pot. In accordance with this metaphor, then, characters as diverse as Madonna's titular Susan, Meg Ryan's Sally Albright and Diane Keaton's Annie Hall can all live together in New York in the spirit of camaraderie. While film has contributed to the articulation of notions of American pluralism, the constancy that sustains such a schema has, arguably, become increasingly difficult to maintain. If the events of 9/11 fractured the romanticism of New York, the impact of Trump's presidency and, more recently, the COVID-19 pandemic have also lessened the comfort level offered by familiar imagery. *Musical Chairs* can be viewed as an example of a romance narrative that takes place in the aftermath of the events of September 2001. Although there is no explicit mention of the attacks, the film mines several issues magnified by the tragedy. We learn, for instance, about the immigrant history of Armando's family, their impoverished arrival in the city and the precarious position of their restaurant during increasing hardship. We witness the family trying to maintain a clear Puerto Rican identity within the diversity of New York. In addition to clear differences in social class, we observe different levels of cultural capital available to the eclectic characters who are united by residing in the ever-evolving location. If it appears crude to suggest that the foregrounding of these elements is in direct response to 9/11, it is, however, possible to identify a partially restorative subtext to the narrative, with New York promoted as an accepting and inclusive space. By virtue of the setting, the uniqueness of wheelchair dancing is normalized, allowing for a focus on character and relationships, rather than a heavy-handed study of the activity in isolation. While audiences may not have seen wheelchair dancing, New York becomes the place where this could – and does – happen in the name of inclusivity. Moreover, the recurring motif of wheelchair dancing can be regarded as an allegory for all people endeavoring to find the steps of movement most suitable for them. The clear visual distinctions between wheelchair and standing dancers evoked in the first act of the narrative are unimportant at its close, reaffirming the city as replete with unifying potential.

Against such a backdrop, then, it can be argued that Seidelman's films, particularly *Musical Chairs*, continue to resonate precisely because the texts have never fully invested in New York's presented mythology and have actively sought to create their own. While her films display a profound affection for New York, they also simultaneously rupture and reimagine the reverence in which the city is steeped. As a result, Seidelman's work can be seen to acknowledge the influence of more canonically classic filmmakers before she imparts a revisionist quality, sharpened by what she terms "New York juice."[43] Seidelman draws on her background in fashion and music to help build a vision of New York that is forever vibrant. "Part of what I love about New York" is the diversity, Seidelman says: "You're not in a rich, all-white enclave."[44] Seidelman continues: "No matter your financial situation, your cultural background, your physical diversity, your gender diversity, everyone is kind of forced to interact with each other because the island is so small."[45]

In *Musical Chairs*, for instance, the collision of the diversity loved by Seidelman is utilized to optimum and tender effect. The invasion of an army of drag artists into the rehabilitation facility poised to ready service users for the wheelchair ballroom championships is an amusing testament to Seidelman's claim that New Yorkers "just adapt"[46] to presenting situations.

Moreover, "that edge" that Seidelman is keen "never to lose"[47] is cultivated through both the film's narrative theme and a romantic subplot pairing lonely, older man Wilfredo (Nelson Landrieu) with a transgender woman. "Let's just say, I'm your perfect woman with a little something extra," Chantelle (Laverne

Cox) remarks, fighting back tears as Wilfredo declares his love. As unlikely as their union may appear, Seidelman's assured orchestration of the couple's union in her vision of New York renders it plausible. Seidelman herself concedes that, if *Musical Chairs* had been relocated and passed through more traditional avenues of production, "there may not have been space for characters like Laverne Cox's."[48]

Musical Chairs' evocation of New York as an accepting, inclusive space is, however, managed by a parallel, more urgent, saltier pulse that provides the grittiness. In the opening scene, for instance, we meet Isabel (Priscilla Lopez), Armando's mother, walking intently towards a Brooklyn-based psychic in search of divine guidance for her son's romantic life. While the soundtrack conveys a brash determination, the cluttered mise-en-scène and surrounding activity encodes the location as a space marked by relative socio-economic disadvantage. We would be unlikely to find *Sex and the City*'s Carrie Bradshaw here, or indeed Leah, the film's female protagonist, whose white genteel femininity serves to signal multiple points of difference from Armando and his family. Where Mia is employed as an instructor at a dance school, Armando works as a janitor, occasionally "teaching old ladies to dance tango." Where Mia is affluent, Armando's extended relatives are of limited means, all involved in the family restaurant business from immigrant lineage.

"Some unfortunate Bloomingdales incident?" quips Chantelle, when attempting to ascertain the cause of Mia's injury. Although Mia's response is more prosaic ("A car accident, actually"), the inquiry reinforces her white, class-based otherness within the confines of the rehabilitation facility. If Mia is not yet aware of the tacit differences between herself and other patients, the film is more cognizant. Alongside "black transexual cripple" Chantelle, injured soldier Kenny (Morgan Spector) and street-smart Nicky (Auti Angel), Mia retains considerable privilege.

The changes that Mia is forced to make following her accident are at least configured as manageable by virtue of her ethnicity and economic status. Furthermore, Mia's rejection of her father's offer for her to live with her family demonstrates a degree of choice in the decisions she makes. Mia is closer to the character of Philip (Bryan Cranston) in *The Upside* (dir. Neil Burger, 2017). A remake of the 2011 French text *Intouchables* (dir. Olivier Nakache and Eric Toledano), here we meet a quadriplegic millionaire who is in search of a caregiver to attend to his needs and help him realize life ambitions that are largely possible because of his immense wealth. If Mia is not able to purchase a range of luxury cars or participate in assisted power sports, she is an affluent woman with a career, an apartment and supportive family. The implication, therefore, is that she has more resources to potentially "pass" as non-disabled or not be defined by her impairment in ways not available to her fellow wheelchair dancers. "How would you like to have a wheelchair stuck to your ass?" retorts

Nicky when she meets a group of inquisitive children on a New York sidewalk. "You better not mess with me. Or I will become your nightmare, bitch," vows Chantelle, after derogatory comments are made about her gender identity. The preemptive defenses employed by both characters emphasize their differences from Mia, for whom these may not be so readily necessary. The characters may share commonalities on account of their impairments and eventual passion for dancing, but their subsequent navigation of life in New York is likely to follow different trajectories. Through grit and magic, material reality and romantic fantasy, *Musical Chairs* optimistically shows how disabled people's stories could be depicted on screen – either with or without ballroom dancing.

"YOU ARE A DANCER!" VISUALIZING DISABILITY IN *MUSICAL CHAIRS*

Having already proposed that *Musical Chairs* is a progressive text in its treatment of disability-related themes, it is now vital to discuss some ways in which this is demonstrated. As obvious as it may appear, the sustained presentation of a group of disabled adults on film can be considered radical. Neither reduced nor framed as dependent upon others, Mia and her friends are always afforded dignity. Unlike some narratives covering physical disabilities that focus on changes to the body, *Musical Chairs* opts for a less invasive visual style. While standard filmic techniques such as close-ups are used, Seidelman routinely uses long shots to fully present the characters in their wheelchairs. Rather than the mobility aid of a wheelchair being presented as a symbol of reduction in status, the film challenges this notion by highlighting the liberating possibilities that can be accessed through a vehicle. "The dancing queen has arrived," declares Chantelle upon entering the first organized dance session, with the ease of the camera mirroring the mood: "Beyonce, eat your heart out." Chantelle later pouts prior to the championships, acting as an amanuensis for the contestants.

If wheelchair usage, then, is explicitly aligned with a newfound independence, the film's most progressive content is displayed pointedly during the major wheelchair dancing competition. While the sedate nature of the dancing sequences is typically commented on in reviews, such comments miss the point, considering *Musical Chairs* on the same terms as other similarly themed narratives, typically featuring a full cast of standing dancers. Filming *Musical Chairs'* wheelchair dance sequences, for example, in the style of *Flashdance* or *Dirty Dancing* would have been both a betrayal of its principal theme and conventionally ableist. As wheelchair ballroom dancing is different from standing dancing, a visual acknowledgement of that difference is crucial. Nonetheless, wheelchair ballroom dancing is imbued with an equal value, where time is given to highlight its uniqueness. "Wheelchair ballroom dancing," Seidelman says, "is actually very beautiful to watch."[49] To maximize that beauty, Seidelman uses assured long shots to capture the grace of wheelchair dancing. Here, Seidelman is reworking conventions in a manner that is fully congruent with the narrative, displaying the movement and requiring scrutiny from non-disabled viewers. Both the placing of wheelchair ballroom dancing in the film and the nature of the movement itself function to command attention. The slower nature of wheelchair ballroom dancing invites a close examination of the practice on screen. In this way, the audience is expected to watch this under-presented style of movement. Furthermore, the sequences eclipse all other narrative components for a time and reaffirm the raison d'etre of the film. Bolstered by the generic signifiers of a film dance sequence, *Musical Chairs* boldly shows what dancing can look like in all its diverse glory through a reverent gaze. The high esteem in which the wheelchair ballroom dancing is held by the narrative is conveyed through the anticipation generated by the rehearsal process. Although the initial formation of the dancing troupe is played for comedy, we see little dancing outside the context of the formal championships. In filmic terms, then, the reveal of the narrative itself is the moment when the movement unfolds in the ballroom.

The progressive facets of the text extend to the film's conclusion where it remains ambiguous as to whether Mia and Armando win the wheelchair ballroom dancing championship. Both screenwriter Madden and Seidelman acknowledge a deliberate lack of clarity, which is highly effective. As an exit note, the film avoids yet another cliché and prioritizes participation – being seen – over winning. A participant in a final regal, embracing pose, Leah is in full ascent. Leah may have had to adapt to unforeseen trauma, but she is what she always was: a dancer.

It has been argued throughout this chapter that Seidelman is largely responsible for harnessing the progressive qualities within the text. *Musical Chairs* proves that disability and its related themes can at least be presented on film without always being problematized. Yet, Madden's deft script is a major ingredient to *Musical Chairs*' effectiveness. Attuned to the importance of authentic, affecting dialogue and narrative pace, Madden gives life to characters whose impairments are ultimately part of their identity, rather than the defining feature. While this is most clearly reflected in the character of Chantelle, a Black transgender woman who happens to be a wheelchair user, other characters are humanely drawn. "I thought she'd be an uptight white bitch, but she's alright," says Rosa (Angelic Zambrama) of Mia, conceding defeat in her pursuit of Armando's affection. Like fellow dancers, Mia is far more than the usually crude stereotypes permitted to live on screen.

Musical Chairs explores both themes and styles that have characterized Seidelman's work to date, but the film is not merely a retread of where she has been before. More significantly, *Musical Chairs* continues to showcase Seidelman's ability to incorporate potentially challenging issues into unashamedly accessible texts. *Musical Chairs* can be considered a film addressing disability that does not disguise its clear intentions, but also permits us to envision future possibilities through a prism in which realities of disability, of New York, are entwined with generic subversion embedded in magic and romance. If the film proves an ideal vehicle for Seidelman's sensibilities as a director, it is resoundingly indicative of what she can bring to a project. In an age that is dependent on a degree of homogeneity in output, Seidelman appears to be the ideal guide for showing us new and innovate sights of what is possible in New York and beyond.

NOTES

1. A Zoom Musical Chat: Interview with Susan Seidelman, May 2021.
2. Roger Ebert, "Musical Chairs," *RogerEbert.com*, 28 March 2012.
3. Maria San Felippo, "Introduction: Love Actually: Romantic Comedy since the Aughts," in *After "Happily Ever After": Romantic Comedy in the Post-Romantic Age* (Detroit: Wayne State University Press, 2021), 3.
4. A Zoom Musical Chat.
5. Zoom interview with Marty Madden, May 2021.
6. Ibid.
7. A Zoom Musical Chat.
8. *Desperately Seeking Susan*, DVD commentary.
9. Michael Oliver, cited in Carol Thomas, *Sociologies of Disability and Illness: Contested Ideas in Disability Studies and Medical Sociology* (London: Palgrave MacMillan, 2007), 13.
10. A Zoom Musical Chat.
11. *Musical Chairs: The Idea*, DVD Extras.
12. San Felippo, "Introduction," 3.
13. Ibid.
14. Zoom interview with Aubree Marchione, Summer 2021.
15. Ibid.
16. Stephen Fairclough, "Disability: Ballet Dancer Joe Powell-Main as 'Wrong Type'," *BBC News*, 2 December 2021.
17. A Zoom Musical Chat.
18. Ibid.
19. Ibid.
20. Zoom interview with Madden.
21. Ebert, "Musical Chairs."
22. A Zoom Musical Chat.
23. A Zoom Musical Chat; Zoom interview with Mario Grigorov, May 2021.
24. Katharine Quarmby, *Scapegoat: Why We Are Failing Disabled People* (London: Portobello, 2011), 237.
25. Ibid. p. 237.
26. Ibid. p. 237.
27. A Zoom Musical Chat.
28. Zoom interview with Marchione.

29. Ibid.
30. Ibid.
31. Nathan Rabin, "Musical Chairs," *AV Club*, 22 March 2012.
32. Ibid.
33. Dreadguacamole user comment on Rabin, "Musical Chairs."
34. MJD user comment on Rabin, "Musical Chairs."
35. Benjamin Lee, "Viola Davis: 'I Stifled Who I Was to Be Seen as Pretty. I Lost Years'," *The Guardian*, 20 October 2018.
36. Nicole Markotić, *Disability in Film and Literature* (Jefferson: McFarland, 2016), 3.
37. Annie Elainey, "Me before You: Better DEAD than Disabled? [CC]," *YouTube.com*, 2017.
38. "Auti Angel," *Musical Chairs* DVD Extra.
39. Tom Shakespeare, *Disability: The Basics* (London: Routledge, 2018).
40. Deborah Jermyn, *Falling in Love Again: Romantic Comedy in Contemporary Cinema* (London: I. B. Tauris, 2009).
41. A Zoom Musical Chat.
42. Diane Negra, *Off-White Hollywood: American Culture and Ethnic Female Stardom* (London: Routledge, 2001), 3.
43. A Zoom Musical Chat.
44. Ibid.
45. Ibid.
46. Ibid.
47. Ibid.
48. Ibid.
49. Ibid.

CHAPTER 13

Death, Illusion and the Hijab in Susan Seidelman's *Cut in Half*

Stacy Thompson

OPENING CREDITS: POSSIBLE PATHS

As the climactic scene begins in Susan Seidelman's short film *Cut in Half*, one sister, Sareen, interrogates the other, Layla, who has recently lost her hair to chemotherapy: "Why are you still wearing the hijab? Your hair's grown back in." Layla responds: "I can't explain it. It just makes me feel better." The sisters immediately leave the topic of the hijab behind and continue their conversation. The scene concludes with Layla confessing her fear to Sareen that her childhood leukemia has returned, and she asks Layla to respect her wishes in refusing a second round of chemotherapy. In the essay that follows, I will argue that the film *Cut in Half* stages a pair of differing psychological strategies for coping with trauma and death, both of which run through the hijab. These strategies rely on specific acts or behaviors that seem to be tied to specific beliefs but that, in fact, work even though no one believes. The film demonstrates that many simple acts that we take for granted are, in fact, complicated by the fact that they are carried out without anyone believing in their efficacy. What is most striking about these acts is that they are still effective. They still provide genuine relief from suffering, for instance, regardless of whether anyone rationally believes in their efficiency. Even with belief subtracted or suspended, the affect remains.

Before working with the connections between acts and belief, however, it is worth thinking about the film's manifest content. *Cut in Half* focuses on a four-member Muslim-American family that lives in Brooklyn, New York. As viewers, we know little about the family, although we can infer that Layla and Sareen were born in the US or immigrated with their parents when they were very young. The girls' father, Sammy, speaks English with an American accent, as do both of his daughters. The actor who plays Sammy, Naser Faris, was born in Egypt but has lived in the US for decades. Déa Julien (Sareen) is from New York City, and Ajna Jai (Layla) has lived in New York for most of her life. Maya, the sisters' mother, speaks English with an Indian accent (the actress, Anna George, is Indian American). The film is composed of nine scenes and takes place over the course of a few days.

From the film's small sampling of the family's life, we learn that the younger daughter Sareen, who is roughly sixteen years old, does not wear the hijab at home or at school; Maya (her mother) does not wear it at home, which is not unusual, even for muhajibh (Muslim women who wear the hijab); Layla, who is eighteen and recovering from cancer, wears the hijab in bed at home but not at the table for dinner; and Sareen keeps Layla's hijab when the latter is being wheeled outside the home to an ambulance in the film's penultimate scene. In short, Layla wears the hijab in the film only at a time when many Muslim-American women would not feel that they needed to (at home in bed) and does not wear it outside her home, when it would most likely be worn. Although she does not wear the hijab at all times, Layla does always wear a smaller scarf that covers her hair. I am differentiating here between a wrap that only covers the hair; the hijab that covers the hair, ears, head and neck; and the nikab, which covers all that the hijab does plus the mouth and nose. The hijab thus does not equate with the English word "veiling." In fact, the one indisputable claim that can be made about what piece or pieces of clothing the word "hijab" references is that no indisputable claim can be made. Following Vashi and Williams, I will use "hijab to refer to the scarf that covers head, hair, neck, and ears, but leaves the face uncovered [. . .] and nikab to refer to the face covering."[1] This aligns with the practice of contemporary US scholarship on the hijab.[2]

Cut in Half was written by seventeen-year-old Arab-American Leen Shumman. The non-profit organization Scenarios USA chose her screenplay to produce and paired her with Susan Seidelman, who directed the film. In 1999, Scenarios USA began asking teens to write screenplays "about the issues that shape their lives," and the "winning writers are partnered with some of Hollywood's finest filmmakers" to turn their screenplays into short films.[3] The non-profit then makes the films available to schools for educational purposes and distributes them via YouTube. In addition to crediting Scenarios USA, the closing credits of *Cut in Half* include a thank you to the Arab-American Family Support Center in Brooklyn, New York, where Leen Shumman works.

In an online interview with Esraa Saleh, from the same Center, Saleh offers her version of the film's message: "Hey. . . Muslims have cancer. . . and live in middle-class neighborhoods, and go to the school that you go to, so there's not really. . . much of a difference."[4] In a sense, Saleh seems to be right about the film. It largely avoids the obvious signifiers – for non-Muslim US audiences – of

Muslim-ness. There are no scenes of prayer or mosque scenes, and no Arabic – the language of Islam – is spoken. This careful avoidance or limitation of signs of Muslim-ness seems aimed at sidestepping any commentary on what Saleh, in the same interview, refers to as "the Arab or Muslim experience"[5] in the US. Thus, the film's lack of "Muslim-ness" would seem to echo Saleh's claim: there is "not really. . . much of a difference"[6] between Muslim-Americans as the potential others in relation to a non-Muslim-American subject's standpoint. The film's message of a lack of difference is redoubled by its focus on living with cancer, if we read disease as a mode of universal human experience, a vector that cuts across differences of religion, ethnicity, culture, class and race to unite us as humans who suffer. It seems important that it is cancer, and childhood leukemia in particular, that afflicts Layla, because this specific disease seems to afflict children without regard for race, class, gender or ethnicity. Leukemia could thus be seen as operating in the film as a great leveler and therefore as a great humanizer.

Nevertheless, it is possible to read the film's surface refusal to make a positive statement about the "Muslim-American experience"[7] as a negative proposition: that the Muslim-American experience is no different from the non-Muslim American experience. The film's comment is that there is nothing to comment on. But the film is more complicated than what this surface reading suggests. For one thing, it undermines Saleh's claim that there is not much of a difference by situating the hijab at a crucial moment in the film's narrative. The hijab is probably the object most recognized and commented on as separating Muslims from non-Muslims. And the hijab itself can suggest separation, hiddenness and difference. There might not be much of a difference between women who wear the hijab and those who do not, but even if the hijab does not signify a positive difference, it could at least signify the act of hiding itself. Or, put differently, if the hijab does not hide any positive content, then it at least hides the fact that it is not hiding anything. In other words, in the context of the film, the hijab hides the fact that there is nothing to hide.

A further message is also possible in addition to "there's not really. . . much difference."[8] Layla's wearing of the hijab coupled with her admission that she is not certain why she wears it opens up the possibility that there is a difference between women who wear the hijab and those who do not, but not necessarily a knowable one. In other words, the film can be read as saying that the hijab does not objectify Muslim-ness as a knowable, sensible thing, but neither is it the site of an impenetrable, spiritual mystery. Rather, the hijab operates as the sign of pure difference without meaning. This is why Layla's use of it is inexplicable, not only to the viewer, but also to Layla herself. The film thus adopts an interesting stance toward ethnic and religious difference: rather than erasing difference through assimilating (Americanizing) it or mystifying it (as metaphysical), the film insists on difference as an absolute impasse, as beyond the scope of positive knowledge.

However, this essay will not be developing any of the three readings that I have touched upon so far: Muslims and non-Muslim as much the same; the hijab as hiding the fact that nothing is hidden; and (perhaps no different from the second argument) the hijab as a sign of pure difference. But what these possible interpretations share is the importance of the hijab. Maybe its meaning is as inscrutable to us as viewers as it is to Layla, but I will take a different tack here. Instead, I will claim that the film's use of the hijab connects it directly to issues of belief and trauma. In *Cut in Half*, each sister finds a psychological strategy for surviving Layla's likely approaching death. In both cases, the sisters mitigate their suffering by acting in accordance with – maintaining – an illusion. Each behaves as if she believes in her illusion. The psychoanalytical names for these two forms of believing in an illusion are fetishism and the transitional object, and each of the sister's strategies for confronting death and suffering is mediated through the hijab. These two paths unite in the hijab, regardless of the fact that neither sister wholly believes in the hijab's religious significance.

TRACKING BACK: HIJAB AS SHIFTING SIGNIFIER

Before considering how the sisters in *Cut in Half* deploy the hijab, it is first necessary to think about the proliferation of possible meanings that are assigned to the hijab. There are multiple, conflicting significations for the wearing of the hijab. Leila Ahmed, Egyptian-American scholar of Islam and the history of Middle Eastern feminism, writes in 1982:

> It consequently seems necessary here to briefly state the obvious: It is the idea of the veil much more than the veil's material presence that is the powerful signifier: of women's proper seclusion and relegation to a private world, of their non-participation, passivity, and even invisibility – metaphorically signified by the veil – in the public domain. And so as long as the veil is notionally present [...] then that society is as surely riven in two, and women – whenever possible in practice, and always on the ideal plane – are non-participant, passive, and invisible.[9]

For Ahmed, the hijab "obviously" and also universally (globally) signifies the presumed subordination of the women who wear it to men.

However, at the other end of the spectrum, numerous contemporary analyses of the hijab as it is worn in the US and Canada and, perhaps more importantly, studies not of the hijab but of women in the US and Canada who wear it, arrive at far different meanings. Muhammad Rahman and Aini Firdaus, for example, conclude from their fieldwork with women who wear the hijab in Norfolk,

Virginia, that the "practice of hijab [. . .] is more complicated than is implied in the simple concepts of male dominance and social segregation."[10] They add that their observations demonstrate that, for the women whom they observed at the Old Dominion University (ODU) mosque in Norfolk, "the hijab does not only represent piety or seclusion or subordination but [. . .] in the context of America [. . .] is also a tool to express individuality and [a] demand for social change."[11] The hijab also allows women connected to the ODU "to be more involved in the public sphere and be more socially accepted."[12]

In her study of Canadian women who wear the hijab, Tabassum Ruby's conclusions advance a step further in thinking of the progressive possibilities of wearing the hijab. She argues that . . .

> Many Muslim women [. . .] claim that the hijab empowers them in numerous ways: making their identities distinct, taking control of their bodies; and giving them a sense of belonging to a wider Muslim world. Thus the discussion on the hijab is contentious, revealing the complexity of the issue.[13]

She also notes a further complication that her research reveals: "Immigrant Muslim women perceive the hijab in a variety of ways and associate it with diverse meanings that range from covering of the head to modest behavior."[14] Also touching on the interrelations between women in North America who wear the hijab and the global Muslim community, Gira Vashi and Rhys Williams' study of second-generation Muslim women in the US argues that "American society puts great emphasis on equality, independence, and the establishment of autonomous personal identity"[15] and that . . .

> . . .the decision to wear hijab can work in just this way for many second-generation American Muslim women. They are creating cultural space for the development of autonomous selves through the use of this potent religious symbol. It emphasizes their Muslim identity and gives them some measure of autonomy, depending upon their personal circumstances, from: a) dominant American non-Muslim culture; b) their Westernized, assimilating parents; or c) their non-assimilating parents who hold expectations for them rooted in Arabic or Indo-Pakistani culture. Wearing hijab is, for them, a practical and useful response to living as young women in a nexus between two cultures and as members of a minority faith.[16]

Because *Cut in Half* concerns two second-generation Muslim women, Vashi and Williams' findings are particularly relevant to the present chapter.

Also germane is Rachel Anderson Droogsma's study of American women who wear the hijab. Her fieldwork leads her to conclude that, for the US Muslim women whom she interviewed, there are "six major functions of hijab,"[17] which include "defining Muslim identity, functioning as a behavior check, resisting sexual objectification, affording more respect, preserving relationships, and providing a source of freedom."[18] She adds that . . .

> Americans often associate the presence of a headscarf with the subjugation of Muslim women. More than anything else, the women [in her study] articulated their desire to challenge this stereotype in the hope of being recognized as free Americans who just happen to wear hijab.[19]

One of her informants echoes Esraa Saleh's comment that I cited earlier – that is, "Muslims have cancer. . . there's not really much of a difference."[20] Droogsma's interviewee says: "I'd hope that somehow [hijab] fosters tolerance, you know, tells people that Muslim women are people just like you. . . we laugh, we cry, [wearing hijab] is just our expression of faith."[21]

In contrast to the academics cited above, Mahmudul Hasan claims in a 2018 article on the relations between feminism and hijab that there is a "mainstream feminist reluctance to accept and appreciate positive meanings or associations of hijab,"[22] adding that "[f]eminist scholars, cultural commentators, media pundits, social scientists and even security experts do not seem tired of the hype and semantic apparatuses to theorize or stereotype hijab and its wearers as hindrances to modernity."[23] But his conclusion strikes me as more intuited than demonstrated. Even a quick glance over the scholarship of the past two decades reveals hundreds of analyses that grant "positive meanings or associations" with hijab. The ones that I have cited here are only a small slice but seem to me more representative of the work being done today than the early condemnation of the hijab that Ahmed offered forty years ago, or that Hasan claims for contemporary "feminist scholars."

RISING ACTION: THE HIJAB AND ITS CONFLICTS

However, to state the obvious, the hijab is an incredibly complicated signifier, throwing off conflicting meanings faster than one can follow. For this reason, this chapter will concern itself with how the hijab functions psychoanalytically in a specific context rather than with its semantic possibilities. To flesh out this psychoanalytical option, we need to look carefully at the climactic scene, which appears about two-thirds of the way through the fifteen-minute film and think about how the scene situates Layla's practice of wearing the hijab. As the scene begins, Sareen returns home from high school and enters Layla's bedroom. After exchanging pleasantries about their day apart from one another (Layla is home-schooling while she recovers from leukemia and a round of chemotherapy that sent her into remission), Layla comments on how beautiful Sareen's hair is. Sareen responds: "Layla, why are you still wearing the hijab? Your hair's grown back in." Sareen's accusatory tone points us toward a couple of possible readings. First, we can infer that Layla probably started wearing the hijab after she was diagnosed with leukemia. We can imagine an exchange between Sareen and Layla in which Layla explained that she was wearing the hijab to hide the fact that her hair was falling out. This excuse might have protected her from admitting to Sareen that her cancer had also led her to a sudden awareness of her mortality and to contemplate eschatological issues. This reading also suggests that, even if Sareen unconsciously understood that Layla wore the hijab as a response to the possibility of her death, Sareen still preferred to maintain the fantasy that her sister wore it to hide her lack of hair. In any case, Layla's choice to wear the hijab was not something that Sareen necessarily expected of her sister. It therefore seems likely that their mother, Maya, chooses not to wear the hijab, perhaps was not expected to wear it upon reaching maturity and did not expect her daughters to do so. In all likelihood, her children did not express a desire to wear it before Layla became ill. Sareen's slightly accusatory tone therefore suggests that she associates the hijab with Layla's concerns over dying and resents the reminder of her sister's illness. Thus, both sisters associate the hijab with the possibility of death. This is not surprising: we expect that, confronted by their own mortality, many people will embrace or at least become more open to religious practices and thinking. *Cut in Half* offers this well-known and unsurprising statement as one of the film's possible meanings, but it is almost immediately cast into doubt by the rest of the scene between the sisters.

CLIMAX: DEATH, FETISHISM AND THE HIJAB

Layla explains to Sareen: "It's not about my hair anymore. I can't explain it; it just. . . makes me feel better. . . I'm just trying to find a good way to tell you. . ." Then, she trails off. Sareen nudges her on: "Just tell me what's wrong." But when Layla says "Why, what's the point?" Sareen quickly interjects with "Don't talk like that!" And when Layla continues: "I'm gonna die either way," Sareen counters, "Please don't say that, okay?!" No doubt this is not an unusual conversation. As anyone who has been close to someone who is terminally ill knows, there are moments when a person confronting death wants to talk about that experience. Why? And, more importantly, why are many people tempted in these moments, like Sareen, to brush aside these requests to talk about the end of life from those whom they care about the most? First, consider Layla's near-knee-jerk responses: "Don't talk like that!" and then "Please don't say that." No doubt these seem like caring responses on the surface and from Sareen's perspective. It is as if she is saying: "You don't need to think about the possibility of dying because that is not going to happen." If she thought about it, Sareen would probably imagine that she is reassuring Layla that morbid talk is not warranted – it is, in fact, totally unnecessary. Received knowledge also holds that a person who has accepted their own death will not fight for life, so perhaps we imagine that we are pushing our loved ones away from a fatal defeatism when we refuse to countenance their imagining of their own deaths.

In psychoanalytical terms, we can describe what is happening here differently, in terms of what is often called magical thinking. "Magical thinking" appears in Freud's work as the belief in the "omnipotence of thought," which he defines as "the over-valuation of mental processes as compared with reality."[24] Drawing a parallel between what he imagines as the advancement of civilization with the mental development of the individual person (a common trope in Freud's work that has not aged well), he writes:

> The animistic phase [of civilization] would correspond to narcissism [in the individual] both chronologically and in its content; the religious phase would correspond to the stage of object-choice of which the characteristic is a child's attachment to his parents; while the scientific stage would have an exact counterpart in the stage at which an individual has reached maturity, has renounced the pleasure principle, adjusted himself to reality and turned to the external world for the object of his desires.[25]

Ignoring Freud's parallelism between civilizational and individual stages of advancement, I want to seize on his notion that a person's desire is initially oriented internally, during the primary narcissism phase that occurs before the infant distinguishes between subject and object, self and other, or self and world. The child later orients her desire outward, toward the parents and, finally, having "adjusted [herself] to reality," the child aims her desire outside the family at objects external to it. In this process of the development of the individual, which is also the transitioning of desire from self to object, magical thinking belongs to the narcissistic phase. It marks a refusal to accept the gap between internal and external, between ego and object, between what one desires and what exists in reality. Freud always insists that phenomena that he tracks in child sexuality and in neurosis – neurotic narcissism, for instance, or an obsessive neurosis – exist in all people to some extent. They are merely exaggerated in neuroses. Thus, in our everyday lives we practice magical thinking in a variety of forms, and when we do so, we construct an illusion that guides our behavior, even though we do not consciously believe in the reality of the illusion. We might know it to be an illusion but behave in accordance with it anyway.

In her wish not to hear Layla talk about the possibility of her death, Sareen exhibits a behavior that is supported by an illusion that she has likely long given up believing in, which is the belief in the omnipotence of thought or speech. She behaves as if the mere verbal expression of a relapse will make it occur. Sareen behaves as if she believes that, if no one thinks that death is a possible outcome or acknowledges it in language, then it ceases to be. Not thinking or speaking about it prevents it from happening, from becoming reality. In other words, she is embracing the omnipotence of thought, or magical thinking. In psychoanalysis, the omnipotence of thought is a holdover from infant mental life, a practice that once proved effective and is therefore nearly impossible to renounce completely, especially at the level of the unconscious. The infant desired the breast (or bottle) and, if she was well-parented, the breast appeared. If that first object were inserted at the proper moment into the infant's mental fantasy of desiring and being able to satisfy its desire by conjuring the breast and vocalizing, then the illusion of the omnipotence of thought was established. What the infant wanted, she seemed able to summon for herself. Magical thinking thus becomes a vanishing mediator on the child's path from the early, pleasure principle-dominated narcissistic phase of development toward a reality principle-dominated and object-oriented phase of reluctant but accepted dependence on the external world for the satisfaction of many desires.

We can thus describe as literally illusory the rationales for Sareen's quick denial of Layla's potentially impending death. Although it might also be true that Sareen is unthinkingly attempting to avoid the pain of thinking about or working through Layla's death for herself. Sareen's denial might be aimed at helping shield Layla from this eventuality, but, perhaps more importantly, it can also be aimed at protecting Sareen from the pain of contemplating the traumatic likelihood of her sister Layla's relapsing. Sareen tries to postpone the moment when she might need to confront this trauma in Layla's presence. But clearly her refusal to do so does not satisfy Layla. She interrupts Sareen's refusal to listen: "Okay just hear me out. 'Cuz Mom and Dad never do anymore." She tells Sareen – who listens – that, if she is relapsing, then she will not be undergoing a second round of chemotherapy. She notes that it is her newly acquired legal right to refuse: "I'm over eighteen. Whatever I decide to do, I'll do. It's my choice." Sareen then scolds Layla for her selfishness in deciding against chemotherapy – for not thinking about her parents' or Sareen's needs – and the scene ends with Layla holding Sareen and attempting to comfort her.

It is easy enough to imagine why it is so important to Layla that Sareen listen to her. First, Layla knows that she might be relapsing, and this likelihood has become a part of her reality. What would it be like to live with such a profound fact when everyone around one denies or refuses to accept it? In a sense, her family is unintentionally gaslighting her, treating her as if she is crazy every time she raises the very real possibility that she might be dying. To maintain one's sense of living a shared social life – living in a collectively established reality – one needs to share with those around one the facts of life in the literal sense: the facts that comprise one's life, which in Layla's case means its new precarity. If Sareen or her parents cannot talk to Layla about the reality that she is experiencing directly (and which they are experiencing at some level, regardless of how much they resist it) – if they cannot allow Layla's reality its space in language, in the stuff of reality and facticity itself – then they risk driving her to feel as if she is cut off from reality. She is particularly vulnerable to what her immediate family thinks and knows, because she is being home-schooled and rarely leaves the house.

In the one home-schooling scene, Layla's teacher also maintains the fiction that Layla is perfectly fine and need not concern herself with death or dying. When Layla asks her why she needs to learn about Christopher Columbus, her teacher tells her: "You need to pass your history test. You want to go to college, right?" In voice-over, Layla comments: "I can't even go to regular school. Why does everyone assume that I'm going to college?" Although her teacher presses on with the lesson, Layla's nose starts bleeding, and the teacher abruptly halts the lesson, as if receiving a kind of answer from the Real itself – a purely biological sign of vulnerability that the teacher takes as an authentic signifier of Layla's sickness, in contrast to Layla's merely symbolic protestations. The house and its inhabitants and occasional visitor are thus Layla's complete reality, and to have her disease denied within that reality no doubt shakes Layla's confidence in what she takes to be factual and knowable. Consequently, Layla needs Sareen to acknowledge that Layla might be dying in order to allow that possibility to exist in the Symbolic Order that is social reality. For Layla, that fact needs to be established in reality next to the Real but meaningless – literally without meaning – biological possibility of her death.

To return to the bedroom scene, Sareen wants Layla's acknowledgement of her possible death. Why? There are at least two options. First, as mentioned above, Layla needs to feel as if she can trust the reality presented to her by her environment and her place within it. This cannot happen if no one acknowledges what she assumes to be true. Second, Layla wants to talk about her possible relapse because, at some un- or semi-conscious level, she probably wants to work through it in the psychoanalytical sense: she wants to talk it through. At the most elementary level, therapy creates a space in which the analysand talks about – or around – that which they cannot articulate and thereby repeats an experience that happened (or is happening) at the level of the Real within the Symbolic. Something traumatic bothers the analysand, and it is its traumatic kernel itself which resists symbolization, resists entering the symbolic order of knowable reality. Counterintuitively, it is the very effort to translate unspeakable trauma into the reality of language, within the parameters of the therapeutic session, that ultimately allows the trauma to touch reality, at least as that which cannot be fully grasped but can be pointed to or circumscribed (if not penetrated) by language. In other words, even if the trauma in its fully traumatic nature cannot be grasped, its unknowability can be registered and that unknowability can itself be known. In the clinic, the analyst endeavors to aid the analysand in using language to take the place of unspeakable trauma, to translate trauma into a narrative that can be inserted into the analysand's Symbolic understanding of herself. The Real of a trauma never disappears completely, but language can attenuate it until it becomes less symptom-producing. The analyst therefore makes possible the modification of unspeakable trauma into ordinary unhappiness. Sareen's acknowledgment of Layla's awareness of her own impending death is thus necessary in order to aid Layla in transforming the trauma of confronting her death into an unhappiness with which she can live.

But how does the hijab connect to Layla's concerns about leukemia and relapse, and how does it participate in the necessary illusions that Layla and Sareen harbor? On the one hand, as mentioned above, it could be that Layla is newly open to religion as a strategy for dealing with the possibility of her own death. The hijab would then signify Layla's burgeoning spirituality or religiosity. The other option that I have presented – the psychoanalytical one – seems to sidestep the hijab. In this one, Layla seems to be spontaneously placing herself in the role of the analysand and Sareen in the role of analyst. In this scenario, Layla feels that Sareen's acknowledgment of and belief in Layla's relapse might grant it reality for her and force it at least partially out of the Real of trauma and into the discursive world of language and knowing, where it will not bother her as deeply as it otherwise might. But recall what Layla tells Sareen when asked directly why she wears the hijab: "It's not about my hair anymore. I can't explain it; it just... makes me feel better... I'm just trying to find a good way to tell you..." The sentence about her hair and the hijab leads Layla directly to telling her sister about her likely relapse and her intimations of her impending death. In this case, the hijab is not a sign of religiosity but plays a different role, a more complicated one. As mentioned above, what strikes the reader about research on the hijab, and more specifically on the women in the US who wear it, is the hijab's polysemous character. In Droogsma's research cited above, there are "six major functions of hijab [... which include ...] defining Muslim identity, functioning as a behavior check, resisting sexual objectification, affording more respect, preserving relationships, and providing a source of freedom."[26] In short, women offer a surplus of reasons for wearing the hijab, some of which they link to specific affects: in Droogsma's account, women feel more Muslim, more respected, more in control and more secure when wearing the hijab. What we do not find in the research is the opposite: wearing the hijab for no particular reason but feeling good about it anyway. For Layla, however, why she wears it is inexplicable, even when she tries to explain it to her sister who feels somewhat affronted or shut out by it. But even though Layla does not know why she wears it, she still feels better when she does. In other words, even though she does not assign it a meaning or believe something concrete about it, it works anyway. In one sense, we are back to an earlier interpretation: what the hijab hides is that there is nothing to hide. But there is more to it than this, because, ultimately, the hijab allows Layla to endure her life.

As the bedroom scene continues, and invoking a seeming contradiction, Layla explains that she simultaneously wants to wear the hijab and refuse further chemotherapy that she believes will only serve to remind Sareen and herself of her disease. She reminds Sareen that her doctor warned her that, if she relapses, the chances of death are high. She then adds, regarding chemotherapy: "I don't always want to be reminded that I'm sick. I want to spend whatever good days I have with you. Not days when you know I'm sick and everyone takes pity on me." On the surface, it seems as if the hijab would serve as a continual reminder for her and Sareen of her disease, but Layla clearly sees it as the opposite – as the substantiation of her concern over the cancer that allows her to forget about it herself. It is as if the hijab takes on the responsibility and weight of concern attached to dying and bears it for her, regardless of what tradition or lack thereof Layla associates with it. In this sense, it operates like a fetish in the psychoanalytical sense. It allows Layla to engage in disavowal, to say: "I know very well that I have a terminal illness that will probably kill me, and yet, I will go on behaving as if I do not believe it." The fetish is the object that stands in within the Symbolic Order – within social reality – and allows the fetishist to focus on it and cathect it (invest it with libidinal energy) while ignoring the Real trauma that lies behind it, even though she knows that the trauma is there. As with the omnipotence of thought, we are again dealing with an illusion that no one believes in but that still has genuine affective results. Layla can admit, with some bitterness, that she will likely die of a relapse, but, in the same sentence, she can imagine good days in which that knowledge never surfaces for her, and the hijab is the hinge that allows those options to coexist. Because it operates as a fetish, it makes perfect sense that Layla does not know why the hijab works for her. The fetish is an illusion that the fetishist maintains but does not believe in, and only by doing so can it serve as the link that connects "Layla is dying" and "Layla is not dying."

THE THIRD ACT: HIJAB AS TRANSITIONAL OBJECT

There is one final and interesting way in which the hijab functions in relation to illusions and belief in *Cut in Half*. The film is bookended by two scenes of Sareen at school. In the first, she slips into an unhappy reverie in a math class and comments wistfully, in voiceover, that she enjoyed coming to school before her sister became ill. In the film's final scene, Sareen is about to take the SAT. As she listens to the proctor's instructions, the camera tracks along a row of students seated at desks and keeps a small stack of SAT tests in focus as it is being passed hand-to-hand down the row. The camera pauses at Sareen as her test arrives, and she places both palms on it. The camera tilts up to her face and then down slightly to follow one of her hands as it drops alongside and behind her desk, where it squeezes Layla's fuchsia hijab, which is now knotted around one of the straps of Sareen's backpack. After a direct cut to the teacher, the camera cuts back to Sareen's face as the teacher says, "You may now open your test booklets... and begin." Sareen, shown in close-up, takes a deep breath after the word "begin," releases it, nods to herself and leans in to start her test as the screen cuts to black and the credits roll. The manifest message is that the SAT is a new beginning for Sareen. It represents her renewed interest in both school and her studies, in the short term – this test, this day – and the long term – at college, in the near future. The camerawork in this scene emphasizes that she is now capable of imagining a future that might not include Layla, either because Sareen will leave home for college, because the relapse will occur and Layla will die, or both.

Somehow, the hijab's transference from Layla to Sareen has made this final moment possible for Sareen. The hijab operates as a transitional object. It is another vanishing mediator, like the omnipotence of thought, that begins in infancy as a psychological technique for shifting desire from the internal world of the self to the external world of objects. This fact is illustrated by child psychoanalyst D. W. Winnicott's description of the transitional object:

> It is assumed here that the task of reality-acceptance is never completed, that no human being is free from the strain of relating inner and outer reality, and that relief from this strain is provided by an intermediate area of experience (cf. Riviere, 1936) which is not challenged (arts, religion, etc.) [. . .]. In infancy this intermediate area is necessary for the initiation of a relationship between the child and the world [. . .]. Essential to all this is continuity (in time) of the external emotional environment and of particular elements in the physical environment such as the transitional object or objects. The transitional phenomena are allowable to the infant because of the parents' intuitive recognition of the strain inherent in objective perception.[27]

Winnicott adds that adults, on the other hand, maintain the psychical pleasures and comforting support of transitional objects through "art or religion or philosophy."[28] Even so, he notes, no one is free from the strain of relating "inner and outer reality,"[29] which is to say the strain of resolving the subjective life of desire with the objective life of possibilities for satisfying desire. But one interesting technique for bridging that gap is by carrying a "transitional object" embedded in an emotional or physical space in which one feels relatively dominant over one's desires over to a new emotional or physical space in which one feels less in control. Winnicott also recognizes the necessary role that illusion plays in the transitional object. The illusion that must be maintained at all costs is that we have the same degree of control over the external world that we seemed to possess over the internal world of our infancy. As infants, we demanded the breast (broadly understood rather than literally – the breast meaning the first object, whatever it was), and it appeared; our desire flared up, was vocalized and seemed to produce its own near-immediate satisfaction. Gradually, through parenting, the infant and then toddler becomes capable of transitioning from the breast to the thumb to the stuffed animal and so on. In each case, the infant moves a step further from the internal fantasy world of a desire that demands and immediately receives the desired object to the acceptance of an external world in which the desired object is external and does not appear immediately. The role of the transitional object is thus to carry over some portion of a person's infantile illusion of control over the satisfaction of desire. The transitional object makes the externality and deferment of desire's satisfaction bearable.

But this is not true only for the developing child. For Winnicott, the transition from internal desire to external satisfaction is always in process and never complete. We never become completely reconciled to our loss of control over the satisfaction of our desire; we never wholly abandon our illusory early ability to satisfy our desire autonomously. Therefore, we often invest certain objects with a degree of illusory power over desire to aid in bridging the gap between internal and external. Winnicott admits that, as adults, we are not allowed to confess to our dependence on transitional objects and their obviously illusory powers.[30] But he also notes in the above passage that certain frameworks, one of which is religion, allow one to openly acknowledge such objects without fear of being considered crazy. There are other objects, however, that we do not acknowledge, even to ourselves. They work anyway, and they produce authentic affects for us.

As I have argued above, it is not exactly religion that Layla and Sareen embrace in order to bear the possibility of Layla's relapse. It seems doubtful that either of them would see the hijab as a sign of Islam's presence in their lives. And probably neither of them would accept a purely rational description of their behavior, or, in other words, admit that the transitional object operates as a kind of contemporary magic. If either of them were directly asked if she believed, based on reason, that wearing the hijab or tying it to a backpack strap would have any appreciable effect on Layla's health or Sareen's peace of mind, I doubt that either would accept it as fact. But that is precisely the nature of illusions of this sort – and of transitional objects, fetishes and magical thinking. They allow for the maintenance of an illusion in which no one believes. They allow for knowledge based on reason to sit side by side with contradictory behaviors and affects. For Layla, the hijab functions as a fetish, which is not believed in literally, a veil that shields her from the trauma of a relapse and of a likely death about which she manifestly knows. For Sareen, however, the hijab functions as a transitional object. Importantly, however, in both cases, the hijab *works* psychologically. Without either sister believing in the hijab's supposed powers rationally, it still makes Layla feel better and allows Sareen to recommit to her education and her life apart from Layla. Carrying Layla's hijab with her allows Sareen to reconcile opposed desires, both of which must be lived with. She knows that Layla is probably dying, and she behaves at school as if Layla were fine and both of their lives were moving forward normally. She simultaneously wants to give all of her time to Layla and to live her own life. In sum, the hijab does not solve the problem of Layla's death; rather, it makes it bearable, both for Layla and for Sareen. For both sisters, it links getting what they want to making do with what they can have.

NOTES

1. Rhys H. Williams and Gira Vashi, "'Hijab' and American Muslim Women: Creating the Space for Autonomous Selves," *Sociology of Religion*, 68, no. 3 (Fall 2007), 270.
2. Vashi and James also note, in relation to the hijab, that "[t]here is no uniformly accepted set of terms for the clothing/covering we discuss here" (270). Ruby writes that, internationally, "regional and global terms differ in classifying the diverse articles of women's clothing and the word *hijab* varies from culture to culture [. . .]. Thus, while a Saudi woman may wear a *niqab* and call it *hijab*, a Canadian Muslim woman could use a headscarf and also identify it as a *hijab* [. . .]. The veil, which is often interpreted in Western traditions as a covering of the head, does not illuminate the complexity of the practice in a Muslim context" (56).
3. Scenarios USA, *YouTube.com*, 23 July 2020.
4. Esraa Saleh, "A Look Behind 'Cut in Half' Pt. 2," Scenarios USA, *YouTube.com*, 2017.
5. Ibid.
6. Ibid.
7. Ibid.
8. Ibid.
9. Leila Ahmed, "Feminism and Feminist Movements in the Middle East: A Preliminary Exploration: Turkey, Egypt, Algeria, People's Democratic Republic of Yemen," *Women's Study International Forum*, 5, no. 2 (1982), 160.
10. Muhammad Sigit Andhi Rahman and Aini Firdaus, "The Practice of Wearing Hijab in a Multicultural Mosque of America," *Humaniora*, 9, no. 2 (July 2018), 138.
11. Ibid. p. 138.
12. Ibid. p. 138.
13. Tabassum F. Ruby, "Listening to the Voices of Hijab," *Women's Studies International Forum*, 29 (2006), 54.
14. Ibid. p. 54.

15. Williams and Vashi, "'Hijab' and American Muslim Women," 285.
16. Ibid. p. 285.
17. Rachel Anderson Droogsma, "Redefining Hijab: American Muslim Women's Standpoints on Veiling," *Journal of Applied Communication Research*, 35, no. 3 (August 2007), 301.
18. Ibid. p. 301.
19. Ibid. p. 313.
20. Saleh, "A Look Behind 'Cut in Half'."
21. Droogsma, "Redefining Hijab," 313.
22. Mahmudul Hasan, MD, "The Feminist 'Quarantine' on Hijab: A Study of its Two Mutually Exclusive Sets of Meanings," *Journal of Muslim Minority Affairs*, 38, no. 1 (2018), 25.
23. Ibid. p. 25.
24. Sigmund Freud, *Totem and Taboo: Some Mental Points of Agreement Between the Mental Lives of Savages and Neurotics*, translated by James Strachey (London: Routledge Classics, 2001), 101.
25. Ibid. p. 105.
26. Droogsma, "Redefining Hijab," 301.
27. D. W. Winnicott, *Playing and Reality* (New York: Routledge Classics, 2005), 18.
28. Ibid. p. 18.
29. Ibid.
30. Ibid.

Bibliography

Adriaens, Fine, and Sofie Van Bauwel. "*Sex and the City*: A Postfeminist Point of View? Or How Popular Culture Functions as a Channel for Feminist Discourse". *The Journal of Popular Culture*, 47, no. 1 (September 2011): 174–95.

Ahmed, Leila. "Feminism and Feminist Movements in the Middle East, A Preliminary Exploration: Turkey, Egypt, Algeria, People's Democratic Republic of Yemen." *Women's Study International Forum*, 5, no. 2 (1982): 153–68.

Ahmed, Sara. *Living a Feminist Life*. Durham: Duke University Press, 2017.

Anderman, Joan. "Wordplay's the Name of the Game on New Electric Company." *The Boston Globe*, 19 January 2009. http://archive.boston.com/ae/tv/articles/2009/01/19/wordplays_the_name_of_game_on_new_electric_company/.

Anderson, Melissa. "Wrecks and the City: A Downtown-NYC Classic Surveys the Damage." *The Village Voice*, 26 July 2016. https://www.villagevoice.com/2016/07/26/wrecks-and-the-city-a-downtown-nyc-classic-surveys-the-damage/.

Andersson, Johan. "Landscape and Gentrification: The Picturesque and Pastoral in 1980s New York Cinema." *Antipode*, 49, no. 3 (2017): 539–56.

Armstrong, Jessica Keishin. *Sex and the City and Us*. New York: Simon & Schuster, 2018.

Bale, Miriam. "Persona Swap PT. 1: Past." *Joan's Digest: A Film Quarterly*, Spring 2012. http://www.joansdigest.com/issue-2/persona-swap-pas-by-miriam-bale.

Bañón, Raquel Medina, and Barbara Zecchi. "Technologies of Age: The Intersection of Feminist Film Theory and Aging Studies." *Investigaciones Feministas* (*Feminist Research*), 112 (2020): 251–62.

Bargainier, Earl. F. "Hissing the Villain, Cheering the Hero: The Social Function of Melodrama." *Studies in Popular Culture*, 3 (1980): 47–56.

Beale, Lewis. "Film Maker Star in Her Own Dream." *Los Angeles Times*, 9 January 1983.

Beecher, Catherine E. *A Treatise on Domestic Economy*. New York: Harper & Bros, 1849.

Behrent, Megan. "Suburban Captivity Narratives: Feminism, Domesticity, and the Liberation of the American Housewife." *Journal of Narrative Theory*, 49, no. 2 (Summer 2019): 247–86.

Bengal, Rebecca. "Famous for Being Famous in Downtown '80s New York: Susan Seidelman on *Smithereens*." *Vogue*, 27 July 2016. https://www.vogue.com/article/susan-seidelman-smithereens-film-interview-1980s-new-york-richard-hell.

—. "Smithereens: Breakfast at the Peppermint Lounge." *Criterion Collection*, 20 August 2018. https://www.criterion.com/current/posts/5823-smithereens-breakfast-at-the-peppermint-lounge.

Bergman, Ingmar, dir. *Persona*. 1966. New York: The Criterion Collection, 2014. Blu-ray.

Brady, Susan. "Seeking Madonna's Double." *Washington Post*, 31 May 1985: B2.

Brooks, Peter. "The Uses of Melodrama." In *Imitation of Life: A Reader on Film and Television Melodrama*, edited by Marcia Landy, 58–67. Detroit: Wayne State University Press, 1991.

Burnetts, Charles. "Sentiment and the 'Smart' Melodrama." In *Improving Passions: Sentimental Aesthetics and American Film*, 142–57. Edinburgh: Edinburgh University Press, 2017.

Butler, Simon Hardy. "Interviewing Susan Seidelman: From Madonna to Menopause." *Curnblog*, 7 March 2014. http://curnblog.com/2014/03/07/interviewing-susan-seidelman-madonna-menopause/.

Callahan, Dan. "A Woman's Face: Bibi Andersson & Persona at BAM." *Slant Magazine*, 21 November 2007. https://www.slantmagazine.com/film/a-womans-face-bibi-andersson-and-persona-at-bam/.

Caulfield, Deborah. "Film Maker, Not a Deal Maker." *Los Angeles Times*, 2 April 1985. https://www.latimes.com/archives/la-xpm-1985-04-02-ca-19510-story.html.

Champlin, Charles. "Critic at Large: Anything Wrong With 'Mr. Right'?" *Los Angeles Times*, 18 April 1987. https://www.latimes.com/archives/la-xpm-1987-04-18-ca-906-story.html.

Chastagner, Claude. "The Parents' Music Resource Center: From Information to Censorship." *Popular Music*, 18, no. 2 (May 1999): 179–92.

Chivers, Sally. *The Silvering Screen*. Toronto: University of Toronto Press, 2011.

Cole, Janis, and Holly Dale. *Calling the Shots: Profiles of Women Filmmakers*. Kingston: Quarry Press, 1993.

Collar, Cammila. "Can You Spot All the Underground Music Cameos in *Desperately Seeking Susan*?" *Medium.com*, 30 June 2017. https://medium.com/outtake/can-you-spot-all-the-underground-music-cameos-in-desperately-seeking-susan.

Conaboy, Kelly. "Being a Male Jerk in the *Sex and the City* Pilot: An Oral History." *The Cut*, 7 June 2018. https://www.thecut.com/2018/06/male-jerks-in-the-sex-and-the-city-pilot-an-oral-history.html.

Cook, Pam. "Making Mr. Right." *Monthly Film Bulletin*, 1 May 1988.

D'Angelo, Mike. "*The Hot Flashes*." *The AV Club*, 11 July 2013. https://film.avclub.com/the-hot-flashes.

Darke, Paul. "No Life Anyway: Pathologizing Disability on Film." In *The Problem Body: Projecting Disability on Film*, edited by Sally Chivers and Nicole Markotić, 97–108. Columbus: Ohio State University Press, 2010.

"David Bowie Criticizes MTV for Not Playing Videos by Black Artists." *MTV News*, 11 January 2016. https://www.youtube.com/watch?v=XZGiVzIr8Qg.

Denisoff, R. Serge. *Inside MTV*. New Brunswick: Transaction, 1988.

"'Desperately Seeking Susan' Turns 30: An Oral History of the Downtown Classic." *Yahoo! News*, 27 March 2015. https://www.yahoo.com/entertainment/desperately-seeking-susan-turns-30-an-oral-114699999372.html.

Desta, Yohana. "Meet the Women Who Molded *Sex and the City*'s Very First Season." *Vanity Fair*, 6 June 2018. https://www.vanityfair.com/hollywood/2018/06/sex-and-the-city-directors-interview.

Dika, Vera. *The (Moving) Pictures Generation: The Cinematic Impulse in Downtown New York Art and Film*. New York: Palgrave MacMillan, 2012.

Dolan, Josephine. *Contemporary Cinema and "Old Age": Gender and the Silvering of Stardom*. London: Palgrave Macmillan UK, 2018.

Dow, Bonnie J. "Prime-Time Divorce: 'The Emerging Woman' of *One Day at a Time*." In *Prime-Time Feminism: Television, Media Culture, and the Women's Movement Since 1970*, 59–85. Philadelphia: University of Pennsylvania Press, 1996.

Droogsma, Rachel Anderson. "Redefining Hijab: American Muslim Women's Standpoints on Veiling." *Journal of Applied Communication Research*, 35, no. 3 (August 2007): 294–319.

Ebert, Roger. "Aches on a Pain." *Rogerebert.com*, 17 August 2006. https://www.rogerebert.com/reviews/boynton-beach-club-2006.

—. "Making Mr. Right." *Rogerebert.com*, 10 April 1987. https://www.rogerebert.com/reviews/making-mr-right-1987.

—. "Musical Chairs." *Rogerebert.com*, 28 March 2012. https://www.rogerebert.com/reviews/musical-chairs-2012.

Edelman, Rob. "Susan Seidelman: Director." *Filmreference.com*, [n. d.]. http://www.filmreference.com/ Directors-Sc-St/Seidelman-Susan.html.

Edmond, Maura. "Deracination, Disemboweling and Scorched Earth Aesthetics: Feminist Cinemas, No Wave and the Punk Avant Garde." *Senses of Cinema*, 80 (September 2016). https://www.sensesofcinema.com/2016/american-extreme/feminist-cinemas/.

Elainey, Annie. "Me before You: Better DEAD than Disabled? [CC]." *Youtube.com*, 2017. https://www.youtube.com/watch?v=AVVQb0x0A6I.

Elley, Derek. "Confessions of a Suburban Girl." *Variety*, 3 September 1992. https://variety.com/1992/film/reviews/confessions-of-a-suburban-girl-1200430696/.

Fairclough, Stephen. "Disability: Ballet Dancer Joe Powell-Main as 'Wrong Type'." *BBC News*, 2 December 2021.

Faulkner, Joanne. *The Importance of Being Innocent*. Cambridge: Cambridge University Press, 2011.

Federici, Silvia. *Revolution at Point Zero: Housework, Reproduction, and Feminist Struggle*. Oakland: PM Press, 2012.

Fiske, John. "MTV: Post-Structural Post-Modern." *Journal of Communication Inquiry*, 10, no. 1 (Winter 1986): 74–79.

Ford, Jessica. "Feminist Cinematic Television: Authorship, Aesthetics, and Gender in Pamela Adlon's *Better Things*." *Fusion Journal*, 14 (2018): 16–29.

Forsburg, Myra. "Susan Seidelman's Recipe for 'Cookie'." *The New York Times*, 29 May 1988. https://www.nytimes.com/1988/05/29/movies/film-susan-seidelman-s-recipe-for-cookie.html.

Freud, Sigmund. *Totem and Taboo: Some Mental Points of Agreement Between the Mental Lives of Savages and Neurotics*, translated by James Strachey. London: Routledge Classics, 2001.

Friedan, Betty. *The Feminine Mystique*. New York: Dell Publishing Company, 1963.

—. *The Feminine Mystique*. New York: W. W. Norton & Company, 2001.

Frosty. "Interview with Ann Magnuson: The Actor, Musician and Performance Artist on Club 57, Bongwater and New York's Downtown New Wave Scene." *Red Bull Music Academy*, 10 October 2017. https://daily.redbullmusicacademy.com/2017/10/interview-ann-magnuson.

Gaines, Jane. "The Genius of Genre and Ingenuity of Women." In *Gender Meets Genre in Postwar Cinema*, edited by Christine Gledhill, 15–28. Chicago: University of Illinois Press, 2012.

Garcia, Laia. "The Lenny Interview: Susan Seidelman." *Lenny Letter*, 9 September 2016. https://www.lennyletter.com/story/the-lenny-interview-susan-seidelman.

Garfield, Rachel. *Experimental Filmmaking and Punk: Feminist Audio Visual Culture in the 1970s and 1980s*. London: Bloomsbury, 2005.

Garland-Thomson, Rosemarie. *Extraordinary Bodies: Figuring Physical Disability in American Culture and Literature*. New York: Columbia University Press, 2017.

Gates, Marya. "*Female Filmmaker Friday: Smithereens* (Dir. by Susan Seidelman)." *Cinema-fanatic.com*, 31 January 2014. https://cinema-fanatic.com/2014/01/31/female-filmmaker-friday-smithereens-1982-dir-susan-seidelman/.

—. "Female Filmmaker Friday: *Cookie*, 1989 (Dir. by Susan Seidelman)." *Cinema-Fanatic. com*, 21 February 2014. https://cinema-fanatic.com/2014/02/21/female-filmmaker-friday-cookie-1989-dir-susan-seidelman/.
Genzlinger, Neil. "Back From the '70s, without the Zaniness." *The New York Times*, 19 January 2009. https://www.nytimes.com/2009/01/19/arts/television/19elec.html.
Gill, Rosalind. "Postfeminist Media Culture: Elements of a Sensibility." *European Journal of Cultural Studies*, 10, no. 2 (2007): 147–66.
Gledhill, Christine. "Prologue: The Reach of Melodrama." In *Melodrama Unbound: Across History, Media, and National Cultures*, edited by Christine Gledhill and Linda Williams, ix–xxv. New York: Columbia University Press, 2018.
Godfrey, Nicholas. *The Limits of Auteurism: Case Studies in the Critically Constructed New Hollywood*. New Brunswick: Rutgers University Press, 2018.
Goldberg, Jonathan. *Melodrama: An Aesthetics of Impossibility*. Durham: Duke University Press, 2016.
Goodman, Ellen. "Parents: Do Kids a Favor – Start Losing Your Cool." *Chicago Tribune*, 7 June 1985: D2.
Goodman, Robin Truth. *Gender Work: Feminism After Neoliberalism*. New York: Palgrave MacMillan, 2013.
Goodwin, Andrew. "Fatal Distractions." In *Sound and Vision: The Music Video Reader*, edited by Simon Frith, Andrew Goodwin and Lawrence Grossberg, 37–56. London: Routledge, 2005.
Grant, Catherine. "Secret Agents: Feminist Theories of Women's Film Authorship." *Feminist Theory*, 2, no. 1 (2001): 113–30.
Gruson, Lindsey. "'Susan' Draws Spirit from the Sidewalks of New York." *The New York Times*, 14 April 1985. https://www.nytimes.com/1985/04/14/movies/susan-draws-spirit-from-the-sidewalks-of-new-york.html.
Harmetz, Aljean. "2 Women Succeed as Producers, But Easy Street Is Down the Road." *The New York Times*, 14 September 1988. https://www.nytimes.com/1988/09/14/movies/2-women-succeed-as-producers-but-easy-street-is-down-the-road.html.
—. "Behind Five Top Films, Five Obsessions." *Los Angeles Times*, 10 April 1988. https://www.nytimes.com/1988/04/10/movies/behind-five-top-films-five-obsessions.html.
Harrington, Erin. *Women, Monstrosity and Horror Film: Gynaehorror*. London: Taylor & Francis, 2017.
Hasan, Mahmudul, MD. "The Feminist 'Quarantine' on Hijab: A Study of its Two Mutually Exclusive Sets of Meanings." *Journal of Muslim Minority Affairs*, 38, no. 1 (2018): 24–38.
Hawkins, Joan, ed. *Downtown Film & TV Culture 1975–2001*. Chicago: Intellect, 2015.
Heap, Chad. *Slumming: Sexual and Racial Encounters in American Nightlife, 1885–1940*. Chicago: University of Chicago Press, 2009.
Hesse, Monica. "'Electric' Is Rewired For the 'oos." *The Washington Post*, 23 January 2009.
Hogeland, Lisa Marie. *Feminism and Its Fictions: The Consciousness-Raising Novel and Women's Liberation Movement*. Philadelphia: University of Pennsylvania Press, 1998.
Hutchinson, Pamela. "Smithereens." *Sight & Sound*, 28, no. 10 (October 2018): 87.
Indie Memphis Film Festival. "Virtual Discussion with Susan Seidelman (Desperately Seeking Susan)." *YouTube.com*, 2 June 2020. https://youtu.be/do0Uv-A5ud8.
Insdorf, Annette. "'Smithereens' – The Story of a Cinderella Movie." *New York Times*, 26 December 1982. https://www.nytimes.com/1982/12/26/movies/smithereens-the-story-of-a-cinderella-movie.html.
Jermyn, Deborah. *Falling in Love Again: Romantic Comedy in Contemporary Cinema*. London: I. B. Tauris, 2009.
Joyrich, Lynne. "All that Television Allows: TV Melodrama, Postmodernism, and Consumer Culture." In *Private Screenings*, edited by Lynn Spigel and Denise Mann, 226–51. Minneapolis: University of Minnesota Press, 1992.

Jurca, Catherine. *White Diaspora: The Suburb and the Twentieth-Century American Novel*. Princeton: Princeton University Press, 2001.

Juzwiak, Rich. "Susan Seidelman on How the 'Woman Director' Label Went from Pejorative to Political." *Jezebel.com*, 24 August 2018. https://jezebel.com/susan-seidelman-on-how-the-woman-director-label-went-fr-1828551112.

Kakoudaki, Despina. "Melodrama and Apocalypse: Politics and the Melodramatic Mode in Contagion." In *Melodrama Unbound: Across History, Media, and National Cultures*, edited by Christine Gledhill and Linda Williams, 311–24. New York: Columbia University Press, 2018.

Kaplan, Ann E. *Feminism and Film*. Oxford: Oxford University Press, 2000.

Kase, Juan Carlos. "The Centre Cannot Hold: *Blank City* (2010) and the Problems of Historicizing New York's Independent Cinema of the Late 1970s and Early 1980s." In *Downtown Film & TV Culture*, edited by Joan Hawkins, 315–30. Chicago: Intellect, 2015.

Kastor, Elizabeth, and Chris Spolar. "Loading Up on Lace in Tribute to Their Idol's Material Whirl." *Washington Post*, 3 June 1985: C1.

Koblin, John. "HBO Max Orders a *Sex and the City* Revival." *The New York Times*, 10 January 2021. https://www.nytimes.com/2021/01/10/business/media/sex-and-city-revival.html.

Kracauer, Siegfried. *Theory of Film: The Redemption of Physical Reality*. Introduction by Miriam Bratu Hansen. Princeton; Princeton University Press, 1997.

Kuhn, Annette. *Women's Pictures: Feminism and Cinema*. New York: Verso, [1982] 1994.

Laderman, David. *Punk Slash! Musicals: Tracking Slip-Sync on Film*. Austin: University of Texas Press, 2010.

Lane, Christina. *Feminist Hollywood: From Born in Flames to Point Break*. Detroit: Wayne State University Press, 2000.

———. "Susan Seidelman's Contemporary Films: The Feminist Art of Self-Reinvention in a Changing Technological Landscape." In *Indie Reframed: Women's Filmmaking and Contemporary American Independent Cinema*, edited by Linda Badley, Claire Perkins and Michelle Schreiber, 70–86. Edinburgh: Edinburgh University Press, 2016.

Lang, Robert. *American Film Melodrama*. Princeton: Princeton University Press, 1989.

Lee, Benjamin. "Viola Davis: 'I Stifled Who I Was to Be Seen as Pretty. I Lost Years'." *The Guardian*, 20 October 2018. https://www.theguardian.com/film/2018/oct/20/viola-davis-stifled-who-was-lost-years-the-help.

Lemire, Christine. "Susan Seidelman: Survivor." *Rogerebert.com*, 12 July 2013. https://www.rogerebert.com/features/susan-seidelman-survivor.

Levy, Emanuel. "Smithereens." *EmanuelLevy.com*, 1 May 2006. https://web.archive.org/web/20210422143826/https://emanuellevy.com/review/smithereens-9/.

———. *Cinema of Outsiders: The Rise of American Independent Film*. New York; London: New York University Press, 2001.

Lewis, Lisa A. "Female Address on Music Television: Being Discovered." *Jump Cut: A Review of Contemporary Media*, 35 (April 1990): 2–15.

———. *Gender Politics and MTV: Voicing the Difference*. Philadelphia: Temple University Press, 1990.

London, Michael. "Strong-Willed Women Behind 'Seeking Susan'." *Los Angeles Times*, 2 April 1985. https://www.latimes.com/archives/la-xpm-1985-04-02-ca-19508-story.html.

Longworth, Karina. "Polly Platt: The Invisible Woman." *You Must Remember This*, 25 May–27 July 2020. http://www.youmustrememberthispodcast.com/episodes/2020/7/pollyplattarchive28.

Lotz, Amanda D. *Redesigning Women: Television After the Network Era*. Chicago: University of Illinois Press, 2006.

Loufbourow, Lili. "The Male Glance." *Virginia Quarterly Review*, March 2018. https://www.vqronline.org/essays-articles/2018/03/male-glance.

Maffi, Mario. *Gateway to the Promised Land: Ethnicity and Culture in New York's Lower East Side*. New York: New York University Press, 1995.
"Making Mr. Right (1987)." *Turner Classic Movies*, 23 October 2019. https://www.tcm.com/tcmdb/title/82474/making-mr-right#articles-reviews?articleId=1542315.
Markotic, Nicole. *Disability in Film and Literature*. Jefferson: McFarland, 2016.
Maslin, Janet. "At the Movies." *The New York Times*, 22 March 1985. https://www.nytimes.com/1985/12/20/movies/at-the-movies.html.
—. "John Malkovich in *Making Mr. Right*." *The New York Times*, 10 April 1987. https://www.nytimes.com/1987/04/10/movies/film-john-malkovich-in-making-mr-right.html.
—. "Smithereens." *The New York Times*, 19 November 1982. https://www.nytimes.com/1982/11/19/movies/smithereens.html.
Massey, Doreen. *Space, Place, and Gender*. Minneapolis: University of Minnesota Press, 1994.
Mayne, Judith. *The Woman at the Keyhole: Feminism and Women's Cinema*. Bloomington: Indiana University Press, 1990.
McRobbie, Angela. *The Aftermath of Feminism: Gender, Culture, and Social Change*. London: Sage Publishing, 2008.
McRoy, Jay. "Italian Neo-Realist Influences." In *New Punk Cinema*, edited by Nicholas Rombes, 39–55. Edinburgh: Edinburgh University Press, 2005.
Metelmann, Jörg, and Scott Loren. *Melodrama after the Tears: New Perspectives on the Politics of Victimhood*. Amsterdam: Amsterdam University Press, 2015.
Mittell, Jason. *Complex TV: The Poetics of Contemporary Television Storytelling*. New York: New York University Press, 2015.
Montañez-Smukler, Maya. *Liberating Hollywood: Women Directors and the Feminist Reform of 1970s American Cinema*. New Brunswick: Rutgers University Press, 2018.
Moore, Suzanne. "Let's See Menopausal Women on Screen – In All Their Glory." *The Guardian*, 15 March 2018. https://www.theguardian.com/commentisfree/2018/mar/15/menopausal-women-screen-glory-representation-menopause-popular-culture.
Mulvey, Laura. "Visual Pleasure and Narrative Cinema", *Screen*, 16, no. 3 (Autumn 1975): 6–18.
Negra, Diane. *Off-White Hollywood: American Culture and Ethnic Female Stardom by Diane Negra*. London: Routledge. 2001.
Nixon, Richard. "Radio Address on the Federal Responsibility to Education (25 October 1972)", *The American Presidency Project*, by Gerhard Peters and John T. Woolley, University of California Santa Barbara, [n. d.]. https://www.presidency.ucsb.edu/documents/radio-address-the-federal-responsibility-education.
Norden, Martin F. *The Cinema of Isolation: A History of Physical Disabilities in the Movies*. New Brunswick: Rutgers University Press, 1994.
Nussbaum, Emily. "Difficult Women: How *Sex and the City* Lost Its Good Name." *The New Yorker*, 22 July 2013. https://www.newyorker.com/magazine/2013/07/29/difficult-women.
Paszkiewicz, Katarzyna. *Genre, Authorship, and Contemporary Women Filmmakers*. Edinburgh: Edinburgh University Press, 2019.
Patterson, Richard. "An Interview with Susan Seidelman on the Making of *Smithereens*." *American Cinematographer*, 64, no. 5 (May 1983): 70.
Petroski, Alex. "'Pink House' in Belle Terre Village Torn Down." *TBR News Media*, 13 December 2017. https://tbrnewsmedia.com/pink-house-belle-terre-village-torn/.
Pinedo, Isabel. *Difficult Women on Television Drama: The Gender Politics of Complex Women in Serial Narratives*. New York: Routledge, 2021.
Polson, Helen. "'The Dance is in Your Body and Not in Your Crutches': Technique, Technology, and Agency in Disability Movement Performance." PhD dissertation, New York University, 2013.

Powell, John A. "How Government Tax and Housing Policies Have Racially Segregated America." In *Taxing America*, edited by Karen Brown and Mary Louise Fellowes, 80–117. New York: New York University Press, 1997.

Premiere Presents. "She-Devil Behind the Scenes 1989." *YouTube.com*, 3 December 2017. https://youtu.be/jCv64p9ALms.

Pribram, E. Deidre. "Melodrama and the Aesthetics of Emotion." In *Melodrama Unbound*, edited by Christine Gledhill and Linda Williams, 237–52. New York: Columbia University Press, 2018.

Quarmby, Katherine. *Scapegoat: Why We Are Failing Disabled People*. London: Portobello Books, 2011.

Rabin, Nathan. "Musical Chairs." *AV Club*, 22 March 2012. https://www.avclub.com/musical-chairs-1798172071.

Rahman, Muhammad Sigit Andhi, and Aini Firdaus. "The Practice of Wearing Hijab in a Multicultural Mosque of America." *Humaniora*, 9, no. 2 (July 2018): 129–40.

Rea, Steven X. "Susan Seidelman's Not Punk." *Philadelphia Inquirer*, 8 May 1983.

Redding, Judith M. and Victoria A. Brownworth. *Film Fatales: Independent Women Directors*. Seattle: Seal Press, 1997.

Rombes, Nicholas, ed. *New Punk Cinema*. Edinburgh: Edinburgh University Press, 2005.

Rosenblum, Constance. "Drop-Dead Clothes Make the Working Woman." *New York Times*, 26 February 1989. https://www.nytimes.com/1989/02/26/movies/drop-dead-clothes-make-the-working-woman.html.

——. "Making Mr. Right." *New York Times*, 3 January 1988. https://www.nytimes.com/1988/01/03/movies/home-video-movies-848788.html.

Ross, Harling. "Patricia Field on What It Was Like to Style Carrie Bradshaw." *Repeller.com*, 4 May 2018. https://repeller.com/patricia-field/.

Rowe Karlyn, Kathleen. *Unruly Girls, Unrepentant Mothers: Redefining Feminism on Screen*. Austin: University of Texas Press, 2011.

——. *The Unruly Woman: Gender and the Genres of Laughter*. Austin: University of Texas, 1995.

Ruby, Tabassum F. "Listening to the Voices of Hijab." *Women's Studies International Forum*, 29 (2006): 54–66.

Sabin, Roger. *Punk Rock: So What? The Cultural Legacy of Punk*. London: Routledge, 1999.

Salamon, Julie. "On Film: Love and the Single Android." *Wall Street Journal*, 9 April 1987. https://go.openathens.net/redirector/colum.edu?url=https://www.proquest.com/newspapers/on-film-love-single-android/docview/398001910/se-2.

Saleh, Esraa. "A Look Behind 'Cut in Half'. Pt. 2." *Scenarios USA*, 2017. https://www.youtube.com/watch?v=nc66_uLUb54 8/7/20.

San Felippo, Maria. "Introduction: Love Actually: Romantic Comedy since the Aughts." In *After "Happily Ever After": Romantic Comedy in the Post-Romantic Age*, 1–24. Detroit: Wayne State University Press, 2021.

Sapirstein, Pat. "*Desperately Seeking Susan* Director Susan Seidelman on Casting Madonna and Shooting the *Sex and the City* Pilot." *Variety*, 16 March 2021. https://variety.com/2021/film/features/susan-seidelman-desperately-seeking-susan-madonna-sex-and-the-city-1234930984/.

Savage, Jon. "Cinema of Punk: The Filth and the Fury." *Sight & Sound*, 26 (2016): 20–23.

"Scenarios USA." *YouTube.com*, 23 July 2020. https://www.youtube.com/c/scenariosusa/about.

Schubach, Alanna. "Stop Blaming the Hipsters: Here's How Gentrification Really Happens (And What You Can Do About It)." *Brick Underground*, 15 February 2018. https://www.brickunderground.com/rent/what-causes-gentrification-nyc.

Seger, Linda. *When Women Call the Shots: The Developing Power and Influence of Women in Television and Film*. New York: Henry Holt and Co., 1996.

Seidelman, Susan, "DVD Audio commentary." Moderated by David Gregory. Blue Underground, 2004.
—. "How I Made *Smithereens*, the Cult 80s NYC Punk Film." Interview by Laura Jacobs. *Dazed*, 21 August 2018. https://www.dazeddigital.com/film-tv/article/41058/1/smithereens-susan-seidelman-the-seminal-new-york-punk-film.
—. Interview by Maya Montañez Smukler, *Academy of Motion Picture Arts and Sciences: Visual History*, 22 September 2016.
—. "Smithereens Q&A with Director Susan Seidelman." Interview by Lars Nilsen, *Austin Film Society*, February 2020. https://www.youtube.com/watch?v=DPaffFwrxmI.
Seidelman, Susan, dir. *And You Act Like One Too.* 1976; New York: Criterion Collection, 2018. Blu-ray Disc.
—. *A Cooler Climate.* 1999; SHOWTIME. *Youtube.com*.
—. *Boynton Beach Club.* 2005; Snow Bird Films. Streaming.
—. *Confessions of a Suburban Girl.* 1992; BBC Scotland. *Youtube.com*.
—. *Cookie.* 1989; Lorimar. Streaming.
—. *Cut in Half.* 2017; New York: Scenarios USA. https://www.youtube.com/watch?v=r7dZWXD3m8Q&t=568s/.
—. *Desperately Seeking Susan.* 1985; Orion. Streaming.
—. *Gaudi Afternoon.* 2001; Lolafilms. DVD.
—. *Making Mr. Right.* 1987; Orion. DVD.
—. *Musical Chairs.* 2011; JMC Independent. Streaming.
—. *Power and Beauty.* 2002; SHOWTIME. DVD.
—. *Sex and the City*, season 1, episode 1: "Sex and the City." Aired 6 June 1998. HBO. HBO GO.
—. *Sex and the City*, season 1, episode 5: "The Power of Female Sex." Aired 5 July 1998. HBO. HBO GO.
—. *Sex and the City*, season 1, episode 10: "The Baby Shower." Aired 9 August 1998. HBO. HBO GO.
—. *She-Devil.* 1989; Orion. Streaming.
—. *Smithereens.* 1982; New York: Blue Underground, 2004. DVD.
—. *Smithereens.* 1982; New York: Criterion Collection, 2018. Blu-ray Disc.
—. *The Dutch Master.* 1993; Regina Zeigler. Digital file.
—. *The Electric Company*, season 1, episode 22: "The Flube Whisperer." Aired 16 September 2009. Six Point Harness, 2009. Streaming.
—. *The Electric Company*, season 1, episode 27: "Mighty Bright Fight." Aired 30 September 2009. Six Point Harness, 2009. Streaming.
—, *The Electric Company*, season 2, episode 11: "Jules Quest." Aired 30 April 2010. Six Point Harness, 2010. Streaming.
—, *The Electric Company*, season 2, episode 12: "Revolutionary Doughnuts." Aired 7 May 2010. Six Point Harness, 2010. Streaming.
—. *The Hot Flashes.* 2013; Vertical Entertainment. Streaming.
—. *The Ranch.* 2004; SHOWTIME. DVD.
—. *Yours Truly, Andrea G. Stern.* 1979; New York: Criterion Collection, 2018. Blu-ray Disc.
Seidelman, Susan, and Susan Berman, "Inside the Making of Post Punk Classic Smithereens." *Little White Lies*, *YouTube.com*, 25 August 2018. https://www.youtube.com/watch?v=GX4vQ942504.
Shakespeare, Tom. *Disability: The Basics*. London: Routledge, 2017.
Sharrock, Thea, dir. *You, Me Before*. Warner Bros, 2016.
Shary, Timothy, and McVittie, Nancy. *Fade to Gray: Aging in American Cinema*. Austin: University of Texas Press, 2016.

Silver, Jocelyn. "Mr. Big Did Drag, and It Is Glorious." *InStyle.com*, 7 May 2020. https://www.instyle.com/celebrity/sex-and-the-city-chris-noth-drag-mr-big.

Silverman, Jeff. "Hottest Director in a Town Full of Directors Is – GASP – Female." *Chicago Tribune*, 7 April 1985: 5. https://www.chicagotribune.com/news/ct-xpm-1985-04-07-8501190902-story.html.

Silverman, Kaja. *The Acoustic Mirror: The Female Voice in Psychoanalysis and Cinema*. Bloomington: Indiana University Press, 1988.

Snyder, Sharon L., and David T. Mitchell. "Body Genres: An Anatomy of Disability in Film." In *The Problem Body: Projecting Disability on Film*, edited by Sally Chivers and Nicole Markotić. Columbus: Ohio State University Press, 2010.

Solomon, Stefan. "The Feminist Possibilities of Unfinished Film." *Society for Cinema and Media Studies Conference*, Roundtable Discussion, 20 March, 2021.

Sones, Melissa. "Fans Scream for Lauper's Clothes Source." *Chicago Tribune*, 1 May 1985. https://www.chicagotribune.com/news/ct-xpm-1985-05-01-8501260614-story.html.

Sontag, Susan. "Persona Review." *Sight and Sound: Scraps from the Loft*, 16 October 2016. https://scrapsfromtheloft.com/2016/10/16/persona-review-susan-sontag/.

Spiegel, Lynn. *Make Room for TV: Television and the Family Ideal in Postwar America*. Chicago: University of Chicago Press, 1992.

Stacey, Jackie. "Desperately Seeking Difference." *Screen*, 28, no. 1 (Winter 1987): 48–61.

Stevens, Kyle. *Mike Nichols: Sex, Language, and the Reinvention of Psychological Realism*. New York: Oxford University Press, 2015.

Stoever-Ackerman, Jennifer. "Reproducing U.S. Citizenship in *Blackboard Jungle*: Race, Cold War Liberalism, and the Tape Recorder." *American Quarterly*, 63, no. 3 (September 2011): 781–806.

"Susan Seidelman and Susan Berman on Smithereens." *The Criterion Channel*, 2018. https://www.criterionchannel.com/videos/susan-seidelman-and-susan-berman-on-smithereens.

Thomas, Carol. *Sociologies of Disability and Illness: Contested Ideas in Disability Studies and Medical Sociology*. London: Palgrave Macmillan, 2007.

Thompson, Kristen. *Storytelling in the New Hollywood: Understanding Classical Narrative Technique*. Cambridge: Harvard University Press, 1999.

Thompson, Stacy. "Punk Cinema." In *New Punk Cinema*, edited by Nicholas Rombes, 21–38. Edinburgh: Edinburgh University Press, 2005.

—. *Punk Productions*. Albany: SUNY Press, 2004.

Thomson, Rachel, and Lisa Baraitser. "Thinking Through Childhood and Maternal Studies: A Feminist Encounter." In *Feminism and the Politics of Childhood: Friends or Foes?* edited by Rachel Rosen and Katherine Twamley, 66–82. London: University College London, 2018.

Tzioumakis, Yannis. *American Independent Cinema*. Edinburgh: Edinburgh University Press, 2006.

—. "Major Status, Independent Spirit: The History of Orion Pictures, 1978–1992." *New Review of Film and Television Studies*, 2, no. 1 (2004): 87–135.

Weaver, Jimmy. "Making a Scene: The Female Punk Narrative in Lou Adler's *Ladies and Gentlemen, The Fabulous Stains* and Susan Seidelman's *Smithereens*." *Punk & Post-Punk*, 2, no. 2 (2013): 179–95.

Weeks, Kathi. *The Problem with Work: Feminism, Marxism, Antiwork Politics, and Postwork Imaginaries*. Durham: Duke University Press, 2011.

Weldon, Fay. *The Life and Loves of a She-Devil*. New York: Ballantine Books, 1983.

Welter, Barbara. "The Cult of True Womanhood: 1820–1860." *American Quarterly*, 18, no. 2, Part 1 (Summer 1966): 151–74.

White, Edmund. "Why Can't We Stop Talking About New York in the Late 1970s?" *New York Times*, 10 September 2015. https://www.nytimes.com/2015/09/10/t-magazine/1970s-new-york-history.html.

White, Patricia. *Women's Cinema, World Cinema: Projecting Contemporary Feminisms.* Durham: Duke University Press, 2015.

Williams, Rhys H., and Gira Vashi. "'Hijab' and American Muslim Women: Creating the Space for Autonomous Selves". *Sociology of Religion*, 68, no. 3 (Fall 2007): 269–87.

Winnicott, D. W. *Playing and Reality*. New York: Routledge Classics, 2005.

Wood, Robin. *Hollywood from Vietnam to Reagan. . .and Beyond*. New York: Columbia University Press, 2003.

Wright, Frank Lloyd. "Frank Lloyd Wright Interview". Interview by Mike Wallace, *The Mike Wallace Interview*, 1957. *YouTube.com*, [n. d.]. https://youtu.be/DeKzIZAKG3E.

Yakir, Dan. "Celine and Julie Golightly". *Film Comment* 21, no. 3 (May/June 1985): 16–21.

—. "Susan Seidelman Preaches Rebellion". *Boston Globe*, 3 December 1989.

Yoshida, Emily. "What *Persona* is Still Teaching Us About Women Onscreen, 50 Years Later". *Vulture*. 12 May 2017. https://www.vulture.com/2017/05/persona-and-the-persistent-horror-of-women-alone-together.html.

Zavarzadeh, Mas'ud. "Review: *Smithereens* by Susan Seidelman". *Film Quarterly* 37, no. 2 (1983): 54–60.

Index

References to images are in italics; references to notes are indicated by n.

9/11 attacks, 193–4
2001: A Space Odyssey (Kubrick, 1968), 52

A Beautiful Mind (Howard, 2001), 192
A Cooler Climate (Seidelman, 1999), 4, 58–9
Academy Awards, 4, 20, 32, 46, 57, 59, 64, 189, 191
Acker, Kathy, 127
actors, 2–3, 33–4, 51–4, 192–3; *see also* casting
Adam (Mayer, 2009), 189
advertising, 2, 5–6, 89, 94, 96, 120, 127, 142, 143, 145, 147
    and *Desperately Seeking Susan*, 111, 113–14, 115–18
Affinity Enterprises, 15
age, 7, 21, 30, 52, 88, 182
    and *Boynton Beach Club*, 61–2, 172–5
    and *The Hot Flashes*, 179–82
agency, 29–30, 40, 177, 182–3
    and MTV, 3, 124–5
Ahmed, Leila, 203, 205
Ahmed, Riz, 191
Ahmed, Sara, 31
Alien (Scott, 1979), 52
Allen Jr, James E., 160
Allen, Woody, 40, 193
Altman, Robert, 90, 112
And You Act Like One, Too (Seidelman, 1976), 12, 46, 64
Anderson, Kevin, 59
Andersson, Bibi, 88
Andersson, Johan, 71

Landscape and Gentrification, 136
Angel, Auti, 192, 195
anti-domesticity, 112–13, 124
Arab-American Family Support Center, 201
Arlen, Alice, 53
Armando (character, *Musical Chairs*), 175–8, 185, 189, 194–5
Armstrong, Jessica Keishin, 32, 34
Arquette, Rosanna, 1, 38, 48, 50, 51, 52, 56, 81, 89, 111, 116, 118, 131
Askin, Peter, 13, 70
auteurism, 6, 28–31, 34–6, 40–1

Baby Boom (Shyer, 1987), 17, 61, 144
Baby It's You (Sayles, 1983), 116
Bale, Miriam, 86–90, 131
Barefoot Executive, The (Seidelman, 1995), 4, 58
Barish, Leora, 16, 49, 112, 132
Barr, Roseanne, 2, 19, 20, 53, 54, 96, *98*, *99*, 134
Barrow, Michael, 100
BBC Scotland, 4, 56, 161
beauty, 38, 54
Beckett, Brenda, 91
Beecher, Catharine
    A Treatise on Domestic Economy, 120
Begley Jr, Ed, 19, 134
belief, 161, 200–5, 206–7, 212
Belle Terre (NY), 134

INDEX 227

Benatar, Pat, 112, 121, 122
Bergman, Ingmar, 88, 90, 112
Berman, Susan, 13, 14, 70, 75, *81*, 91, *92, 93*, 102, 143
Beth (character, *The Hot Flashes*), 102, 179–81
Big, Mr. (character, *Sex and the City*), 32, 33
Bigelow, Kathryn, 30, 127
Billie Jean (music video, 1982), 119
bodies, 171, 172, 173–5, 179–81, 182–3; *see also* disability; nudity
Bonilla, E. J., 175, 185, 190
Borden, Lizzie, 12, 69, 127
Borderline (music video, 1984), 50, 116, 122, 125
Bowie, David, 119
Boyle, Barbara, 16, 50, 114
Boynton Beach Club (Seidelman, 2005), 2–3, 5–6, 7, 39, 56, 101–2
  and age, 61–2, 171–5, 181–2, 189
Bramon, Risa, 51
Breakfast at Tiffany's (Edwards, 1961), 18
breast cancer, 63, 179, 180
Brett, Jonathan, 57, 58
Broadcast News (Brooks, 1987), 17, 23, 144
Brooks, Peter, 163
Brown, Christy, 192
Buggles, The, 119
Burnetts, Charles, 166
Burns, Mark R., 105
Bushnell, Candace, 57

cable films, 4–5, 15–16
camera work, 26, 72–4, 76, 80, 86, 93, 99, 100, 137, 145, 150, 153, 162, 165, 167, 173, 175, 179, 212
Campbell, Judith *see* Exner, Judith
cancer *see* breast cancer; leukemia
Cannes Film Festival, 2, 11, 15, 49, 69–71, 78, 91, 138
Cannon, Dyan, 2, 33
capitalism, 17
career women, 17, 21–2, 96, 143
  and *Making Mr. Right*, 146–9, 151–2, 153–4
Cariou, Len, 62, 101, 172
Carlisle, Ann, 51
Carrie (character, *Sex and the City*), 2, 33, 34, *35*, 36, 38, 46, 57, 81, 100–1, *101*, 195
  and New York City, 135, 136–8
Carrus, Janet, 187, 188

casting, 2–3, 20, 51, 53–4, 62–3, 70, 129
  and Madonna, 50, 114–17
  and *Making Mr. Right*, 142–3
  and *Sex and the City*, 32–3, 138
celebrity, 112, 114–15, 123–4
  and *Desperately Seeking Susan*, 116–17, 118, 123
Celine and Julie Go Boating (Rivette, 1974), 90
Champlin, Charles, 23
Chantelle (character, *Musical Chairs*), 2, 62, 177, 194–6, 197
Charlotte (character, *Sex and the City*), 2, 137–8
chemotherapy, 8, 200, 206, 208, 211
Cher, 116
childhood, 4, 159–62
  and *The Electric Company*, 162–9
  and leukemia, 200, 202
  and magical thinking, 207, 208
  and transitional object, 212–13
Chinn, Lori Tan, 135–6
Chivers, Sally, 174, 181
Chytilova, Vera, 89
Cinema of Transgression, 69
cinematography, 50, 71–3, 100, 162
class, 17, 113, 115, 120
Clear and Present Danger (Noyce, 1994), 149
clothing *see* costume; fashion; hijab
CODA (Heder, 2021), 191
Coen, Joel, 13
Collier, Zena, 59
color, 145–6, 149
comedy, 2, 25, 54, 176; *see also* romantic comedy; screwball comedy
communication, 7–8
community, 5, 8, 13, 16, 61, 64, 79–80, 114, 121, 133–6, 179, 204
Confessions of a Suburban Girl (Seidelman, 1992), 4, 51, 56–7, 58, *87*, 93, 100, 131
  and childhood, 160, 161–2, 168
  and guerrilla filming, 131
  and New York City, 127
  and suburbia, 85–8
Cook, Pam, 146–7, 154
Cookie (character, *Cookie*), 1, 3–4, 11, 17, 23–4, 25, 26, 36, 37, 38, 52–3, 55, 81, 84, 125, 130, 187
Cookie (Seidelman, 1989), 3–4, 11, 36, 57
  and gangsters, 17, 23–4, 26

Cookie (Seidelman, 1989), *(cont.)*
   and New York City, 128, 132, 133
   and production, 53
   and suburbia, 86
costume, 38, 45, 51, 75, 77, 95, 164; *see also* fashion
COVID-19 pandemic, 64, 193
Cox, Laverne, 2, 62, 177, 194–5
Crip Camp (Lebrecht, 2020), 191
critics *see* film critics
crowd-sourcing, 5
Cut in Half (Seidelman, 2017), 7–8, 64, 200–2
   and death, 206–11
   and hijab, 203–6, 211–14

Daisies (Chytilova, 1966), 98
D'Angelo, Mike, 180
Daniel (character, *Musical Chairs*), 175–7
Darke, Paul, 178
Dash, Julie, 29
Davis, Judy, 55, 59
Davis, Viola, 191
Day Lewis, Daniel, 192
death, 112, 163, 172, 175, 176, 200, 203, 206–11
Deficit (Seidelman, 1975–6), 45–6
Deleau, Pierre-Henri, 15, 70–1
Demme, Jonathan, 49
Denisoff, R. Serge, 119
Designing Women (TV series), 144
Desperately Seeking Susan (Seidelman, 1985), 1, 2, 6–7, 11, 48, 82, 185
   and casting, 50–1, 116–17
   and ending, 56
   and fashion, 38–9
   and female celebrity, 112, 114–15
   and female friendship, 39, 51
   and feminism, 111–12
   and freeze frame, 26
   and genre, 53
   and Madonna, 117, 118, 142
   and music culture, 124–5
   and New York City, 32, 34, 73, 127–9, 131–2, 133
   and Orion Pictures, 16–17
   and people trading, 79
   and persona swaps, 89–91, 94–5
   and plot, 28
   and pop culture, 25
   and Seidelman, 49–50
   and *Sex and the City*, 37
   and sexuality, 38, 122–4
   and space navigation, 140–1
   and style, 17, 50–1
   and suburbia, 86, 92, 93–4
   and unruly woman narrative, 18–19, 115–16
   and urban landscape, 113–14
Desta, Yohana, 136
devil, 96–7
Dez (character, *Desperately Seeking Susan*), 94, 95, 124, 132
Dick, Vivienne, 69
disability, 5, 7, 191–3
   and *Musical Chairs*, 62–3, 175–9, 186–91, 195–8
Disney, 4, 58, 64
distribution, 5–6, 24, 62, 118
   and *Musical Chairs*, 186, 187
   and *Smithereens*, 15–16, 71
Dolan, Josephine, 173, 174
domesticity, 19, 20, 30, 114, 120
   and *Desperately Seeking Susan*, 111, 112, 113, 115
   and *Making Mr. Right*, 141
   and television, 118, 121
doubles, 6, 86
Dow, Bonnie J., 112
Downtown Cinema, 69
Driver, Sarah, 13
Droogsma, Rachel Anderson, 204–5, 210
drugs, 113, 129
Dryburgh, Stuart, 32
DuArt Film Laboratories, 14
Dutch Master, The (Seidelman, 1994), 4, 7–8, 56, 57, 99–100

Early Edition (TV series), 4
East Village (NYC), 13, 34, 47, 127, 129
   and *Smithereens*, 48, 130, 131–2
Ebert, Roger, 54, 57, 143–4, 171, 185, 188
Edmond, Maura, 127–8
Edson, Richard, 51
education, 91, 123, 160, 161, 186, 201, 214
El Khadem, Chirine, 72
Electric Company, The (TV series), 7, 160–1, 169
   and "Jules Quest," 165–7
   and "Mighty Bright Fight," 164–5
   and "Revolutionary Donuts," 167–8
   and "The Flube Whisperer," 162–4

Ephron, Nora, 53, 193
Eric (character, *Smithereens*), 13, 15, 18, 70, 72, 76, 77, 78–80, 82, 93, 131
erotic thrillers, 17
ethnicity, 7, 195, 200, 201, 202; *see also* hijab
Exner, Judith, 37, 58, 59

Falk, Peter, 23, 33, 53, 133
Faris, Naser, 201
fashion, 12, 24, 30, 38–9, 45, 48, 59, 117, 118, 129, 194
Fast Times at Ridgemont High (Heckerling, 1982), 34
Fatal Attraction (Lyne, 1987), 17, 21
Feelies, The, 48–9, 74
Fellini, Federico, 76, 93
female beauty, 38
feminism, 7, 11, 17, 46, 57
  and auteurism, 29–31
  and *Desperately Seeking Susan*, 94, 111–12, 113
  and hijab, 205
  and *Making Mr. Right*, 140–4, 153, 154–5
  and *She-Devil*, 97–9
fetishism, 203, 206–11, 214
Field, Patricia, 38, 43n
Field, Sally, 61
film critics, 3, 23, 54, 69, 75–7, 154, 190; *see also* Ebert, Roger
financing, 5, 12, 14, 15, 16, 58, 60, 63, 187
Firdaus, Aini, 203
First Wives Club (Wilson, 1996), 21
Florine (character, *The Hot Flashes*), 179–80, 181
Ford, Jessica, 28
Forrest Gump (Zemeckis, 1994), 192
Frank, Jillian, 47
Frankie Stone (character, *Making Mr. Right*), 7, 19, 21–2, 23, 26
  and color, 145–9
  and feminism, 140–4
  and romance, 152–3
  and *Sex and the City*, 37
  and spaces, 150–2
  and television, 144–5
  and work, 149–9
freeze frames, 26, 36, 80
French New Wave, 114, 127
Freud, Sigmund, 207

Friedan, Betty, 89
  The Feminine Mystique, 85–6, 90–1, 93, 96, 115
Friedbergh, Mark, 32
friendship, 39, 52–3, 56–7, 59, 61, 63, 65–6, 79, 80, 86, 88–90

Gaines, Jane, 30
gangster films, 17, 23–4, 36, 53, 133
Garland-Thomson, Rosemarie, 7, 171, 172, 175, 176, 182
Gary (character, *Desperately Seeking Susan*), 93–5, 113, 116, 119, 123–4
Gates, Marya, 32
Gaudi Afternoon (Seidelman, 2001), 4, 5, 55, 56, 60–1, 182
gender, 4–5, 6–7, 17, 61–2, 182–3
  and *Desperately Seeking Susan*, 114
  and *The Electric Company*, 163–4
  and MTV, 121–2
  and work, 149
  see also transgender narratives; women
genre, 3, 6, 7, 12, 17–19, 21, 23, 24, 25–6, 30, 40, 53–4, 72, 86, 87, 88, 89, 90, 111, 119, 135, 136, 141, 143, 146, 186; *see also* erotic thrillers; gangster films; melodrama; romantic comedy; science fiction; soap opera
gentrification, 130, 135–8
George, Anna, 201
Giancana, Sam, 59
Gill, Rosalind, 144
girl bonding, 51, 56
Girlfriends (Weill, 1978), 127
Girls Just Want to Have Fun (music video, 1983), 117, 121–2, 125
Gitlow, Shelly, 61
Giuliani, Rudy, 138
Gledhill, Christine
  Melodrama Unbound, 159, 166
Godfather, The (Coppola, 1972), 133
Godfrey, Nicholas, 40
Golden, Annie, 132
Goldin, Nan, 127
Good Luck to You, Leo Grande (Hyde, 2022), 174
Goodfellas (Scorsese, 1990), 133
Goodman, Mark, 119
Gordon, Betty, 12
Graduate, The (Nichols, 1967), 64

Grant, Catherine, 30
Grigorov, Mario, 186, 188
guerrilla filming, 75, 130–1
Guggenheim Museum (NYC), 134–5

Hannah, Daryl, 3
Hanover, Donna, 138
Harrington, Erin, 180, 182
Harron, Mary, 130
Harry (character, *Boynton Beach Club*), 172–3
Hasan, Mahmudul, 205
Hawking, Stephen, 192
Hawn, Goldie, 116
HBO, 28, 29, 32, 33, 34, 39, 57, 58
Headly, Glenne, 2, 25, 52, 143
Heap, Chad, 120
Heckerling, Amy, 13, 29, 34
Hell, Richard, 13, 14, 70, 93, 129, 132
Hell's Kitchen (NYC), 131
Help, The (Taylor, 2011), 191
Hepburn, Audrey, 18
hijab, 200, 201, 202–6
    and fetishism, 210–11
    and transitional object, 211–14
Hoffman, Dustin, 99
Hogeland, Lisa Marie, 112
Holiday (music video, 1983), 50, 116
Holland, Agnieszka, 4
home video, 11, 15–16
Hopkins, Billy, 51
Hot Flashes, The (Seidelman, 2013), 3, 5, 6, 7, 33–4, 171
    and agency, 180–2
    and bodies, 179–80
    and female friendship, 39, 56–7, 63
    and housewives, 102
    and location, 63
housewives, 6, 85, 90–1, 96, 97
    and *Boynton Beach Club*, 101–3
    and *Desperately Seeking Susan*, 93–4, 111–12, 113, 115
    and *The Dutch Master*, 99–100
    and *Sex and the City*, 100–1
Hutchinson, Pamela, 75–6

I Am Sam (Nelson, 2001), 189
I Love New York campaign, 127
immigration, 120, 200–1, 204
Independent Feature Project, 16
Independent Film Market, 11

independent films, 2, 4, 5–6, 11, 12–13, 15–16
indirect authorship, 36
industrialization, 120
Insdorf, Annette, 71
Into the Groove (music video, 1985), 118
Isabel (character, *Musical Chairs*), 177, 195

Jack (character, *Boynton Beach Club*), 101–2, 172–4, 181
Jackson, Michael, 119
Jacob, Gilles, 15, 71
Jai, Ajna, 8, 201
Jailhouse Rock (Thorpe, 1957), 117
James, Rick, 119
Jarmusch, Jim, 13, 69
Jermyn, Deborah, 193
Jetsons, The (TV series), 22, 52
Joyrich, Lyn, 159
Julien, Déa, 201
Jurca, Catherine, 114

Kauffmann, Stanley, 76
Keaton, Diane, 116, 193
Kellerman, Sally, 2, 62, 101, 172
Kennedy, John F., 37, 58, 59
Kern, Richard, 69
King, Michael Patrick, 31
Kotsur, Troy, 191
Kracauer, Siegfried, 72–3

L Word, The (TV series), 60
Lachman, Ed, 50
Laderman, David, 75
Ladies and Gentleman, the Fabulous Stains (Adler, 1982), 14
Lane, Christina, 3, 5, 6, 39
    and *Boynton Beach Club*, 174
    and creative agency, 29–30
    and female characters, 79
    and *Sex and the City*, 82
    and *She-Devil*, 21
    and *Smithereens*, 80
Lang, Robert, 169
Last Picture Show, The (Bogdanovich, 1971), 40
Lauer, Dorene, 119
Lauper, Cyndi, 112, 117, 121–2, 125
Layla (character, *Cut in Half*), 8, 200–1, 202, 203, 205–11, 212, 213–14
Lebrecht, James, 191

Lee, Spike, 13, 17
Leslie (character, *Desperately Seeking Susan*), 93–4, 113, 115, 119, 123
leukemia, 200, 201, 202, 205–6, 207–10
Levinson, Barry, 40
Levy, Emanuel, 76
Lewis, Juliette, 58
Lewis, Lisa, 114–15, 121, 122
LGBTQIA+ community, 7, 60, 64
Like a Virgin (music video, 1984), 117
Lindsey, Arto, 51
Little Rascals, The (Spheeris, 1994), 4
Lloyd, Emily, 23
locations, 30, 34, 63–4, 71, 76, 131, 137–8; see also New York City
Loewy, Raymond, 52
London, Michael, 114
Long Island, 134
Loquasto, Santo, 51, 118
Loren, Scott, 167
Lorimar Film Entertainment Company, 11, 24
Lotz, Amanda D., 36
Loufbourow, Lili, 30, 40
Love Is a Battlefield (music video, 1983), 122
love triangles, 13
Lunch, Lydia, 127
Lurie, John, 51, 132
Lynch, David, 90

McCarty, Bruce, 33
McRobbie, Angela, 144
McRoy, Jay, 72
McVittie, Nancy, 172, 182
Madden, Marty, 186, 188, 197
Madonna, 1, 2, 7, 34, 37, 48, 51, 52, 54, 75, 94, 143, 162, 164
  and appearance, 38
  and casting, 50, 138
  and celebrity, 111, 112, 114, 115, 116–18, 121, 123, 124
  and persona, 54, 92, 93
  and videos, 111, 117–18, 121, 122, 125
Madsen, Virginia, 3, 34
Maffi, Mario, 129
mafia, 53, 55, 133
magazine culture, 25, 91, 93–4, 96, 118, 120
  and *Making Mr. Right*, 142, 145, 147–8, 154
magical thinking, 207–9

Magnuson, Ann, 2, 21, 52, 142–3, 149
Making Mr. Right (Seidelman, 1987), 2, 3–4, 7, 11, 21–3, 51, 59
  and actors, 52
  and color, 52, 146–7
  and feminism, 141–5, 154–5
  and genre, 19, 26, 53, 141
  and pop culture, 25
  and romance, 153–4
  and screwball comedy, 19
  and sexuality, 37–8
  and spaces, 146–50
  and television, 145–6
  and toxic masculinity, 33
  and work, 17, 147–50
male gaze, 18
Malkovich, John, 2, 22, 33, 52
Manheim, Camryn, 3, 63, 179
Mannequin (Gottlieb, 1987), 141
Marchione, Aubree, 187, 190
Marilyn (character, *Boynton Beach Club*), 172, 174–5, 176
marketing, 15, 118–19, 148, 149, 152, 182, 186
Markotić, Nicole, 191
marriage *see* housewives
Marshall, Garry, 60
Mary Fisher (character, *She-Devil*), 19, 20–1, 24–5, 55, 134–5
  and persona swap, 95–6, 97–8, 99
Masina, Giulietta, 76, 93
Maslin, Janet, 71, 76
Massey, Doreen, 152
Mathis, Samantha, 58
May, Elaine, 40
Maya (character, *Cut in Half*), 201, 206
MC Hammer, 119
Me Before You (Sharrock, 2016), 192
Medavoy, Mike, 16, 50
media, 6, 7, 25, 28–9, 36, 39, 113, 117, 118, 121–2, 123–4, 130, 141–2, 144–6, 148–50, 153–4, 155, 159, 186
Medina Bañón, Raquel, 173
Melamed, Lisa, 60
melodrama, 18, 159, 176, 182, 189
  and *The Electric Company*, 160, 162–9
menopause, 179–80, 189
Metcalf, Laurie, 2, 51, 52
Metelmann, Jörg, 167

232 INDEX

Mia (character, *Musical Chairs*), 133, 175–8, 185, 187, 188, 189, 192, 195–6, 197
Miami, 22, 52, 146
Midnight Cowboy (Schlesinger, 1969), 65
Miramax Films, 11, 16
Miranda (character, *Sex and the City*), 2, 32, 37
Mitchell, David T., 177
Mitchell, Eric, 69
Mittel, Jason, 30, 31
Moonstruck (Jewison, 1987), 17
Moore, Demi, 100
Moore, Suzanne, 179
motherhood, 19–20, 58, 61, 91, 96–7, 102, 121, 144, 163–4, 182
MTV, 7, 50, 111, 113–14, 119
  and female celebrity, 112–17, 123–5
  and patriarchy, 121
Mulvey, Laura, 173–4, 181
Murphy Brown (TV series), 144
music, 19, 20, 37, 49, 50, 125, 127, 129, 130, 166, 168, 188; *see also* MTV; punk rock
Music (Sia, 2021), 191
Musical Chairs (Seidelman, 2011), 2, 5, 6, 7, 63–4, 171, 181–2, 185–6
  and disability, 175–9, 187–93, 196–8
  and New York City, 133, 193–6
Muslims *see* hijab
My Big Fat Greek Wedding (Zwick, 2002), 186
My Left Foot (Sheridan, 1989), 192

Nares, Jamie, 69
Negra, Diane, 193
neo-realism, 72
New Line Cinema, 11, 15, 16, 71
New Orleans, 64
New Wave, 13–14, 24, 71, 114, 117, 127, 129
New York City, 1, 2, 7
  and culture, 47–8
  and *Desperately Seeking Susan*, 50–1, 116, 128–9, 131–2
  and fashion, 38
  and gentrification, 134–8
  and *Musical Chairs*, 192, 193–6
  and punk culture, 13, 14, 15
  and Seidelman, 32, 127–8, 129–30, 133–4
  and *Sex and the City*, 34–6, 132–3
  and *Smithereens*, 69–73, 75, 77–8, 79–82, 130–1

New York University (NYU), 11, 12–13, 45–6, 47, 69, 127
Nichols, Mike, 193
Nicholson, Jack, 181
Nights of Cabiria (Fellini, 1957), 71, 76, 93
Nixon, Richard, 160
No Wave, 69, 129–33, 138
Norden, Martin F., 176, 178
Norman, Marsha, 59
nostalgia, 22, 77, 138, 148
Noth, Chris, 32, 33, 43n
Noto, Blaise, 118
nudity, 63, 100, 173–4, 181
Nussbaum, Emily, 37
Nyswaner, Ron, 13, 49, 70

Olesberg, Jonathan, 15
Oliver, Michael, 186
Orion Pictures, 11, 16–17, 19, 50, 114
  and Madonna, 116, 117

Palcy, Euzhan, 4
Panic Room (Fincher, 2002), 149
parallel-protagonist structure, 79, 89
Parker, Sarah Jessica, 38, 57, *101*
Paszkiewicz, Kataryzna, 30
patriarchy, 26, 115, 117, 121–2, 125, 176
Paul (character, *The Hot Flashes*), 180
Paul (character, *Smithereens*), 13, 15, 18, 70, 73, 93
  and character, 76–9, 80, 81–2
Peppermint Lounge, the (NYC), 14, 18, 71, 72, 73
Pereths, Joy, 15
Persona (Bergman, 1966), 86, 88–9, 112
persona swap films, 6, 86–90, 95, 99, 131
Peters, Dr. (character, *Making Mr. Right*), 2, 19, 22, 26, 141, 143, 146, 148, 150–4
Pillsbury, Sarah, 16, 49, 114, 118
Pinedo, Isabel, 29, 31, 36
Pipes, Leah, 133, 175, 185, 190
Pittman, Bob, 119
Platt, Polly, 40, 44n
Poe, Amos, 12, 69
pop culture, 12, 25, 76, 100
post-feminism, 39, 144, 154
Powell, John A., 121
Powell-Main, Joe, 187

power, 38, 46, 53, 54–5, 77, 97–8, 99, 116, 124, 137, 144, 155, 171, 177, 188, 189, 204, 213–14
Power and Beauty (Seidelman, 2002), 4, 37, 58, 59, 182
Presley, Elvis, 117
Pribram, E. Deidre, 169
Prince, 117, 119
production design, 22, 30, 31, 32, 34, 36, 51
promotion, 5–6
prostitution, 37, 60, 70, 76, 82, 94, 122–3
punk cinema, 4, 12, 69, 71–2, 74–6
punk rock, 13, 14, 15, 26n, 47, 75, 77, 89, 92, 93–5
   and *Desperately Seeking Susan*, 136
   and New York City, 129–33, 134

Quarmby, Katharine, 189–90
Queer as Folk (TV series), 60
queer narratives, 5, 7, 60–1; see also LGBTQIA+ community

Rabin, Nathan, 190
race, 4, 7, 17, 62, 63, 127, 128, 187, 195, 197
   and *Desperately Seeking Susan*, 111, 113, 114–15, 125
   and *The Hot Flashes*, 179–80
   and MTV, 119
   and urban landscapes, 120–5
   see also ethnicity
Rahman, Muhammad, 203–4
Rain Man (Levinson, 1988), 192
Ranch, The (Seidelman, 2004), 4, 5, 37, 55, 58–60
   and girl groups, 56
   and othering, 182
Ray, Gary, 132
realism, 20, 37, 50, 72–3, 128
Redglare, Rockets, 51
religion, 7, 200, 201–2, 210, 212, 213; see also hijab
revenge films, 19–21, 26, 53, 134; see also *She-Devil*
Rinn, Brad, 13, 14
Rivette, Jaques, 90
Roberta (character, *Desperately Seeking Susan*), 1, 19, 26, 82
   and domesticity, 118
   and New York City, 131, 132
   and persona swap, 94–5

and sexuality, 123, 124
and suburbia, 93–4, 115, 116
and voyeurism, 112, 113
Roberts, Robin, 180
romantic comedy, 6, 7, 11–12, 17–18, 193
   and *Boynton Beach Club*, 171–4
   and *Making Mr. Right*, 152–3
   and *Musical Chairs*, 186
Roseanne (TV series), 20
Rosefelt, Reid, 128
Rowe Karlyn, Kathleen, 18, 115
Roxie (character, *The Hot Flashes*), 179
Ruby, Tabassum, 204
Ruby Bridges (Palcy, 1998), 4
Run-DMC, 119
Ruth Patchett (character, *She-Devil*), 19, 20–1, 26, 54–6, 134–5
   and persona swap, 95–6, 97–9

Sage, Bill, 33
Salamon, Julie, 23
Saleh, Esraa, 201–2, 205
Samantha (character, *Sex and the City*), 2, 37, 38, 100, 138
Sammy (character, *Cut in Half*), 200–1
San Filippo, Maria, 187
Sandy (character, *Boynton Beach Club*), 176, 177, 178
Sanford, Midge, 16, 50, 116
Sareen (character, *Cut in Half*), 200–1, 205–12, 213–14
Savage, Jon, 129
Savoca, Nancy, 29
Sayles, John, 116
Scenarios USA, 201
science fiction, 7, 12, 19, 21–3, 53, 141, 143, 147, 159; see also *Making Mr. Right*
Scorsese, Martin, 40
Scott and Beth B, 69
screwball comedy, 12, 19, 39, 53, 91, 123, 169, 186
Secret Garden, The (Holland, 1993), 4
Seidelman, Florence, 5–6, 61, 101
Seidelman, Susan, 1–2, 3–5, 11, 12, 57–60
   and actors, 33–4
   and auterism, 28–9, 30
   and casting, 2–3
   and childhood, 159–60, 161–2
   and distribution, 5–6
   and *The Electric Company*, 162–9

234 INDEX

Seidelman, Susan (*cont.*)
   and female characters, 78–9
   and female independence, 17–18
   and genre, 25–6
   and New York City, 47–8, 127–8, 129–30, 131–2
   and NYU, 45–6
   and script choice, 91–2
   and SHOWTIME, 57–60
   and suburbia, 56, 85–6
   and television, 40
   and voiceover, 46–7
   see also *Boynton Beach Club*; *Confessions of a Suburban Girl*; *Cookie*; *Cut in Half*; *Desperately Seeking Susan*; *Hot Flashes, The*; *Making Mr. Right*; *Musical Chairs*; *Ranch, The*; *Sex and the City*; *She-Devil*; *Smithereens*
Sesame Street (TV series), 160, 161
Sex and the City (TV series), 1–2, 4, 7, 30
   and auteurism, 28–9, 41
   and casting, 32–3
   and female characters, 36–7
   and friendship, 39
   and look, 34–6
   and New York City, 72, 81, 128, 131, 133–4, 135–8
   and opening credits, 38, 82
   and pilot, 31–2, 57–8
   and sexuality, 37–8
   and "The Baby Shower" episode, 100–1
sex work, 5, 32, 37, 60; *see also* prostitution
sexuality, 7, 37–8, 182–3
   and *Boynton Beach Club*, 172–4
   and *Desperately Seeking Susan*, 113, 115–16, 123–4
   and disability, 176–7
   and *The Hot Flashes*, 181–2
   and MTV, 112, 122
Shakespeare, Tom, 192
Shary, Timothy, 172, 182
She Bop (music video, 1984), 122
She-Devil (Seidelman, 1989), 2, 6, 11, 25, 185
   and ending, 54–5, 98–9, 105–10
   and female friendship, 39
   and makeover montage, 38
   and New York City, 128, 131, 134–5
   and persona swaps, 90, 95–6, 97–9
   and professional world, 17
   and reception, 54, 58
   and revenge genre, 19–21, 26
   and *Sex and the City*, 37
   and suburbia, 86, 133–4
   and technology, 24–5
   and toxic masculinity, 33
She's Gotta Have It (Lee, 1986), 17, 23
Shields, Brooke, 3, 102, 179
shot-reverse-shots, 73, 94
SHOWTIME, 5, 57, 58–60
Shumman, Leen, 201
Sia, 191
Silver, Joan Micklin, 29
Silver, Jocelyn, 34–5
Silver, Marisa, 12
Silverman, Kaja, 30
Sinatra, Frank, 59
Siskel, Gene, 54, 57
Smithereens (Seidelman, 1982), 1, 2, 6, 11, 14–15, 36
   and camera work, 73–4
   and Cannes, 70–1
   and critics, 76–8
   and distribution, 15–16
   and ending, 81–2
   and Field, 43n
   and music, 49
   and New York City, 34, 47, 48, 69–70, 71–3, 128, 130–1, 133, 135
   and Noth, 32, 43n
   and people trading, 79–81
   and pop culture, 25
   and production, 13–14
   and punk girl narrative, 18, 26n, 75–6, 92–3
   and reception, 71–2
   and space navigation, 141
   and style, 17
   and suburbia, 86
   and toxic masculinity, 33
Snyder, Sharon L., 177
soap opera, 12, 19, 25
social media, 6
SoHo (NYC), 34, 50, 131
Sontag, Susan, 88–9, 102
Sopranos, The (TV series), 29
Sorvino, Mira, 7–8
Sound of Metal (Marder, 2019), 191
spaces, 141, 150–2
Spheeris, Penelope, 4
Spiegel, Lynn, 118, 120

Spielberg, Steven, 40
Stacey, Jackie, 113
Star, Darren, 31–2, 57
Steve Marcus (character, *Making Mr. Right*), 142, 145
Stoever-Ackerman, Lynn, 124
streaming, 6, 64
Streep, Meryl, 2, 19, 20, 33, 53–4
Strugatz, Barry, 105
suburbia, 6–7, 18, 56–7, 85–6, 128
    and *Desperately Seeking Susan*, 93–5, 113, 115
    and housewives, 90–1
    and *Making Mr. Right*, 147, 148
    and race, 120–1
    and *Sex and the City*, 137–8
    and *She-Devil*, 133–4
    and *Smithereens*, 78
Sundance Film Festival, 11, 16
Susan (character, *Desperately Seeking Susan*), 1, 18–19, 24, 26, 37
    and coolness, 148–9
    and New York City, 131–2
    and persona swap, 93–5, 112
    and unruliness, 115–16, 162
    and youth culture, 113
Sykes, Wanda, 3, 63, 179

Tales of Erotica (film compilation, 1993–5), 4, 32
technology, 22, 24–5
television, 4, 6, 39–40, 112
    and auteurism, 29–30
    and children, 159, 160–1
    and domesticity, 118, 121
    and *Making Mr. Right*, 144–5, 153
    see also *Electric Company*; HBO; MTV; *Sex and the City*; SHOWTIME
Telluride Film Festival, 16, 71
Teresa (character, *The Dutch Master*), 7–8, 99–101
Terms of Endearment (Brooks, 1983), 64
Tewkesbury, Joan, 29
That Girl (TV series), 18
Theory of Everything, The (Marsh, 2014), 191–2
Thomas, Marlo, 18
Thompson, Kristin, 79
    Storytelling in the New Hollywood, 89–90

Thompson, Stacy, 74
Three Women (Altman, 1977), 112
Thriller (music video, 1983), 119
#TimesUp movement, 64
Tootsie (Pollack, 1982), 98–9
toxic masculinity, 33
transgender narratives, 5, 62–3, 194–5, 197
transitional object, 203, 211–14
transportation, 132–3
trauma, 203, 208, 209–10
Trish (character, *Making Mr. Right*), 142, 145
Trump, Donald, 193
Turner, Tina, 112, 121
Turturro, John, 51
Tzioumakis, Yannis, 16

Ullmann, Liv, 88
Ulysses (character, *Making Mr. Right*), 2, 19, 22, 23, 150–1, 152–5
United Artists, 17
unruly women, 18–19, 20–1, 24, 115–16
Upside, The (Burger, 2017), 195
urban landscapes, 6–7, 18, 113, 120–1, 122, 123; see also New York City
US Film Festival, 16

Vaccaro, Brenda, 2, 33, 53
Vashi, Gira, 204
veiling see hijab
Velvet Underground, 130
Video Killed the Radio Star (music video, 1981), 119
videos see MTV
Viva Las Vegas (Sidney, 1964), 117
voiceover, 7, 46–7, 209, 212
voyeurism, 51, 56, 111, 112–13, 117, 123–4

Wall Street (NYC), 130, 135
Warhol, Andy, 130
Warner Bros., 24, 114
Weaver, Jimmy, 14
Weeks, Kathi, 149
Weill, Claudia, 29, 127
Weird Science (Hughes, 1985), 140
Weldon, Fay, 97
    The Life and Loves of a She-Devil, 6, 19, 53, 55, 95–6, 105, 134
Westside Highway (NYC), 131
What's Love Got To Do With It (music video, 1984), 121

wheelchair dancing, 63, 176, 176–9, 187, 190, 194, 196–7
When Harry Met Sally (Reiner, 1989), 17
White, Patricia, 30
Wiest, Dianne, 23, 53, 58
Wilfredo (character, *Musical Chairs*), 194–5
Williams, Rhys, 204
Winnicott, D. W., 212–16
women, 4–5, 7, 11–12, 64
   and auteurism, 28–31, 40–1
   and celebrity, 112, 114–15
   and characters, 78–80
   and communication, 7–8
   and directors, 3–4, 16–17
   and domesticity, 120
   and friendship, 39, 52–3, 57–8, 60
   and hijab, 203–5, 210
   and independence, 17–18
   and menopause, 179–80, 182
   and MTV, 121–2
   and New York City, 127–8, 135
   and persona swaps, 86–91
   and punk rock, 14
   and revenge, 19–20
   and romantic comedy, 6
   and *Sex and the City*, 36–7
   and sexuality, 37–8
   and television, 39–40
   and unruly, 18–19, 20–1, 24
   see also career women; feminism; housewives
Wood, Robin, 34
work *see* career women
Working Girl (Nichols, 1988), 17, 143
Wren (character, *Smithereens*), 1, 6, 13, 35, 37
   and age, 52
   and character, 14–15, 18, 24, 70, 71, 73–4, 75–80
   and clothing, 48, 73
   and coolness, 148–9
   and freeze frames, 26
   and New York City, 71–2, 74–5, 130–1
   and people trading, 79–80
   and punk aesthetic, 74–6, 92–3
   and unruliness, 162

Yoshida, Emily, 89, 90
Yours Truly, Andrea G. Stern (Seidelman, 1979), 12, 46–7, 64

Zavarzadeh, Mas'ud, 76–7, 130
Zecchi, Barbara, 173
Zedd, Nick, 69

EU representative:
Easy Access System Europe
Mustamäe tee 50, 10621 Tallinn, Estonia
Gpsr.requests@easproject.com

www.ingramcontent.com/pod-product-compliance
Lightning Source LLC
Chambersburg PA
CBHW051121160426
43195CB00014B/2285